HOUGHTON MIFFLIN HARCOURT
TEXAS JOURNEYS

Program Authors

James F. Baumann · David J. Chard · Jamal Cooks
J. David Cooper · Russell Gersten · Marjorie Lipson
Lesley Mandel Morrow · John J. Pikulski · Héctor H. Rivera
Mabel Rivera · Shane Templeton · Sheila W. Valencia
Catherine Valentino · MaryEllen Vogt

Consulting Author

Irene Fountas

Cover illustration by Tim Jessell.

Printed in the U.S.A.

ISBN 10:   0-54-724087-2
ISBN 13:   978-0-54-724087-9

3456789 - 0914 – 18 17 16 15 14 13 12 11 10
4500226936

HOUGHTON MIFFLIN HARCOURT
School Publishers

Good Citizens

Big Idea People make a community strong.

Unit 2

Express Yourself

Big Idea — We communicate in many ways.

Unit 3

LEARNING LESSONS

Big Idea Facing a challenge helps us to grow.

Welcome, Reader!

You're about to set out on a reading journey that will take you from the streets of Japan to a fossil field in Canada, bursting with dinosaur bones! On the way, you'll learn amazing things as you become a better reader.

Your reading journey begins with a proud principal who decides five days of learning isn't nearly enough for such a fine school.

Many other reading adventures lie ahead. Just turn the page!

Sincerely,

The Authors

Good Citizens

Unit 1

Big Idea

People make a community strong.

Paired Selections

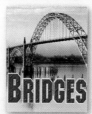

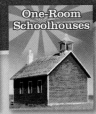

A FINE, FINE SCHOOL
By Sharon Creech · Pictures by Harry Bliss

One-Room Schoolhouses

✓ **TARGET VOCABULARY**

principal

soared

strolled

worried

proud

announced

fine

certainly

Vocabulary Reader

Context Cards

TEKS 3.4B use context to determine word meaning; **ELPS** 4D use prereading supports to comprehend texts

Vocabulary in Context

1 principal

A principal who gets to know the students will be a better leader.

2 soared

Colorful kites soared high in the sky at the school's cultural fair.

3 strolled

Students and their families strolled for miles to raise money for charity.

4 worried

This boy is worried. He is afraid rain will ruin the class field trip.

- **Study each Context Card.**
- **Use two Vocabulary words to tell about an experience you had.**

5 proud

These young actors feel proud of their terrific performance in a school play.

6 announced

Each day, a different student announced school news over a loudspeaker.

7 fine

The sun shines and the air is clear. It is a fine day for the school yard sale.

8 certainly

We certainly should turn off lights when not using them. This surely saves energy.

Background

✓ **TARGET VOCABULARY** **Ways We Learn** Imagine if your principal strolled in and announced you had to go to school all year long. What if you had to sit in class while the summer temperatures soared outside? What if you worried about tests on Saturdays instead of learning to swim? School is certainly important, but you can also be proud of useful things you learn from your family at home, like riding a bike or cooking a fine meal. We can learn new things every day, no matter where we are.

Learning at School	Learning at Home
Math	How to make a sandwich
Science	How to plant a garden
Reading	How to ice skate
Social Studies	How to knit or sew

Comprehension

✓ TARGET SKILL **Story Structure**

Where does *A Fine, Fine School* take place, and who are the characters? What problem do the characters face, and how do they solve it? Use a story map like this to keep track of the characters, setting, and plot of the story.

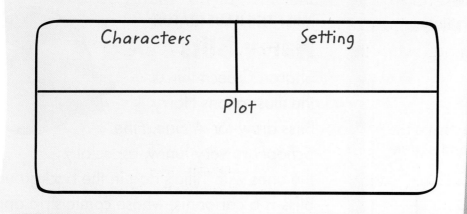

✓ TARGET STRATEGY **Summarize**

Use details about the characters, setting, and plot on your story map to summarize, or retell in your own words, the important parts of *A Fine, Fine School*. As you summarize, you'll better understand how the story parts work together.

Main Selection

A FINE, FINE SCHOOL
By Sharon Creech • Pictures by Harry Bliss

✔ **TARGET VOCABULARY**

principal	proud
soared	announced
strolled	fine
worried	certainly

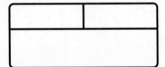

✔ **TARGET SKILL**

Story Structure Name the setting, character, and plot in a story.

✔ **TARGET STRATEGY**

Summarize Tell the important parts of the story in your own words.

GENRE

Humorous fiction is a story that is written to entertain the reader.

MEET THE AUTHOR
Sharon Creech

When Sharon Creech is working on a book, she sometimes gets stuck. She doesn't know what to write next. When that happens, she goes for a long walk, does some laundry, or cleans the bathroom. Then she returns to her computer and starts writing again.

MEET THE ILLUSTRATOR
Harry Bliss

Sharon Creech thinks the illustrations Harry Bliss drew for *A Fine, Fine School* are very funny, especially the ones with Tillie's dog in the background. Bliss is a cartoonist whose comic strip appears in daily newspapers. He and his family live in Vermont.

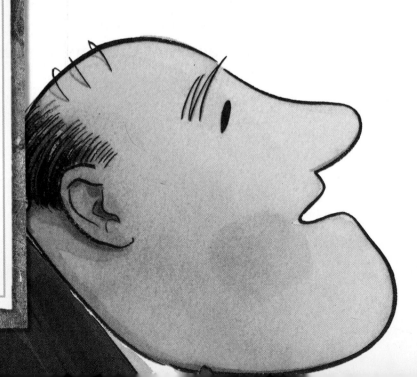

A FINE, FINE SCHOOL

by Sharon Creech 🍎 pictures by Harry Bliss

Essential Question

What are the parts of a story?

Mr. Keene was a principal who loved his school. Every morning he strolled down the hallway and saw the children in their classes. He saw them learning shapes and colors and numbers and letters. He saw them reading and writing and drawing and painting. He saw them making dinosaurs and forts and pyramids.

"Oh!" he would say. "Aren't these fine children? Aren't these fine teachers? Isn't this a fine, fine school?"

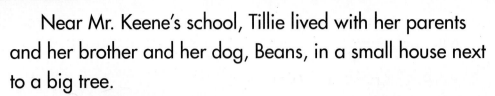

Near Mr. Keene's school, Tillie lived with her parents and her brother and her dog, Beans, in a small house next to a big tree.

On Mondays and Tuesdays and Wednesdays and Thursdays and Fridays, Tillie went off to school.

At school, Tillie learned her shapes and colors and numbers and letters. Sometimes, when she saw Mr. Keene standing in the hallway, he waved.

"Aren't these fine children?" he said to himself. "Aren't these fine teachers? Isn't this a fine, fine school?"

On the weekends—Saturday and Sunday—
Tillie climbed her favorite tree, and she took
Beans on walks and threw him sticks,

and she pushed her brother on a swing
and tried to teach him how to skip.

But on Mondays and Tuesdays and Wednesdays
and Thursdays and Fridays, Tillie went off to school.
Beans and her brother did not like to see her go.
"Hurry, hurry, hurry home!" her brother called.

One day, Mr. Keene called all the students and teachers together and said, "This is such a fine, fine school! I love this school! Let's have more school! From now on, let's have school on Saturdays, too!"

The teachers and the students did not want to go to school on Saturdays, but no one knew how to tell Mr. Keene that. He was so proud of the children and the teachers, of all the learning they were doing every day.

And so, that Saturday, Tillie set off for school.

"But it's Saturday! What about the swings?" her brother called.

The following month, Mr. Keene announced, "This is such a fine, fine school! I love this school! Let's have more school! From now on, let's have school on Sundays, too!"

The teachers and the students did not want to go to school on Sundays, but no one knew how to tell Mr. Keene that. He was so proud of the children and the teachers, of all the learning they were doing every day.

And so, that Sunday, Tillie set off for school.

"But it's Sunday! What about the skipping?" her brother called.

STOP AND THINK

Author's Craft Find places on pages 17–21 where the author repeats words and sentences to make the story more fun to read.

The following month, Mr. Keene called everyone together again and said, "This is such a fine, fine school! I love this school! Let's have more school! From now on, let's have school in the summer, too, all summer long, every single day!"

"How much we will learn!" he said. "We can learn everything! We will learn all about numbers and letters, colors and shapes, the Romans and the Egyptians and the Greeks. We will learn about dinosaurs and castles and—and—everything! We will learn *everything!*"

22

The teachers and the students did not want to go to school on Saturdays and Sundays and holidays and all summer long, every single day. But no one knew how to tell Mr. Keene that. He was so proud of the children and the teachers, of all the learning they were doing every day.

And so, on the first day of summer, Tillie set off for school. "But it's summer! What about summer?" her brother called.

✔ STOP AND THINK

Story Structure What is the main problem in this story? Which story character is responsible for this problem?

TEKS 3.2B; **ELPS** 4I

And that day, Tillie went to see Mr. Keene. She stood in his office, in front of his desk.

"What a fine, fine school this is!" Mr. Keene said. "What amazing things everyone is learning!"

"Yes," Tillie said, "we certainly are learning some amazing things."

"A fine, fine school!" Mr. Keene said.

"But," Tillie said, "not everyone is learning."

"What?" Mr. Keene said. He looked very worried. "Who? Who isn't learning? Tell me, and I will see that they learn!"

"My dog, Beans, hasn't learned how to sit," Tillie said. "And he hasn't learned how to jump over the creek."

"Oh!" Mr. Keene said.

"And my little brother hasn't learned how to swing or skip."

"Oh!" Mr. Keene said.

"And I—" she said.

"But you go to school!" Mr. Keene said. "To our fine, fine school!"

"True," Tillie said. "But I haven't learned how to climb very high in my tree. And I haven't learned how to sit in my tree for a whole hour."

"Oh!" Mr. Keene said.

 STOP AND THINK

Summarize In your own words, summarize the things Tillie and others are not learning because of the extra school days.

 ELPS 4I

That day, Mr. Keene walked up and down the halls, looking at the children and the teachers. Up and down he walked. Up and down, up and down.

The next morning, Mr. Keene called everyone together. The children and the teachers were very worried.

Mr. Keene said, "This is a fine, fine school, with fine, fine children and fine, fine teachers. But not everyone is learning."

The children and the teachers were very, very worried.

Mr. Keene said, "There are dogs who need to learn how to sit and how to jump creeks."

What did he mean? Was he going to make their dogs come to school?

"There are little brothers and sisters who need to learn how to swing and how to skip."

What did he mean? Was he going to make their younger brothers and sisters come to school, too?

The children and the teachers were very, very, very worried.

"And you, all of you—children and teachers—you need to learn how to climb a tree and sit in it for an hour!" Mr. Keene said.

The children and the teachers were very worried.
"And so from now on we will . . . **not** have school on
Saturdays or Sundays or in the summer!"

FREE AT LAST

A GOTTA LOVE IT!

A huge, enormous, roaring cheer soared up to the ceiling and floated out the windows so that everyone in the town heard the fine, fine children and the fine, fine teachers shout, "Fine! Fine! Fine!"

And the fine, fine children and the fine, fine teachers lifted Mr. Keene up, and they carried him down the hallway and out the doors and through the town, up and down, in and out. And everywhere they went, the people said, "What a fine, fine school with such fine, fine teachers and fine, fine children and a fine, fine principal!"

Your Turn

1. The word <u>worried</u> on page 24 most closely means —

   ◯ smart

   ◯ nervous

   ◯ happy

   ◯ tired

   TEKS 3.4C; **ELPS** 1C , 3B, 4F

2. ✔ **TARGET SKILL** ## Story Structure

   Use a story map like this to describe how Tillie's problem begins. Then explain how Tillie solves her problem. **TEKS** 3.8A

   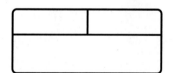

3. ✔ **TARGET STRATEGY** ## Summarize

   Use the information from your story map to help you summarize Tillie's solution to her problem. **TEKS** 3.8A

4. **Oral Language** Work with a partner to retell the major events of the story, using the Retelling Cards. Ask questions to help each other remember what happened. **TEKS** 3.29A

   Retelling Cards

 TEKS **3.4C** identify/use antonyms/synonyms/homographs/homophones; **3.8A** sequence/summarize main events/influence on future events; **3.29A** listen/ask questions/make comments; **ELPS 1C** use strategic learning techniques to acquire vocabulary; **3B** expand/internalize initial English vocabulary; **4F** use visual/contextual/peer/teacher support to read/comprehend texts

Technology

One-Room
Schoolhouses

✔ TARGET VOCABULARY

principal	proud
soared	announced
strolled	fine
worried	certainly

GENRE

Informational text gives factual information about a topic. This is an online encyclopedia article.

TEXT FOCUS

Photographs show true pictures of important text details. **Captions** explain a photo or picture. Look at the photos and captions before you read. Discuss what you think the article will be about. After you read, see if your predictions were correct.

TEKS **3.2A** use ideas to make/confirm predictions; **3.13D** use text features to locate information/make and verify predictions

---

File   Edit   View   Favorites

Encyclopedia 🌐

One-Room Schoolhouses

One-room schoolhouses were once common in America. In the early 1900s, there were more than 250,000. Some children today still attend one-room schoolhouses.

Students of all ages were proud to learn in these small schools. There was usually one teacher and no principal.

Search

Daily Life

A ringing bell often announced the start of each day. Students did chores, such as bringing in wood for cooking and heating or raising a flag that soared in the sky above the schoolyard.

The teacher worked with one or two students at a time. They studied subjects like reading, math, history, spelling, and handwriting. Students wrote on small slates, or blackboards, because paper was too expensive.

Mary McLeod Bethune

Famous Students

Some famous Americans learned in one-room schoolhouses. Mary McLeod Bethune went to one in South Carolina in the late 1800s. She became one of America's great teachers. She fought for civil rights.

Former United States President Lyndon Johnson attended a one-room schoolhouse in Texas. Johnson was born near Stonewall, Texas, in 1908. He was President from 1963 until 1969.

Lyndon Johnson

Schoolhouses Today

Some students still study in a one-room schoolhouse. In winter, fewer than one hundred people live on Monhegan Island, in Maine. It is too far to go to the mainland for classes, so students attend the island's little schoolhouse.

In most places, bigger schools opened when one-room schoolhouses became too small. People became worried about losing the fine old buildings. Some became museums. You can tour a school in South Dakota just like one that writer Laura Ingalls Wilder attended.

Other schoolhouses became stores, restaurants, and homes. These little buildings are certainly important pieces of American history.

Laura Ingalls Wilder, writer of *Little House on the Prairie*, strolled several miles to a school like the one shown in the photo below.

Making Connections

Express Your Opinion How would you feel about going to school on the weekend? Give a speech about this topic. Express your opinion about what you think would be good and bad about going to school on weekends.

Compare and Contrast How is Tillie's school in the story *A Fine, Fine School* different from a real one-room schoolhouse? Make a list of at least three differences. Then list at least two ways they are the same.

Students today write on paper.

...ents ...long ago ...on slates

Connect to Social Studies In some countries, students go to school in summer and on weekends. Work with a group to research more ways in which schools in another country are different from yours. Take notes. Share your results with the class.

TEKS **3.26A(ii)** collect information from experts/reference texts/online searches; **3.26C** take notes/categorize evidence; **3.29A** listen/ask questions/make comments; **3.30** speak coherently/effectively about topics; **RC-3(D)** make inferences/use textual evidence; **RC-3(F)** make connections between texts; **ELPS 3G** express opinions/ideas/feelings

TEKS **3.22A(vii)** use/understand coordinating conjunctions; **3.22B** use complete subject/complete predicate; **ELPS 3C** speak using a variety of grammatical structures; **5E** employ increasingly complex grammatical structures in writing

Grammar

Subjects and Predicates The two main parts of a sentence are the subject and the predicate. The **subject** tells whom or what the sentence is about. The **predicate** tells what the subject does or is.

Academic Language

complete subject
complete predicate

Subject	Predicate
Jessica	went to school.
The sun	was shining.
Her class	went outside for recess.
The children	played on the swings.
They	had fun.

All the words in the subject are called the **complete subject**. All the words in the predicate are called the **complete predicate**.

Turn and Talk **Work with a partner. Find the subject and the predicate in each sentence. Be ready to explain your thinking.**

❶ Tom loves science class.

❷ His class planted seeds.

❸ They watered them.

❹ The seeds grew tall.

❺ The plants have flowers now.

Sentence Fluency Combining sentences can make your writing clearer. When two sentences have the same predicate, you can put the sentences together. Join the subjects and put the word *and* between them to form a compound subject.

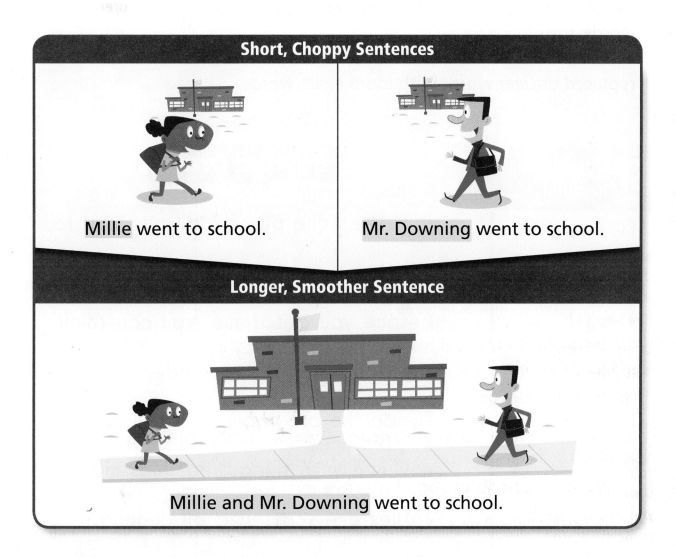

Short, Choppy Sentences

Millie went to school.

Mr. Downing went to school.

Longer, Smoother Sentence

Millie and Mr. Downing went to school.

Connect Grammar to Writing

As you revise your paragraph that describes, look for short sentences that have the same predicate. Try to combine the sentences, using a compound subject.

Write to Narrate

☑ **Word Choice** The author of *A Fine, Fine School* uses exact words. She doesn't just say that children made "things." She says they made "dinosaurs and forts and pyramids." When you write a **description**, use exact words, too.

Sarah wrote a description of an art room. Later, she replaced unclear words with more exact words.

Writing Traits Checklist

☑ **Ideas**
Did I use details for at least two of the five senses?

☑ **Organization**
Is each detail about my main idea?

☑ **Word Choice**
Did I use exact words?

☑ **Voice**
Did I let my feelings come through?

☑ **Sentence Fluency**
Do my sentences flow smoothly?

☑ **Conventions**
Did I edit for spelling, grammar, and punctuation?

Revised Draft

There's one place I always love to go. It's the school art room! Even before you get there, you can smell the ~~art stuff.~~ paint and clay It's a wonderful smell!

Inside the art room, the walls are covered with ~~things~~ pictures, masks, and puppets that kids made.

Tables are scattered all around.

Easels are scattered all around. Jars of red, blue, and yellow paint are stacked up.

40

The Best Place at School
by Sarah Walker

There's one place I always love to go. It's the school art room! Even before you get there, you can smell the paint and clay. It's a wonderful smell! Inside the art room, the walls are covered with pictures, masks, and puppets that kids made. Tables and easels are scattered all around. Jars of red, blue, and yellow paint are stacked up. While we work, Ms. Varga plays music to go with our project. For instance, once she played soft, tinkly music when we made snowflakes. When I'm in the art room, I never want to leave.

I added some exact words. I also combined two sentences to avoid repeating a predicate.

Reading as a Writer

Why did Sarah change "art stuff" to "paint and clay"? Where can you add exact words in your description?

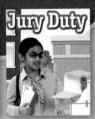

Vocabulary in Context

trial

jury

convinced

guilty

pointed

honest

murmur

stand

Vocabulary Reader

Context Cards

TEKS 3.4B use context to determine word meaning **ELPS** 1E internalize new basic/academic language

trial
In a trial, people in a courtroom review what happened to figure out the truth.

jury
Members of a jury hear the facts of the case and make a decision together.

convinced
The lawyer made the jury members believe her. They were convinced.

guilty
Jurors tell the judge whether they think the accused person is guilty or innocent.

- Study each Context Card.
- Make up a new context sentence that uses two Vocabulary words.

5 pointed

A witness pointed to a map to show where the crime took place.

6 honest

People in court are asked to be honest and tell the truth.

7 murmur

The judge asks for silence when he hears a murmur in the courtroom.

8 stand

When people take the stand in court, they sit down and answer questions.

Background

✓ TARGET VOCABULARY **In a Courtroom** Have you ever watched a trial in a movie? A person is pointed out by someone who yells, "He's guilty!" People in the courtroom murmur in agreement. In real life, however, a trial follows strict rules. Witnesses promise the judge to be honest. Then they take the stand and answer questions about what happened. A jury listens carefully to the facts. The people in the jury must be completely convinced before they find a person guilty or innocent.

Judge's Bench
The judge sits here to direct the trial.

Witness Stand
People who saw and heard key events answer questions here.

Jury Box A group of regular people pay attention to the evidence to reach a decision.

Gallery People sit here to watch the trial.

Comprehension

✔ TARGET SKILL Conclusions

Draw conclusions as you read *The Trial of Cardigan Jones*. Find ways to tie story details together to figure out what really happened. Use a chart like this to describe your conclusions and the details that helped you to draw them.

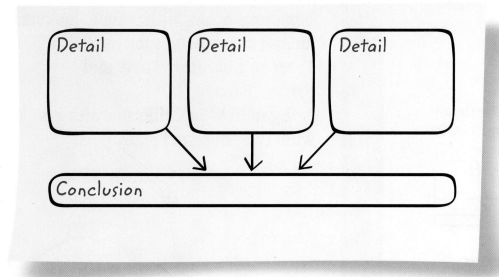

✔ TARGET STRATEGY Infer/Predict

Use the conclusions you draw to infer, or figure out, important details about the judge and jury at Cardigan's trial. You may even be able to predict what the judge finally decides!

The Trial of CARDIGAN JONES
By Tim Egan

✔ **TARGET VOCABULARY**

trial	pointed
jury	honest
convinced	murmur
guilty	stand

✔ TARGET SKILL

Conclusions Use details to figure out ideas that the author doesn't state.

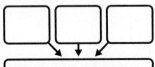

✔ TARGET STRATEGY

Infer/Predict Use clues to figure out more about the selection.

GENRE

A **fantasy** is a story that could not happen in real life.

MEET THE AUTHOR AND ILLUSTRATOR

Tim Egan

Back when Tim Egan was in elementary school, his favorite subject was art. He says he was much better at art than he was at math. Now Egan makes his living as an author and an artist, creating humorous books with serious-looking animal characters, such as *Burnt Toast on Davenport Street* and *Serious Farm*.

Egan lives in California with his wife, two sons, and many pets.

The Trial of CARDIGAN JONES

written and illustrated by **Tim Egan**

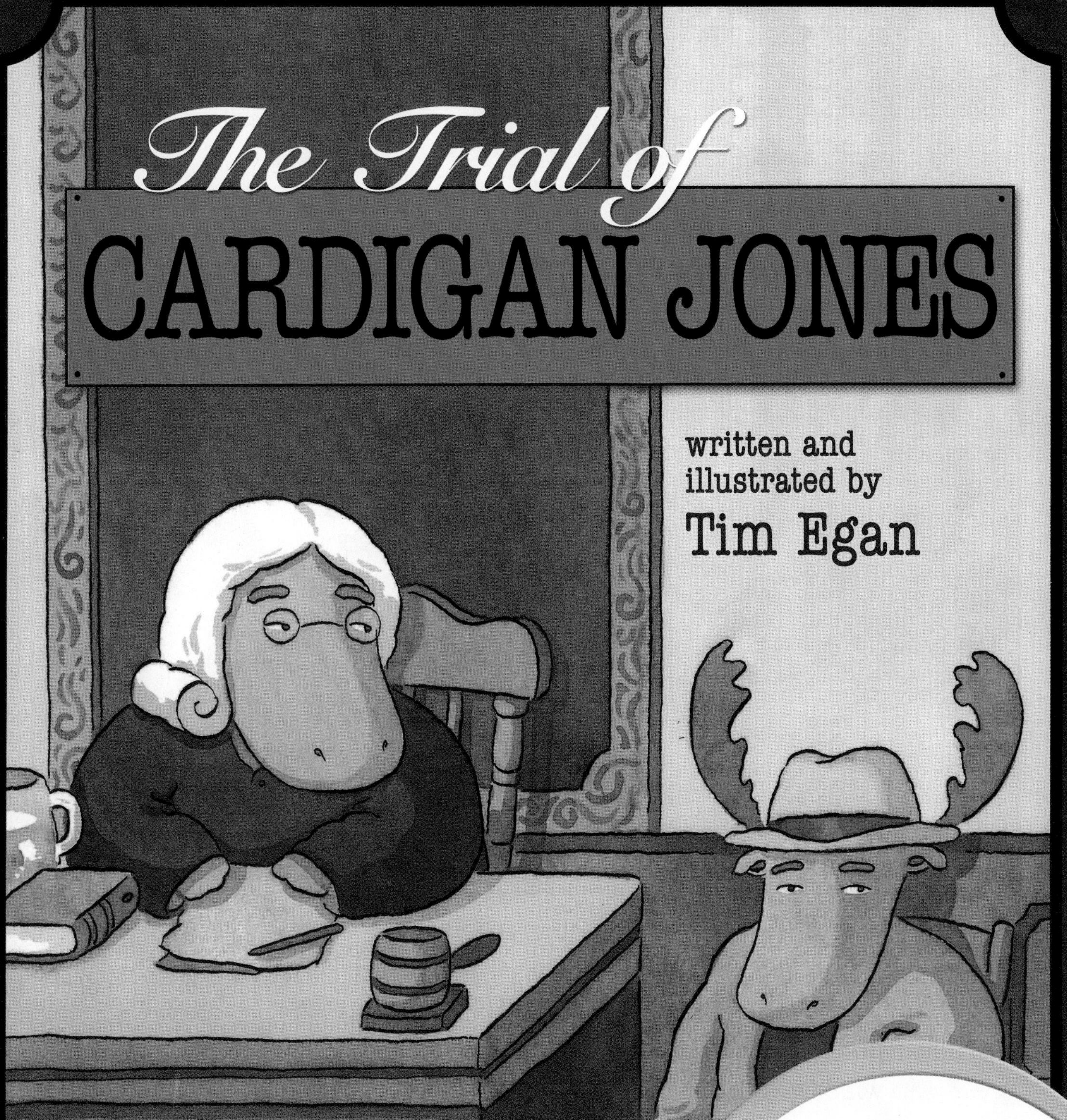

Essential Question

What helps you make decisions about a character?

Cardigan walked by Mrs. Brown's house just as she was putting a fresh-baked apple pie in her window. Cardigan loved pies.

STOP AND THINK

Author's Craft What do the words *fresh-baked* tell you about how the pie probably looked, smelled, and felt?

TEKS 3.10

He walked over and smelled the pie. A neighbor
next door saw him, and a milkman, driving by, saw him
too. Cardigan was new in town, and they weren't sure
what he was up to.

A moment later, Mrs. Brown came back to the window and the pie was gone. She was so upset, she called the police.

She told them that she'd seen a moose just a few minutes before, so they drove around the block and stopped Cardigan.

 STOP AND THINK

Conclusions Why did Mrs. Brown call the police and mention seeing a moose?

TEKS 3.2B

Noticing that he had pie crust on his shirt, they arrested him, even though he insisted he hadn't stolen the pie.

A judge and a jury were chosen to decide if he stole the pie or not. The neighbor and the milkman were called as witnesses.

Cardigan's trial started the next day. Mrs. Brown took
the stand first. "Is there anyone in this courtroom that you
saw the day the pie disappeared?" the judge asked her.

"Yes," she said, "that moose over there." She pointed
to Cardigan.

There was a murmur from the crowd. "He did it.
He's guilty," someone said.

"We don't know that yet," said the judge. The rabbit then took the stand. "Did you see anyone near the pie?" the judge asked the rabbit.

"Sure did," said the rabbit. "That moose right there. He stole it."

"No, I didn't!" shouted Cardigan. "I didn't steal it!
I promise!"

"Order!" shouted the judge. Cardigan turned and his
antlers bumped a statue and sent it crashing to the floor.

It made a really loud noise, and the jury gave Cardigan
dirty looks. "Next witness!" shouted the judge.

The milkman then took the stand. "Who did you see
at the time the pie was taken?" the judge asked.

"The moose," he said, "no question about it. He
walked right up to the window. His face was practically
touching the pie."

By now, some folks were convinced that Cardigan took
the pie, even though the judge kept saying, "We still don't
have any proof."

Finally, Cardigan was called to the stand. As he crossed the courtroom, his antlers got all wrapped up in the flag. It took him over a minute to get untangled.

"He's a troublemaker," declared a gopher.

Others nodded in agreement as the judge asked, "Well, moose. Did you walk up to the pie?"

"Well, uh, yes, but just to smell it . . ." said Cardigan softly.

"I knew it!" shouted a goat. "Lock him up!"

"Order!" commanded the judge. "Order in the court!"

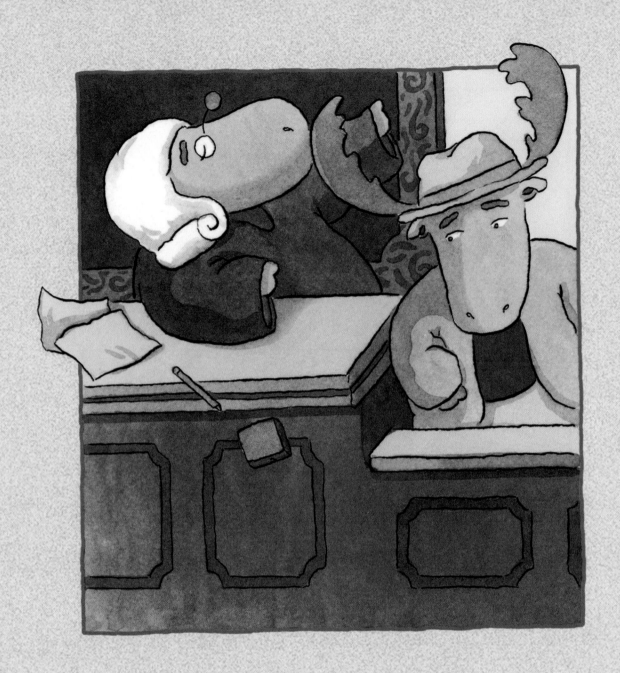

"But I didn't take it!" insisted Cardigan. "Honest!"

He stood up, and his antlers knocked the judge's gavel to the floor.

"Sit down!" shouted the judge. But as Cardigan went to sit, he bumped the judge with his antlers.

The judge fell to the ground.

"He hit the judge!" shouted one of the security guards. They grabbed Cardigan and started taking him away. The jury members had made up their minds.

But the judge stood up and said, "Now just hold on a minute!"

"I'm curious about something," he said. "Follow me."

STOP AND THINK

Infer/Predict Why does the judge stop the jury? Where do you predict he will take them?

TEKS 3.2A

He walked out of the courtroom, and everyone followed him through the town.

They reached Mrs. Brown's house, and the judge walked around the outside to the window where the pie had been.

Sure enough, there, smushed all over the bushes, was the apple pie. It didn't smell very good anymore.

"You knocked it off the window with those giant antlers
of yours, you silly moose," said the judge, laughing. "It was
an accident."

Everyone immediately felt terrible for being so rotten to
Cardigan, and the jury proclaimed him "not guilty" right then
and there.

To make it up to him, they had a party in his honor,
and Mrs. Brown baked a pie especially for him, even after
he broke her favorite vase.

Your Turn

1. On page 53, the word <u>murmur</u> means to —

 ⬭ argue

 ⬭ faint

 ⬭ jump

 ⬭ whisper

2. ✔ **TARGET SKILL** **Conclusions**

 During the trial, many characters draw a conclusion about Cardigan's guilt. Use a chart like this to show their conclusion and the details they used to draw it. **TEKS** 3.2B

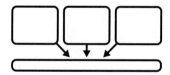

3. ✔ **TARGET STRATEGY** **Infer/Predict**

 How is the judge's conclusion different from the other characters'? What does this tell you about the judge?

4. **Oral Language** In a small group, take turns narrating, or telling, the story's main events. Include specific details about the characters, setting, and story problem. Remember to speak slowly and clearly. **TEKS** 3.8A; 3.30; **ELPS** 3H

TEKS 3.2B ask question/clarify/locate facts/details/use text evidence; 3.8A sequence/summarize main events/influence on future events; 3.30 speak coherently/effectively about topics; **ELPS** 3H narrate/describe/explain with detail

Social Studies

✔ TARGET VOCABULARY

trial	pointed
jury	honest
convinced	murmur
guilty	stand

GENRE

Readers' Theater is a text that has been written for readers to read aloud. What can you tell about the characters in this readers' theater by reading their exact words, or dialogue?

TEXT FOCUS

When people use **persuasion**, they try to get someone to do something. Discuss what the lawyer on page 68 wants jurors to do. Is he convincing? Give reasons for your answer.

 TEKS **3.7** explain plot/character through dialogue in scripts; **3.14** identify author's persuasion

Readers' Theater

Jury Duty

by Ann Rossi

Cast of Characters

Mom	Madison	Victor

Madison: Mom, you got a letter from the state of California.

Victor: What's it about?

Mom: I've been called for jury duty.

Victor: Wow! You're going to be on a jury.

Mom: Not necessarily. Many people get called for jury duty, but not everyone becomes a juror.

Victor: Why not?

Mom: Being on a jury is a big responsibility. In a criminal trial, a jury decides whether an accused person is guilty or innocent. The judge and lawyers want to make sure I will be fair.

Victor: How do they do that?

Mom: The judge will tell me about the case. Then the judge and the lawyers will ask me questions. It's my duty to give clear, honest answers, not to just murmur.

Madison: Is it okay if you know someone in the case?

Mom: No, the judge and lawyers would think I was convinced about the accused person's guilt or innocence before the trial started. They would not let me serve.

Victor: What happens if you *are* picked to be on a jury?

Mom: Well, first I would listen to people who take the stand and testify, or tell what they know. Then the lawyers for each side would try to convince me that their version of what happened is the truth. In the end, I'll make my final decision based on facts, not feelings.

Victor: Mom, what *do* lawyers say to persuade jurors?

Mom: Hmm, let's imagine Goldilocks from *Goldilocks and the Three Bears* is on trial. The lawyer on the three bears' side might say something like this. . .

Jurors, the facts prove Goldilocks is not innocent! The bears pointed to her when asked, "Who did it?" She was found asleep in their home, with porridge on her chin. You must do the right thing, and find Goldilocks guilty!

Making Connections

 Text to Self

On Trial With a small group, act out the *The Trial of Cardigan Jones*. Take turns in the starring role. Afterward, discuss how it might feel to be an innocent person on trial. Give specific details to describe how you would feel.

 Text to Text

TEKS RC-3(F); **ELPS** 4K

Connect to Social Studies Think about the judge in *The Trial of Cardigan Jones* and what you read about judges in *Jury Duty*. What two qualities do you think are most important for being a good judge? Why? Summarize them in a short paragraph.

 Text to World

TEKS 3.20C; **ELPS** 3G

Imagine that you are on the jury at the Cardigan Jones trial. Write, then read aloud, several journal entries about the trial. Tell how your opinion about Cardigan's guilt or innocence changes as the trial goes on.

 TEKS 3.20C write responses to texts that demonstrate understanding; **3.29A** listen/ask questions/make comments; **3.30** speak coherently/effectively about topics; **RC-3(D)** make inferences/use textual evidence; **RC-3(F)** make connections between texts; **ELPS** 3G express opinions/ideas/feelings; 3H narrate/describe/explain with detail; 4K employ analytical skills to demonstrate comprehension

69

Grammar

Kinds of Sentences There are four kinds of sentences. Every sentence begins with a capital letter and ends with an end mark. A **statement** tells something. A **question** asks something. A **command** tells someone to do something. An **exclamation** shows strong feeling, such as excitement, surprise, or fear.

Academic Language

statement

question

command

exclamation

Kind of Sentence	Example
statement	The trial starts today.
question	Who is the judge?
command	Please sit down.
exclamation	Here comes the judge!

Turn and Talk **Work with a partner. Say each sentence aloud. Identify each sentence as a statement, question, command, or exclamation.**

❶ The jury listened to the trial.

❷ They talked about the case.

❸ They cannot decide what to do!

❹ What will happen now?

❺ Tell the jurors to try again.

Sentence Fluency You know that sentences can be statements, questions, commands or exclamations. Make your writing lively by using all four types of sentences.

Paragraph with One Type of Sentence

We all have accidents. We can share those stories with each other. All of us will learn something new. We will be much smarter in the end.

Paragraph with Four Types of Sentences

Don't we all have accidents? Let's share those stories with each other. All of us will learn something new. How much smarter we will be in the end!

Connect Grammar to Writing

As you revise your friendly letter, try to use different kinds of sentences to make your writing lively.

Write to Narrate

☑ **Ideas** In *The Trial of Cardigan Jones*, the author's purpose is to interest readers. That's why the story is full of funny and surprising details. When you revise your **friendly letter**, add details that your audience will enjoy. Travis wrote his sister a letter about a town fair. He wanted to tell Sabrina about the fun day he had. Later, he added details that would make her smile.

Writing Traits Checklist

☑ **Ideas**
Did I include interesting details?

☑ **Organization**
Did I use correct letter form?

☑ **Word Choice**
Did I use lively, vivid words?

☑ **Voice**
Did I show how I feet about events?

☑ **Sentence Fluency**
Did I use different kinds of sentences?

☑ **Conventions**
Did I capitalize and punctuate the parts of a letter correctly?

Revised Draft

Dear Sabrina,

The town fair was a blast! First, Diego and I went to the Dunk the Mayor tank. If you hit a target with a ball, Mayor Lewis dropped into the tank. After that, we went into the moonwalk and bounced like crazy.

He kept saying, "I sure would like a dip in that cool water." We granted his wish!

197 Second Street

Myra, OH 54325

July 20, 2008

Dear Sabrina,

The town fair was a blast! First, Diego and I went to the Dunk the Mayor tank. If you hit a target with a ball, Mayor Lewis dropped into the tank. He kept saying, "I sure would like a dip in that cool water." We granted his wish! After that, we went into the moonwalk and bounced like crazy. Then we went on the roller coaster. Guess who sat right in front of us. Your fifth-grade teacher, Mrs. Huber! She was screaming just like us.

How is camp? I miss you.

Love,

Travis

In my final letter, I added some funny details. I also used different kinds of sentences.

Reading as a Writer

Which details did you enjoy in Travis's letter? Where can you add fun and surprising details in your letter?

Destiny's Gift
Kids Making a Difference

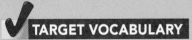
✓ **TARGET VOCABULARY**

afford

customers

contacted

raise

earn

figure

block

spreading

Vocabulary
Reader

Context
Cards

 ELPS 4D use prereading supports to comprehend texts

Vocabulary in Context

1 afford

Kids collect toys for families who can't afford to buy them.

2 customers

Some store owners ask customers to donate a dollar to charity.

3 contacted

This girl contacted neighbors by phone and asked for help with projects.

4 raise

Many groups have bake sales to raise needed money.

COOKIES 50¢

BROWNIES $1.00

- Study each Context Card.
- Ask a question that uses one of the Vocabulary words.

5 earn

These students are trying to earn enough to help buy new library books.

6 figure

Many schools figure out ways to reuse paper instead of throwing it away.

7 block

Neighbors keep this city block pleasant by having a cleanup day each month.

8 spreading

With floodwaters spreading, people had to pitch in and stack sandbags.

Background

✓ TARGET VOCABULARY **Community Helpers** Each year, millions of children figure out ways to raise money for people who can't afford the things they need. Some children have block parties, or neighborhood street fairs. Others earn money by selling lemonade or washing cars. Store owners can be contacted and asked to get customers to donate, or give money to help. Spreading the word is important, too, so make plenty of signs and fliers.

Ways you can raise money

Ways you can get the word out

Ways you can get others to help

Comprehension

✔️ **TARGET SKILL**   **Understanding Characters**

In *Destiny's Gift*, Destiny and Mrs. Wade act like real people. What they say and do are clues to their thoughts, feelings, and motives, or reasons for their actions. On a chart like this one, list story details, your own experiences, and your ideas about why the characters act as they do.

Details About the Character	My Experience	What I Think

✔️ **TARGET STRATEGY**   **Analyze/Evaluate**

As you read, analyze and evaluate what Destiny and Mrs. Wade say and do. This will help you decide on the characters' motives and learn more about what they are like.

Main Selection

TARGET VOCABULARY

afford	earn
customers	figure
contacted	block
raise	spreading

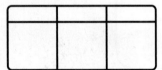
TARGET SKILL

Understanding Characters
Tell why characters act as they do.

TARGET STRATEGY

Analyze/Evaluate Think about what you read. Then form an opinion about it.

GENRE
Realistic fiction is a story with events that could happen in real life.

Natasha Anastasia Tarpley

Natasha Tarpley remembers being very shy as a young girl. "Reading for me was a way to escape into whole other worlds," she says. Some of her favorite authors were Judy Blume, Beverly Cleary, and Laura Ingalls Wilder.

MEET THE ILLUSTRATOR
Adjoa J. Burrowes

To make her illustrations look three-dimensional, Adjoa J. Burrowes cuts out each part of a scene separately. Then she pastes the individual pieces of heavy paper on top of each other. "It makes it almost look like it's jumping out from the page," she says.

Destiny's Gift

by
Natasha Anastasia Tarpley

illustrated by
Adjoa J. Burrowes

Essential Question

What clues in a story tell you about the characters?

My favorite place in the world was Mrs. Wade's bookstore, across the street from my house. Mrs. Wade knew everything there was to know about words, and I loved words!

I went over to Mrs. Wade's every Tuesday and Saturday. As soon as I walked into the store, the wind chimes above the door tinkled a special hello.

"Hey there, Destiny!" Mrs. Wade would call out, and stop whatever she was doing to give me a big hug. She smelled like flowers and peppermint and had long, silver dreadlocks that fell to her waist.

"What's the word?" Mrs. Wade would ask.

"Let's go find out," I would say.

We'd rush over to the big, thick dictionary Mrs. Wade kept on a pedestal in the store. I'd close my eyes, open the dictionary, and point.

Whatever word my finger landed on was our word for the day. Mrs. Wade always helped me with words I didn't understand. We sounded out each word and picked it apart like a puzzle, until I knew all there was to know about the word.

I wrote down everything in my notebook, which I carried everywhere I went.

When I wasn't writing words, I was reading them—
gobbling them up from the pages of books as if they were
candy. Mrs. Wade always gave me new books to read. She even
introduced me to real authors who came to read their books at
her store. I liked to talk to them because they loved words just
like I did.

That's how I decided I wanted to become a writer when
I grew up.

On Saturdays Mama and Daddy let me stay at Mrs. Wade's until closing. I helped Mrs. Wade around the store. I watered the plants and fluffed the big, comfy pillows where people could curl up and read on the floor.

Then Mrs. Wade and I would put the new books on the shelves. Sometimes I'd open a book, stick my nose in between the pages, and take a big whiff. It smelled like ink and grass and the old clothes in my granny's closet. The crisp paper felt like autumn leaves between my fingers.

The part I liked best about these Saturdays was the end of the day, after all the customers had gone. Mrs. Wade would set up a tray with peppermint tea and butter cookies, the kind with a hole in the middle. We would drink our tea and pretend the butter cookies were diamond rings around our fingers.

Then I would read to Mrs. Wade from my notebook. She'd listen to my stories and poems with her eyes closed. I'd imagine I was a famous author, reading to a room full of people. Sometimes, after I finished reading, Mrs. Wade would open her eyes and say, "Words are a very powerful gift."

I wasn't sure what she meant, but I felt very important indeed!

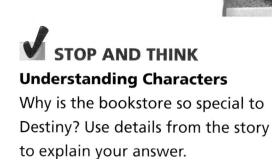

✔️ **STOP AND THINK**

Understanding Characters
Why is the bookstore so special to Destiny? Use details from the story to explain your answer.

Then one Saturday everything was different when I got to Mrs. Wade's store. Instead of talking to her customers or unpacking new books as usual, Mrs. Wade was reading a letter and looking very sad. She put away the letter and smiled when she saw me, but I could tell she wasn't her usual cheerful self.

Later, while we had our tea, Mrs. Wade told me what was wrong. She took my hands in hers, and we sat with our knees touching.

"Have you ever had a really tough assignment in school, but no matter how hard you try you just can't seem to figure it out?" she asked.

I nodded. Math problems were always like that for me.

STOP AND THINK
Author's Craft How does the author create a serious mood and hint that Mrs. Wade has sad news to share with Destiny?

"Well, I've been trying for a long time to figure out a way to keep the bookstore open, but I haven't had much luck," Mrs. Wade said, sighing. "My landlord is raising my rent, and I can't afford to pay the new amount. I may have to close the store." Mrs. Wade sighed again, and I thought I saw a small tear in the corner of her eye.

My heart froze midbeat. Close? No! I couldn't believe it.

"Why? Why do you have to close the store?" I asked, my voice shaking.

"I need to earn more money in order to pay the higher rent, and there just aren't enough customers for that," Mrs. Wade said.

"We can get more!" I shouted.

"We'll see." Mrs. Wade smiled a sad smile. "We'll see."

When I got home, I told Mama and Daddy about
Mrs. Wade's store. I cried so hard, I didn't think I'd ever stop.

Mama and Daddy wrapped me in their arms.

"I know how much the store means to you," Mama said,
stroking my hair.

"Maybe there's something we can do to help," said Daddy.

Mama and Daddy got on the telephone and called all
our neighbors. The next day everybody on our block came
to our house to talk about what we could do to save
Mrs. Wade's store.

The following Saturday, all the kids in the neighborhood passed out fliers to get folks to come to Mrs. Wade's bookstore. The grown-ups contacted the local TV news stations and newspapers and called Mrs. Wade's landlord to ask him to lower her rent so the store could stay open.

On Sunday we made signs that said "Save Our Store" and then marched around the neighborhood. It felt like being in a parade.

The next Saturday we had a huge block party to raise money. There was singing and dancing and tables full of good food. I helped Mrs. Wade at her table, and we sold boxes and boxes of books.

I had so much fun, I almost forgot to feel sad. Almost.

✓ **STOP AND THINK**

Analyze/Evaluate Which idea for saving the store do you think will be the most successful? Why?

TEKS 3.2A

Even with all the signs and the fliers and the block party,
I still wanted to do something special for Mrs. Wade. I wanted
to give her a gift that would be just from me.

I thought and thought, but couldn't come up with any ideas.

"What're you thinking so hard about?" Mama asked.

"I want to make a special gift for Mrs. Wade, but I can't think of anything," I said.

"Well, why don't you close your eyes and take a deep breath," Mama said. "Then remember all the good times you had with Mrs. Wade at the bookstore. I'm sure you'll come up with something."

I closed my eyes and followed Mama's suggestion.
Suddenly I had an idea! I jumped up, got out a new notebook,
and started to write.

I wrote down everything I loved about Mrs. Wade's store,
from the sound of the wind chimes hanging on the door to the
smell of the brand-new books and Mrs. Wade's peppermint tea.

I wrote all afternoon and all evening long. Mama and
Daddy even let me write during dinner.

The next morning I finished writing and ran over to Mrs. Wade's store at its usual opening time. But when I got there, the store was closed!

My heart pounded with fear as I peeked through the front window. Could Mrs. Wade have closed the store without telling me?

I was about to go home to tell Mama and Daddy when I heard Mrs. Wade's voice.

"Destiny, here I am!" Mrs. Wade called from her stoop next door.

"Why isn't the store open?" I asked.

"I just needed some time to think," Mrs. Wade said.

"Will you have to close the store forever?" I whispered.

"I hope not, but I'm just not sure, Destiny," Mrs. Wade said sadly. "It's hard to know if customers will keep coming back."

I didn't know what to say. Then I remembered my notebook.

"I have a present for you," I said and handed the notebook to Mrs. Wade. Her eyes lit up with surprise when she opened it and saw: "Mrs. Wade's Bookstore, by Destiny Crawford."

"Why don't you read it to me?" Mrs. Wade asked, a big smile spreading across her face.

I read every word as Mrs. Wade listened with her eyes closed.

When I finished, Mrs. Wade gave me a big, long hug.

"Destiny, this is the best present anyone has ever given me," she said, beaming. "Words are a powerful gift, indeed."

That time I knew exactly what she meant.

Mrs. Wade and I don't know if the store will close, but until then we are going to keep reading and writing and gobbling up all the words we can!

1. Which word on page 88 means the opposite of the word spend?

   ⬭ afford

   ⬭ close

   ⬭ pay

   ⬭ earn

   TEKS 3.4C

2. 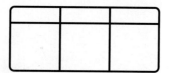 **TARGET SKILL** **Understanding Characters**

   How does Mrs. Wade's mood change after she opens Destiny's gift? Use a chart like this one to record story details that help you figure out how she is feeling. **TEKS** 3.8B

3. **TARGET STRATEGY** **Analyze/Evaluate**

   Do you believe the bookstore will be saved? Give examples from the story to explain your answer. **ELPS** 4K

4. **Oral Language** Work in a small group. Take turns narrating, or telling, the beginning, middle, and end of the story. Include specific details that explain why characters think, feel, and act as they do. **TEKS** 3.8A; **ELPS** 3H

 TEKS 3.4C identify/use antonyms/synonyms/homographs/homophones; **3.8A** sequence/summarize main events/influence on future events; **3.8B** describe characters' relationships/changes; **ELPS** 3H narrate/describe/explain with detail; **4K** employ analytical skills to demonstrate comprehension

Social Studies

GENRE

Informational text gives factual information about a topic. This is a social studies article. After you read, tell a partner what the topic is. Share facts and details you learned about this topic.

TEXT FOCUS

A **map** is a drawing of an area such as a neighborhood, town, or state.

 TEKS **3.2B** ask questions/clarify/locate facts/details/use text evidence; **ELPS** **3H** narrate/describe/explain with detail

Kids
Making a Difference
By Jeremy Stone

National and Global Youth Services Day began in 1988. Celebration of this day is spreading around the world.

A Day to Help

Would you like the chance to figure out fun ways to improve your school, block, or town? Put your ideas into action in April on National and Global Youth Services Day!

On this day, kids across the country work to make their communities safer and cleaner, or to help others. Some collect food for people who can't afford it. Others raise money for local charities. They earn this money by holding fundraisers or getting customers at local shops to make donations.

Texas Kids Help Out

On Youth Service Day in Arlington, Texas, more than 800 kids help their community. Some visit nursing homes. Others plant flowers. In historic Arlington Cemetery, youth baseball teams pick up trash. The cemetery is next to the teams' ball fields.

After a busy day, it's party time in Vandergriff Park! The hard-working kids gather there to celebrate.

Helping with Art

One group of artists in San Francisco is helping children make their city beautiful all year round. Adult artists from a group called Kids Serve go to schools around the city. The artists help students plan special murals. The murals are usually about topics the children are studying in class.

Once the mural is planned, the children work together to create the mural in a public area. When it is done, neighbors are contacted and invited to celebrate and enjoy the mural.

This mural celebrates California's Civil Rights leaders.

Making Connections

Text to Self

Talk About Making a Difference Kids help out in *Destiny's Gift* and "Kids Making a Difference." Take turns telling about a time you helped your community. Listen carefully as others speak. Make sure you understand the general meaning and context of what you hear.

Text to Text

Make a Poster Work in a small group. Review the ways Mrs. Wade's friends helped the bookstore in *Destiny's Gift* and the community projects in "Kids Making a Difference." Then think of a way your group could improve the neighborhood. Make a poster to show your idea.

Text to World

Connect to Poetry Mrs. Wade's bookstore was important to Destiny and her neighbors. Write a poem about a bookstore or library you know. Share it with the class.

TEKS **3.18B** write poems that convey sensory details; **3.29A** listen/ask questions/make comments; **3.30** speak coherently/effectively about topics; **3.31** participate in discussions/build on others' ideas; **RC-3(F)** make connections between texts; **ELPS 2G** understand meaning/main points/details of spoken language; **3E** share information in cooperative learning interactions

Grammar

Sentence Fragments and Run-ons A sentence is a group of words that tells a complete thought. It has a subject and a predicate. A **sentence fragment** is missing its subject or predicate. Two or more sentences that run together are called **run-on sentences**.

Academic Language

sentence fragment

run-on sentence

Sentence Fragment	Complete Sentence
My best friend.	My best friend likes to read.
Owns the bookstore.	Mr. Owen owns the bookstore.

Run-on Sentence	Correct Sentences
Do you like to read it is fun.	Do you like to read? It is fun.
Ty likes books, he buys a lot.	Ty likes books. He buys a lot.

 **Write each sentence fragment as a complete sentence.**

❶ Went to the bookstore.

❷ His new book.

Write two sentences for each run-on sentence.

❸ Will you go to the library with me I'm leaving now.

❹ Dad bought a book, he read it to me.

Sentence Fluency Too many short sentences make writing sound choppy. Good writers combine short, choppy sentences that have ideas that go together into one compound sentence. Use a comma and the conjunction *and*, *or*, or *but* to combine two sentences.

Short, Choppy Sentences

We lined up at the bookstore.

The author signed our books.

Longer, Smoother Sentence

We lined up at the bookstore, and the author signed our books.

Connect Grammar to Writing

As you revise your personal narrative, look for ways to combine choppy sentences. You may be able to make them into a compound sentence using a conjunction.

Write to Narrate

✓ **Voice** In *Destiny's Gift*, when Mrs. Wade says that words are powerful, Destiny tells us her thoughts and feelings: "I wasn't sure what she meant, but I felt very important indeed!" In your **personal narrative** paragraph, you can do the same.

Callie wrote about the time she helped a neighbor. Later, she added some of her thoughts and feelings.

Writing Traits Checklist

✓ **Ideas**
Did I use details that help readers picture the events?

✓ **Organization**
Did I tell the events in order?

✓ **Word Choice**
Did I use clear, vivid words?

✓ **Voice**
Did I share what I thought and felt?

✓ **Sentence Fluency**
Did I write complete sentences?

✓ **Conventions**
Did I leave space between each word in my sentences?

Revised Draft

One day I asked my neighbor Mr. Mazur where his cat was. He said, "I had an operation. Chester has to stay at a shelter till I can take care of him again." Then I had an idea. I asked Mom if I could take care of Chester so Mr. Mazur could keep him at home.

> I felt so sad for Mr. Mazur and for myself, too, because I love Chester!

108

Mr. Mazur, Chester, and Me

by Callie Perakis

One day I asked my neighbor Mr. Mazur where his cat was. He said, "I had an operation. Chester has to stay at a shelter till I can take care of him again." I felt so sad for Mr. Mazur and for myself, too, because I love Chester! Then I had an idea. I asked Mom if I could take care of Chester so Mr. Mazur could keep him at home. When she said yes, I yelled, "Yippee!" So all summer, I went over to Mr. Mazur's every day. I gave Chester his food and water. Then I talked with Mr. Mazur and played with Chester. When I went home, I felt good inside because I knew Mr. Mazur would not be lonely.

> I added thoughts and feelings. I also made sure to write complete sentences.

Reading as a Writer

Which sentences tell you how Callie felt? Where can you add your thoughts and feelings in your paper?

✔ **TARGET VOCABULARY**

crew

tide

cling

balancing

foggy

disappears

stretch

excitement

Vocabulary Reader   Context Cards

 ELPS 4D use prereading supports to comprehend texts

Vocabulary in Context

1 crew

A crew, or group of workers, has just started to build a new bridge.

2 tide

When the sea falls at low tide, it's a good time to make repairs.

3 cling

Painters cling to the bridge when the wind blows. They hold on tightly!

4 balancing

Workers must be good at balancing on high, thin beams without falling.

- Study each Context Card.
- Discuss one picture. Use a different Vocabulary word from the one in the card.

5 foggy

On foggy days, thick mist makes it hard to see. Drivers must go slowly.

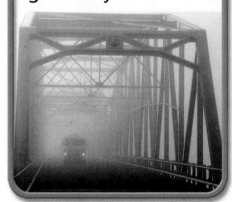

6 disappears

Half of the bridge disappears in this photo. It seems to vanish in the fog.

7 stretch

Bridges may stretch over land or run across large bodies of water.

8 excitement

Marathon runners feel excitement as they cross this bridge. It is a thrill!

Background

Building Bridges What does it take to build a mile-long suspension bridge? The crew must work as a team to stretch giant steel cables from high towers. These cables hold the roadway in place and make it strong. Balancing high above a rushing tide is dangerous work. In foggy weather, workers struggle to see as they cling to the rising bridge. The roadway below disappears in the mist. However, excitement builds as the bridge is finally done.

The Brooklyn Bridge, the first steel-wire suspension bridge in the world, was completed in 1883. It took nearly fourteen years to build!

Comprehension

✔ TARGET SKILL Compare and Contrast

As you read *Pop's Bridge*, find out how a boy compares his pop's job to that of his friend's father. What is the same about the workers' skills and abilities? What is different? Use a Venn diagram like this one to compare story details.

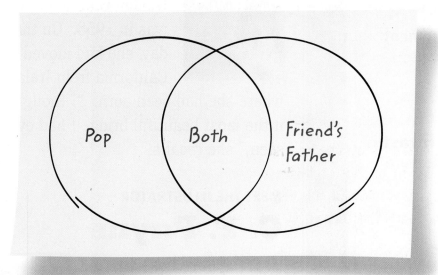

Pop   Both   Friend's Father

✔ TARGET STRATEGY Infer/Predict

Compare and contrast details in *Pop's Bridge*. Then use your ideas to infer, or figure out, more about what it takes to build a bridge. What does the boy learn from watching the Golden Gate Bridge being built?

Main Selection

✔ TARGET VOCABULARY

crew	foggy
tide	disappears
cling	stretch
balancing	excitement

✔ TARGET SKILL

Compare and Contrast
Tell how details or ideas are alike and different.

✔ TARGET STRATEGY

Infer/Predict Use clues to figure out more about the selection.

GENRE

Historical fiction is a story that takes place in a real period of history.

MEET THE AUTHOR

Eve Bunting

The first time Eve Bunting ever saw the Golden Gate Bridge was in 1958. On that day, she had moved to California from Ireland, where she had been born. "I thought it the most beautiful bridge I had ever seen," she recalls.

MEET THE ILLUSTRATOR

C. F. Payne

C. F. Payne, whose initials stand for Chris Fox, is famous for drawing people with very large heads, noses, and ears. Sometimes Payne uses friends as models for his drawings, as he did in *Pop's Bridge*.

POP'S BRIDGE

by Eve Bunting • illustrated by C. F. Payne

Essential Question

How can two bridges be alike and different?

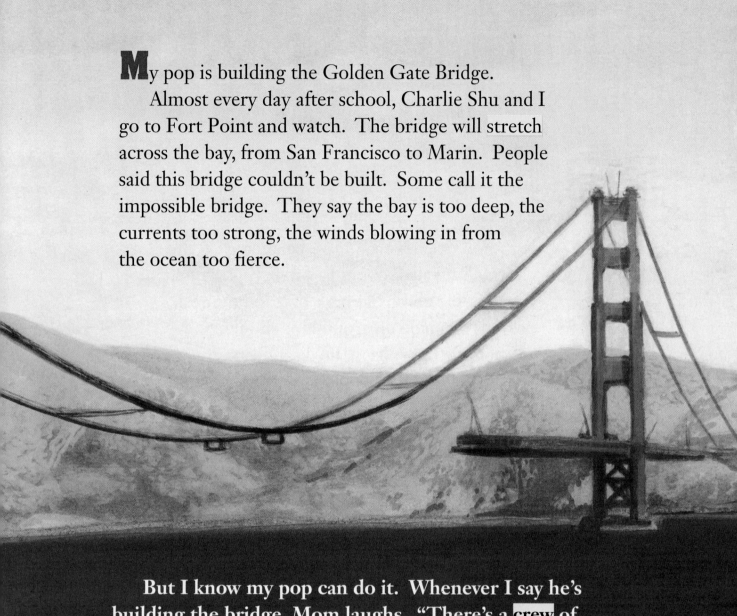

My pop is building the Golden Gate Bridge.

Almost every day after school, Charlie Shu and I go to Fort Point and watch. The bridge will stretch across the bay, from San Francisco to Marin. People said this bridge couldn't be built. Some call it the impossible bridge. They say the bay is too deep, the currents too strong, the winds blowing in from the ocean too fierce.

But I know my pop can do it. Whenever I say he's building the bridge, Mom laughs. "There's a crew of more than a thousand men working on that bridge, Robert. Including Charlie's dad," she reminds me. I know that, but I just shrug.

To me, it's Pop's bridge.

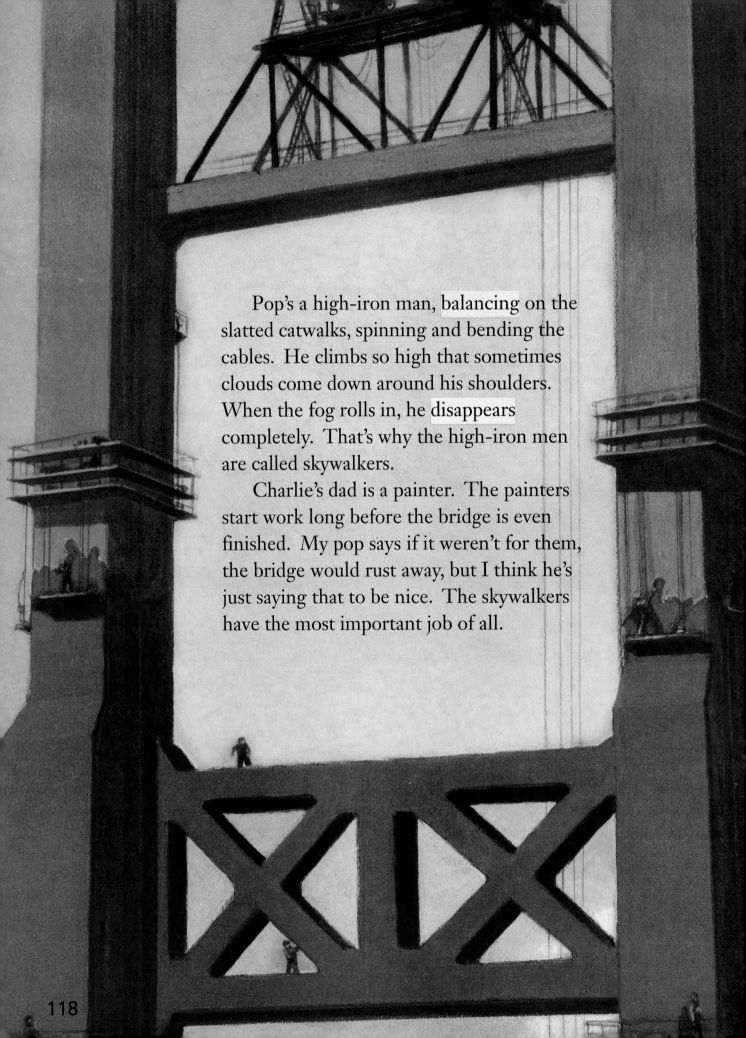

Pop's a high-iron man, balancing on the slatted catwalks, spinning and bending the cables. He climbs so high that sometimes clouds come down around his shoulders. When the fog rolls in, he disappears completely. That's why the high-iron men are called skywalkers.

Charlie's dad is a painter. The painters start work long before the bridge is even finished. My pop says if it weren't for them, the bridge would rust away, but I think he's just saying that to be nice. The skywalkers have the most important job of all.

At Fort Point I look for Pop through the binoculars Mom lends me. The workers look alike in their overalls and swabbie hats, but I can always find my pop because of the red kerchief he ties at his throat. It's our own scarlet signal.

I don't worry much about him on days when the sun sparkles on the water, when sailboats skim below. It's so beautiful I can forget that it's dangerous, too. But when the wind blows through the Golden Gate, the men cling to the girders like caterpillars on a branch. On foggy days my hands sweat on the binoculars. *Where is he?* When I find him, I try not to look away, as though the force of my eyes can keep him from falling.

✔ **STOP AND THINK**

Compare and Contrast What is the same about Robert's father and Charlie's father? What is different?

TEKS 3.2B

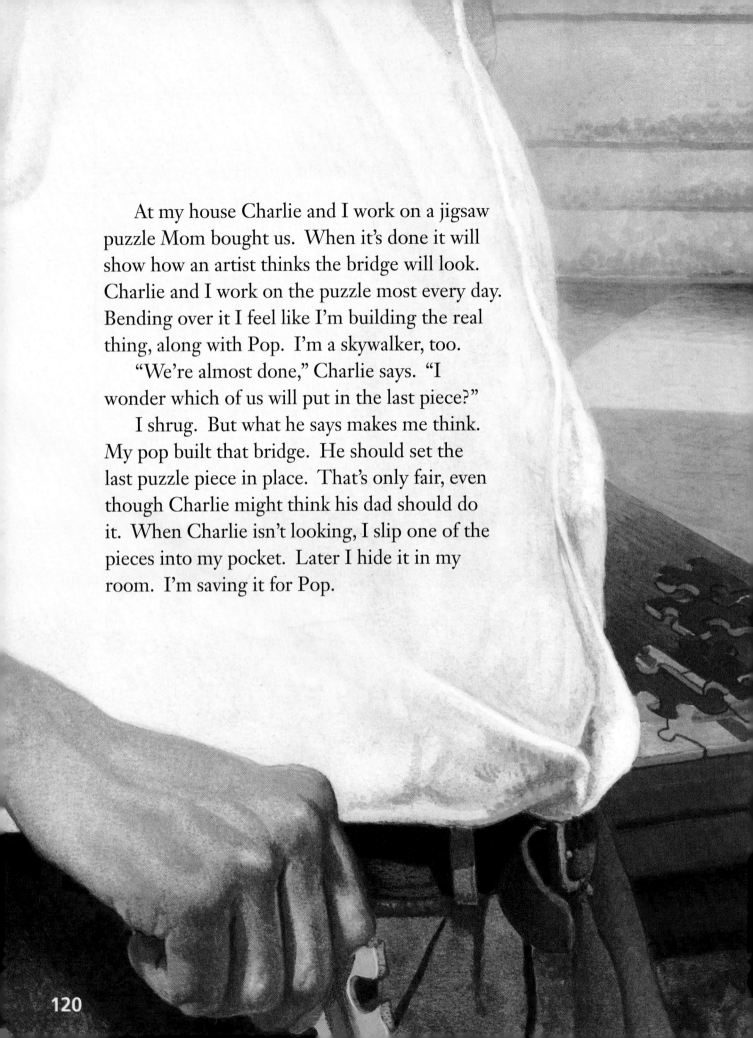

At my house Charlie and I work on a jigsaw puzzle Mom bought us. When it's done it will show how an artist thinks the bridge will look. Charlie and I work on the puzzle most every day. Bending over it I feel like I'm building the real thing, along with Pop. I'm a skywalker, too.

"We're almost done," Charlie says. "I wonder which of us will put in the last piece?"

I shrug. But what he says makes me think. My pop built that bridge. He should set the last puzzle piece in place. That's only fair, even though Charlie might think his dad should do it. When Charlie isn't looking, I slip one of the pieces into my pocket. Later I hide it in my room. I'm saving it for Pop.

The "impossible bridge" is nearly finished.
One evening Mom and Pop and I walk down to
Fort Point. The bridge hangs between stars and sea.
   "It's like a giant harp," my pop says. "A harp for
the angels to play." I look up at him, and I can tell
this wasn't just a job to my pop. He loves the bridge.

STOP AND THINK

Author's Craft What does the author compare the bridge to on this page? What does it tell you about how the bridge looks?
TEKS 3.10; **ELPS** 4J

123

In San Francisco there is great excitement. Everyone is waiting for opening day.

Charlie and I have watched nearly every bit of the bridge go up. We saw the two spans come together from opposite directions. We saw them meet. We saw the roadway go in. And my pop did it. No one can be as proud as I am. Not even Charlie. After all, my dad is a skywalker.

And then one day, something terrible happens. Charlie and I are watching as the scaffolding pulls away from the bridge. There's a noise like a train wreck as the scaffolding crashes down into the safety net. The net tears loose, and men go with it into the swirling tide.

I can't breathe. I can't think.

But then I look hard through the binoculars and see Pop still on the bridge, his red kerchief whipping. "Pop!" I whisper in relief. Beside me Charlie is screaming, "Where's my dad? Where's my dad?"

We had seen him working close to that scaffolding. I can't see him now.

"We'll find him," I promise. "We have to." I sweep the binoculars up and down the bridge cables, looking at every painter hanging high on his Jacob's ladder or swinging in a bosun's chair, like a knot on a rope.

"Be there, Mr. Shu," I plead, and then spot him. "Over by that cross girder!" I yell. Charlie fumbles for the binoculars. I help him. He looks where I point.

"He's there! He's safe!" Charlie gasps.

The next day we find out that only two of the twelve men in the water were saved.

I think and think about that day. At night, half asleep, I see the bridge shake. I hear the crash. One of those men in the water could have been Pop. Or Charlie's dad.

I finally understand, and I feel ashamed. Equal work, equal danger, for skywalkers *and* for painters.

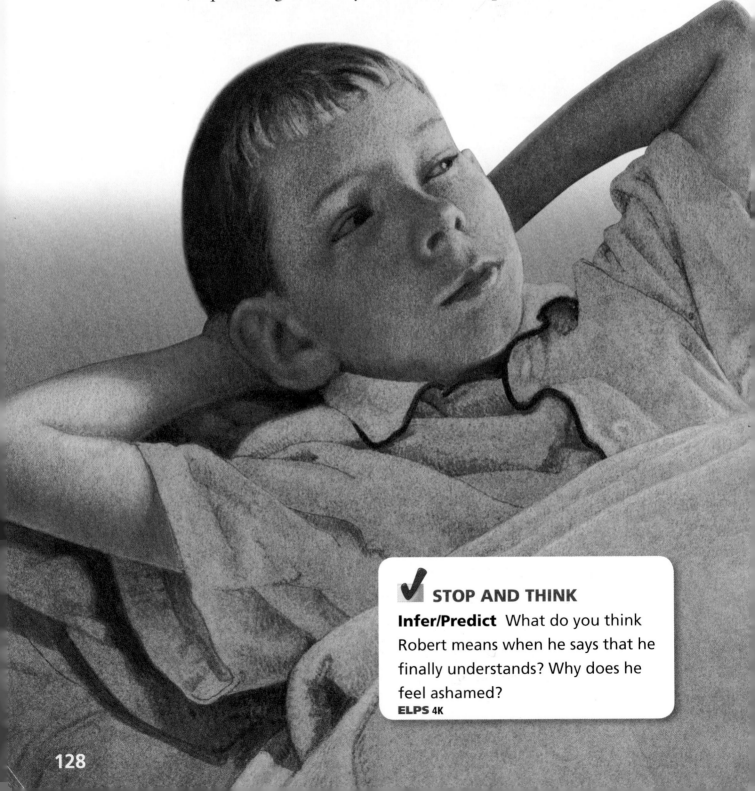

✔️ **STOP AND THINK**

Infer/Predict What do you think Robert means when he says that he finally understands? Why does he feel ashamed?
ELPS 4K

The work goes on. A new safety net is put in place.
Pop says there's less talking and joking now among the men.
There's a remembering.

But the bridge must be finished. And at last it is.
We watch through Mom's binoculars as the golden spike
is drilled in at the center of the main span. Now the
celebration can begin.

On opening day no cars are allowed. Thousands of people walk and dance and roller-skate across the bridge, including us. I wear Pop's kerchief around my neck. There's a man riding a unicycle. There's another on stilts. Navy biplanes fly above the great steel towers. Battleships and cruisers sail below the bridge and into San Francisco Bay. Wind strums its music through the stretch of the cables, and I think of my pop's harp.

That night our family has our own party with Charlie and his dad. There's stewed chicken and a Chinese noodle dish Charlie's dad made and a snickerdoodle pie.

The jigsaw puzzle sits on the coffee table with a gap in the middle. "I've searched and searched for that missing piece," my mother says.

"A good thing we didn't leave our bridge with a space like that," Mr. Shu says.

Pop chuckles. "We'd be working still."

It's time.

I slip upstairs to get the hidden puzzle piece, then find the scissors and cut the piece carefully in half. I go back down and put a half piece in Mr. Shu's hand and the other in my pop's. "Finish it," I say. "It's your bridge. It belongs to both of you."

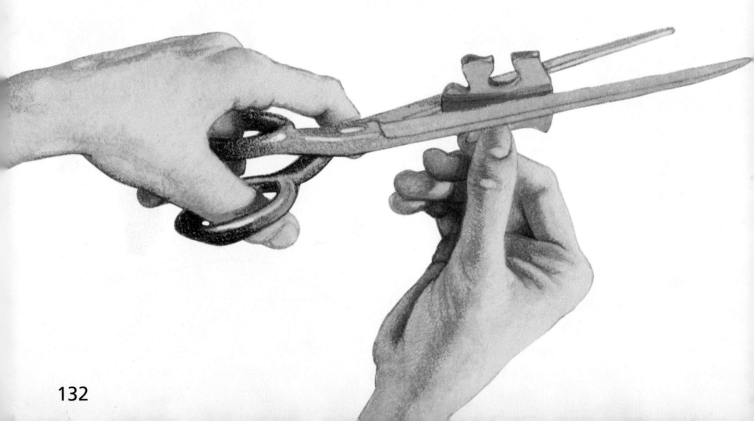

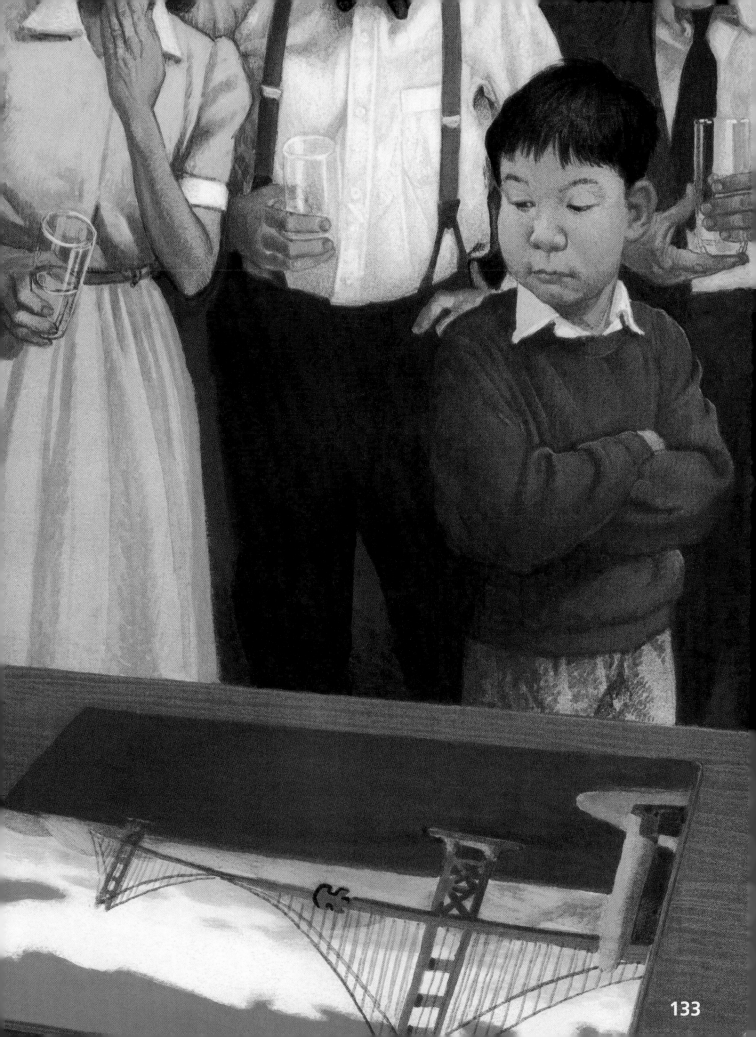

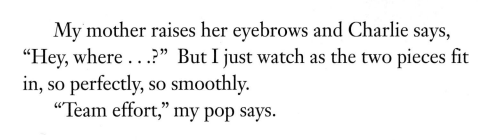

My mother raises her eyebrows and Charlie says,
"Hey, where . . . ?" But I just watch as the two pieces fit
in, so perfectly, so smoothly.

"Team effort," my pop says.

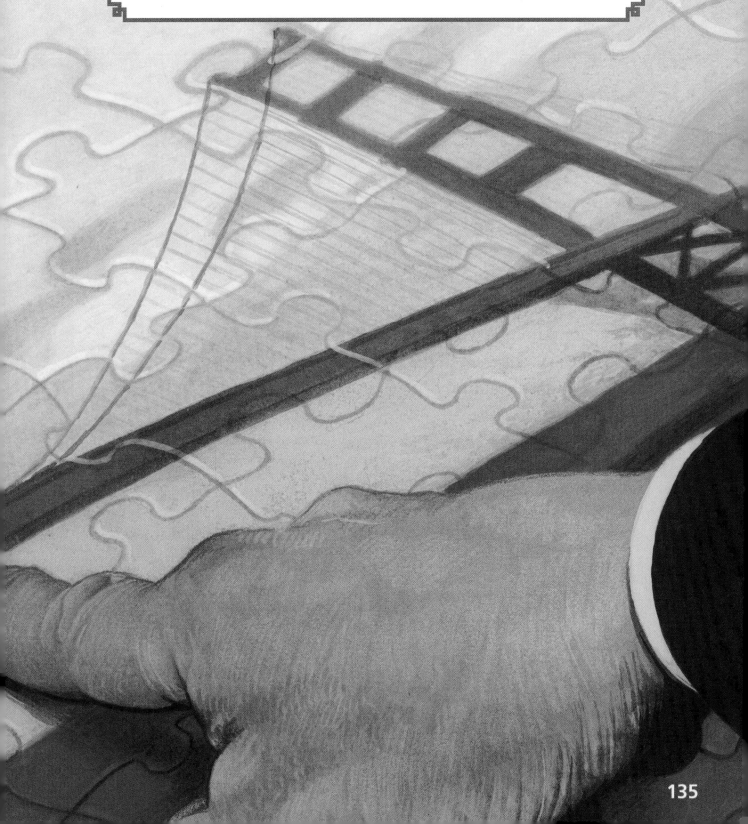

We raise our glasses of sarsaparilla to celebrate the laborers and riveters, the carpenters and the painters and the skywalkers. All the men who worked together to build the most beautiful bridge in the world.

Your Turn

1. Which words from page 117 help the reader understand the meaning of <u>crew</u>?

   ⬭ pop can do it

   ⬭ building the bridge

   ⬭ a thousand men

   ⬭ she reminds me

   ELPS 1F

2. 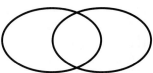✔ **TARGET SKILL** **Compare and Contrast**
   Use a Venn diagram like this one to compare and contrast Robert's character at the beginning and the end of the story. How does he change? **TEKS 3.8B**

3. ✔ **TARGET STRATEGY** **Infer/Predict**
   Do you think Charlie understands what happened to the missing puzzle piece? Do you think his friendship with Robert will change now that he knows the truth? **TEKS 3.8B; ELPS 4J**

4. **Oral Language** Work in a group. Take turns placing story events shown on the Retelling Cards in order. **TEKS 3.8A**

   Retelling Cards

 TEKS **3.8A** sequence/summarize main events/influence on future events; **3.8B** describe characters' relationships/changes; **ELPS 1F** use accessible language to learn new language; **4J** employ inferential skills to demonstrate comprehension

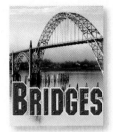

BRIDGES

GENRE

Informational text gives factual information about a topic. This is a science text. What is the topic? How do you know?

Preview the selection before you read. Look at the photos, captions, headings, and diagram, and predict what you might learn about the topic. After you read, see if your predictions were correct.

TEXT FOCUS

A **diagram** is a drawing that shows how something works.

TEKS **3.2A** use ideas to make/confirm predictions; **3.12** identify topic/author's purpose; **3.13D** use text features to locate information/make and verify predictions; **3.15B** locate/use graphic features of text

BRIDGES

by Matthew Danzeris

Bridges help people get from place to place. They join communities. They stretch across waterways and the swirling tide. They take us over roadways and landforms.

People have been building bridges for thousands of years. They think about how long the bridge must be. They think about what the bridge will cost. Then they decide what kind of bridge to build.

The arch bridge shown here is the Bayonne Bridge, which goes from New Jersey to New York. Workers finished building it in 1931.

Arch Bridge

An arch bridge uses sturdy curved structures called arches. The arches rest on strong supports called abutments. Abutments are set firmly in the solid ground below the water.

Beam Bridge

The beam bridge is the simplest kind of bridge for a crew to build. It costs the least, too!

A beam bridge has a beam. It lies across supports called piers. The piers must be close enough together to give the beam strength. That way, the roadway won't bend or sag too much when traffic crosses it. Most beam bridges are less than 250 feet long.

Florida's Rickenbacker Causeway Bridge is a beam bridge. It connects the city of Miami to the island of Key Biscayne.

Suspension Bridge

A suspension bridge can stretch as far as 7,000 feet. That's more than a mile! On a suspension bridge, the roadway hangs from cables. The cables rest on top of towers. At each end of the bridge, an anchorage holds the cables in place.

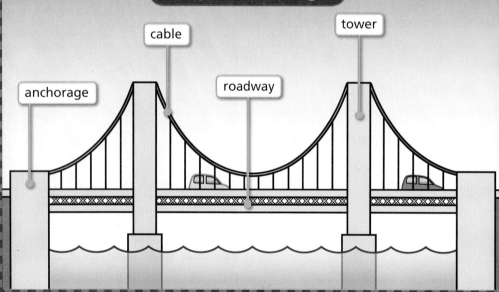

Suspension Bridge

cable

tower

roadway

anchorage

Building Bridges

A large crew of workers builds most bridges. The work is dangerous. Workers wear harnesses to stay safe when they are balancing up high. Strong winds and foggy weather make the work even more dangerous. Builders cling to the bridge. When at last the work is done, excitement grips everyone. A ceremony may be held to celebrate.

St. John's Bridge, in Portland, Oregon, is a suspension bridge. When the fog is heavy, the bridge practically disappears!

Making Connections

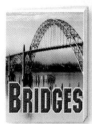

Text to Self — ELPS 5G

Write about Work In *Pop's Bridge*, Robert tells about being both proud of and worried about his father's job. Write a paragraph that tells about the job one of your family members does and how you feel about it.

Text to Text — ELPS 4G

Compare Bridges How is a suspension bridge, like the one Robert's father helped build, different from a beam bridge? Make and label a drawing or make a list to show two ways they are different.

Text to World — TEKS 3.26A(ii); ELPS 4K

Connect to Math Use the Internet or another source to find the lengths of the Golden Gate, Verrazano Narrows, and Akashi Kaikyo bridges. Then make a bar graph to compare the lengths of these suspension bridges.

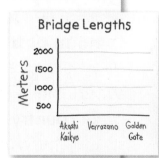

Bridge Lengths — Meters: 2000, 1500, 1000, 500 — Akashi Kaikyo, Verrazano, Golden Gate

TEKS 3.26A(ii) collect information from experts/reference texts/online searches; **ELPS 4G** demonstrate comprehension through shared reading/retelling/responding/note-taking; **4K** employ analytical skills to demonstrate comprehension; **5G** narrate/describe/explain in writing

Grammar

Common and Proper Nouns A **noun** names a person, place, or thing. A noun that names any person, place, or thing is called a **common noun**. A noun that names a particular person, place, or thing is called a **proper noun**.

Academic Language

common noun

proper noun

Common Nouns	Proper Nouns
The bridge is long.	The Golden Gate Bridge is long.
He walked to the fort.	He walked to Fort Point.
My uncle likes to paint.	Uncle Bob likes to paint.

 **Work with a partner. Say each noun aloud. Identify each noun as a common noun or a proper noun.**

1. Ash Road

2. country

3. Mexico

4. David Robinson

5. teacher

6. holiday

Word Choice Use exact nouns to make your writing clearer and more interesting. Exact nouns help your readers picture what you are writing about.

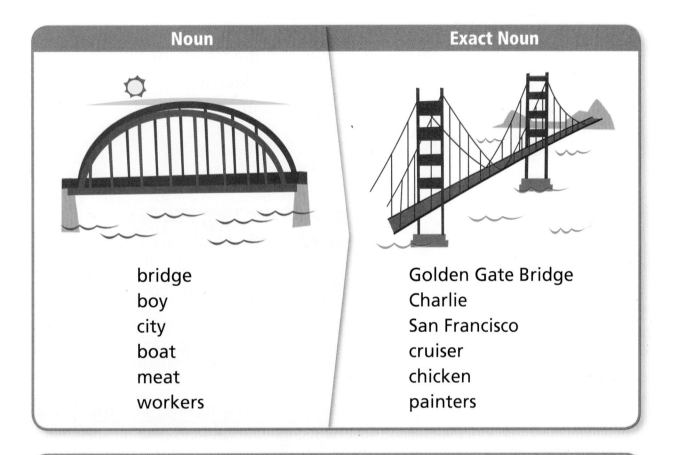

Noun	Exact Noun
bridge	Golden Gate Bridge
boy	Charlie
city	San Francisco
boat	cruiser
meat	chicken
workers	painters

Less Exact Noun: The bridge is painted the color of rust, not gold.

More Exact Noun: The Golden Gate Bridge is painted the color of rust, not gold.

Connect Grammar to Writing

As you revise your personal narrative next week, think of exact nouns you can use. Exact nouns will help make your writing easy to understand.

Reading-Writing Workshop: Prewrite

Write to Narrate

☑ **Ideas** Before drafting a **personal narrative**, writers organize their ideas. Use a chart to put events in order. Then add important, interesting details about each event.

Kelly decided to write about the time she learned to swim. First, she listed ideas. Then she put them into an events chart and added more details.

Writing Process Checklist

▶ **Prewrite**

☑ Did I pick a topic I'll enjoy writing about?

☑ Will my audience like my topic?

☑ Did I write down all the main events?

☑ Did I add details to make the events more interesting?

☑ Did I put the events in order?

Draft

Revise

Edit

Publish and Share

Exploring a Topic

<u>afraid to go in deep end</u>

-everyone swam without me

-couldn't play water games

<u>brother Cal taught me to swim</u>

-treading water

-floating on back

~~-bandage fell off knee~~

<u>first time in deep end</u>

-scared – stayed near side

-wouldn't let go of Cal

-started floating on my own

Events Chart

Event: I was afraid to go in the deep end of the swimming pool.

Details: had to sit out when my friends played games

missed a lot of fun

Event: My brother Cal gave me lessons.

Details: helped me practice strokes

learned to float on back, tread water

Event: I finally swam in the deep end.

Details: scared at first, wouldn't let go of Cal

floated on my own, love deep end now

> When I organized my personal narrative, I added important, interesting details.

Reading as a Writer

Which of Kelly's details did you find most interesting? Where can you add details to your own chart?

✓ **TARGET VOCABULARY**

stands
fans
score
league
slammed
polish
style
pronounced

Vocabulary Reader   **Context Cards**

Mia and Nomar

 ELPS 4D use prereading supports to comprehend texts

Vocabulary in Context

1 stands
Peanut vendors walk up and down through the stands at a baseball game.

2 fans
Happy fans cheer when players on their favorite teams play well.

3 score
Soccer players must work together to score a goal and earn one point.

4 league
These volleyball players are in a league, or group of teams.

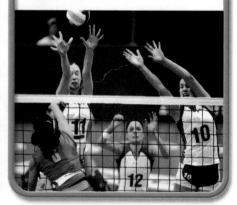

- Study each Context Card.

- Tell a story about two or more pictures, using their Vocabulary words.

5 slammed

This player slammed the puck so hard that it went straight into the net.

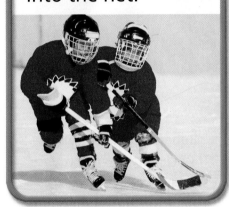

6 polish

Before bowlers play a game, they may polish the ball to remove any dust.

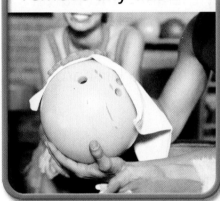

7 style

This fan has her own special style. It's a clever way to show team spirit.

8 pronounced

The announcer pronounced, or said, each player's name loudly and clearly.

Background

✔ **TARGET VOCABULARY** **Baseball Skills** Many players dream of playing Major League Baseball, but few succeed. It takes special talent. You must polish your skills for years and work every day to develop your own special style. Even then, only a small number of players make it.

It's thrilling for players to hear their names pronounced loudly by the announcer after they have slammed a home run out of the park to score a run. Hearing the cheering fans in the stands rewards all their hard work.

Roberto Clemente won 12 Gold Glove Awards for his defense as a right fielder. He also had over 3,000 hits!

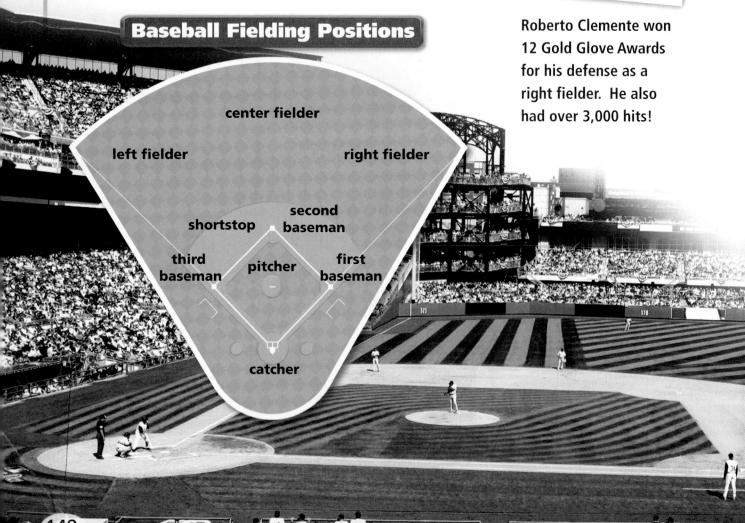

Baseball Fielding Positions

center fielder

left fielder   right fielder

second baseman

shortstop

third baseman   pitcher   first baseman

catcher

Comprehension

✓ TARGET SKILL   Cause and Effect

In *Roberto Clemente,* the author shares events from the life of his hero, Roberto Clemente. Notice which event causes other events to happen. The first event is the cause. The second event is the effect. Use a chart like this one to record causes and effects as you read.

Cause	Effect

✓ TARGET STRATEGY   Visualize

Use details the author gives about each cause and effect on your chart to help you visualize events in *Roberto Clemente.* Which words and phrases help you picture scenes from Clemente's life and baseball career?

TARGET VOCABULARY

stands	slammed
fans	polish
score	style
league	pronounced

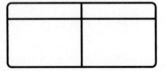
TARGET SKILL

Cause and Effect Tell how one event makes another happen and why.

TARGET STRATEGY

Visualize As you read, use selection details to picture what is happening.

GENRE

The author of a **biography** writes about another person's life. The author of an **autobiography** writes about his or her own life. Is *Roberto Clemente* a biography or an autobiography?

 TEKS 3.9 explain point of view in biography/autobiography

MEET THE AUTHOR
JONAH WINTER

Although Jonah Winter was raised in Texas, as a kid he rooted for the Pittsburgh Pirates and Roberto Clemente. "Growing up, he was my hero," Winter says. Today Winter lives in Pittsburgh, where he plays the clarinet, writes poetry, and watches baseball.

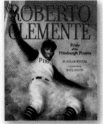

MEET THE ILLUSTRATOR
RAÚL COLÓN

Like Roberto Clemente, Raúl Colón is from Puerto Rico. While Colón is known mainly as an illustrator, his artwork is also familiar to people who ride the New York City subway. An enormous mural he created called *Primavera* (Springtime) fills a whole wall of a subway station.

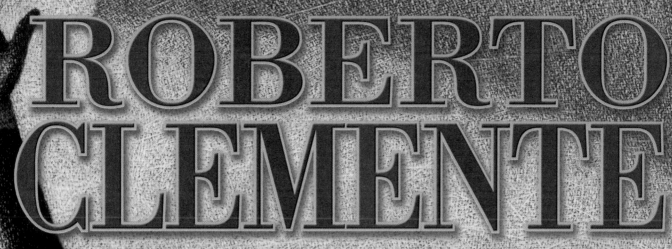

ROBERTO CLEMENTE

PRIDE OF THE PITTSBURGH PIRATES

by
JONAH WINTER

illustrated by
RAÚL COLÓN

Essential Question
What causes someone to be called a hero?

On an island called Puerto Rico,
where baseball players are as plentiful
as tropical flowers in a rain forest, there
was a boy who had very little but a fever
to play and win at baseball.

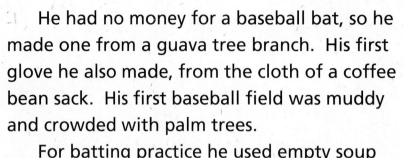

He had no money for a baseball bat, so he made one from a guava tree branch. His first glove he also made, from the cloth of a coffee bean sack. His first baseball field was muddy and crowded with palm trees.

For batting practice he used empty soup cans and hit them farther than anyone else. Soup cans turned into softballs. Softballs turned into baseballs. Little League turned into minor league turned into winter league: professional baseball in Puerto Rico.

STOP AND THINK

Author's Craft What descriptive words does the author use to help you picture Clemente's unusual bat, glove, and balls and the field where he played?

TEKS 3.10

He played so well he received an
invitation to play in . . . the major
leagues in America! What an honor!

But the young man was sent to
a steel-mill town called Pittsburgh,
Pennsylvania, where his new team, the
Pittsburgh Pirates, was in *last place*.
Now this was something very strange,
being on a losing team.

For the young Puerto Rican,
everything was strange. Instead
of palm trees, he saw smokestacks.
Instead of Spanish, he heard English.
Instead of being *somebody*, he
was nobody.

His first time at bat, he heard the announcer stumble through his Spanish name: "ROB, uh, ROE . . . BURRT, um, let's see, TOE CLUH-MAINT?" It echoed in the near-empty stands.

Roberto Clemente was his name, and this is pronounced "Roe-BEAR-toe Cleh-MEN-tay." As if to introduce himself, Roberto *smacked* the very first pitch.

But it went right up the infield . . . and into the second baseman's glove. Still, Roberto ran like lightning—and beat the throw to first base.

The Pittsburgh fans checked their scorecards. Who was this guy, "Roberto Clemente"?

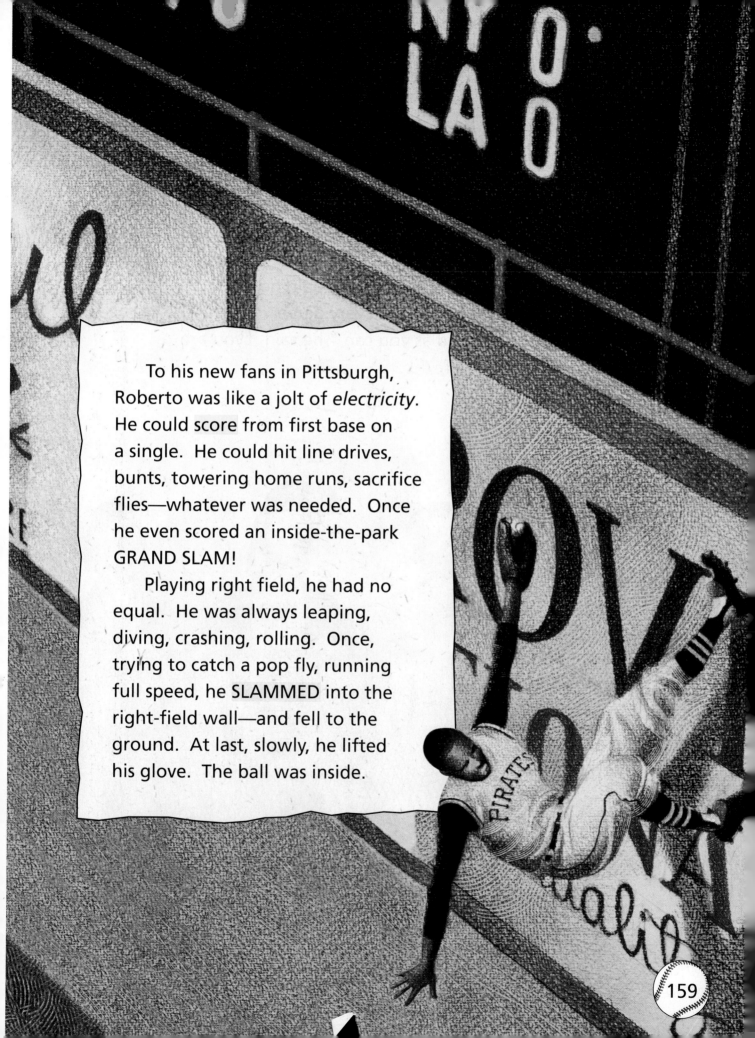

To his new fans in Pittsburgh, Roberto was like a jolt of *electricity*. He could score from first base on a single. He could hit line drives, bunts, towering home runs, sacrifice flies—whatever was needed. Once he even scored an inside-the-park GRAND SLAM!

Playing right field, he had no equal. He was always leaping, diving, crashing, rolling. Once, trying to catch a pop fly, running full speed, he SLAMMED into the right-field wall—and fell to the ground. At last, slowly, he lifted his glove. The ball was inside.

But it wasn't just how he played. He had *style*. He was *cool*.

He had this move he did with his neck before each at bat, creaking it one way, then the other. Soon kids who wanted to be just like Roberto were doing it too, twisting their necks this way and that.

Roberto did it to ease the pain he felt from playing his heart out in every game. "If you don't try as hard as you can," he said, "you are wasting your life."

Roberto tried so hard, he helped the last-place Pirates make it all the way to the World Series where they beat the mighty NEW YORK YANKEES!

After the series, down in the streets of Pittsburgh, Roberto walked alone among his fans, who were so busy celebrating, they didn't even notice him. That didn't bother Roberto. He was happy to feel lost in the crowd of a party he had helped create.

✔ **STOP AND THINK**

Cause and Effect What happens as a result of Clemente's hard work?

TEKS 3.13C

But there was something that would have made Roberto's joy a little sweeter. As much as fans loved him, the newspaper writers did not. When Roberto was in such pain he couldn't play, they called him "lazy." They mocked his Spanish accent, and when Roberto got angry, the mainly white newsmen called him a Latino "hothead."

Roberto swore he would be so good, he would *have* to get the respect he deserved. He would become the greatest all-around baseball player there ever was.

At home that Christmas, Roberto went back to the same muddy field he'd played on as a boy. In his pocket was a bag full of bottle caps that he emptied into the hands of some kids. They threw him the caps, and he hit each one again and again.

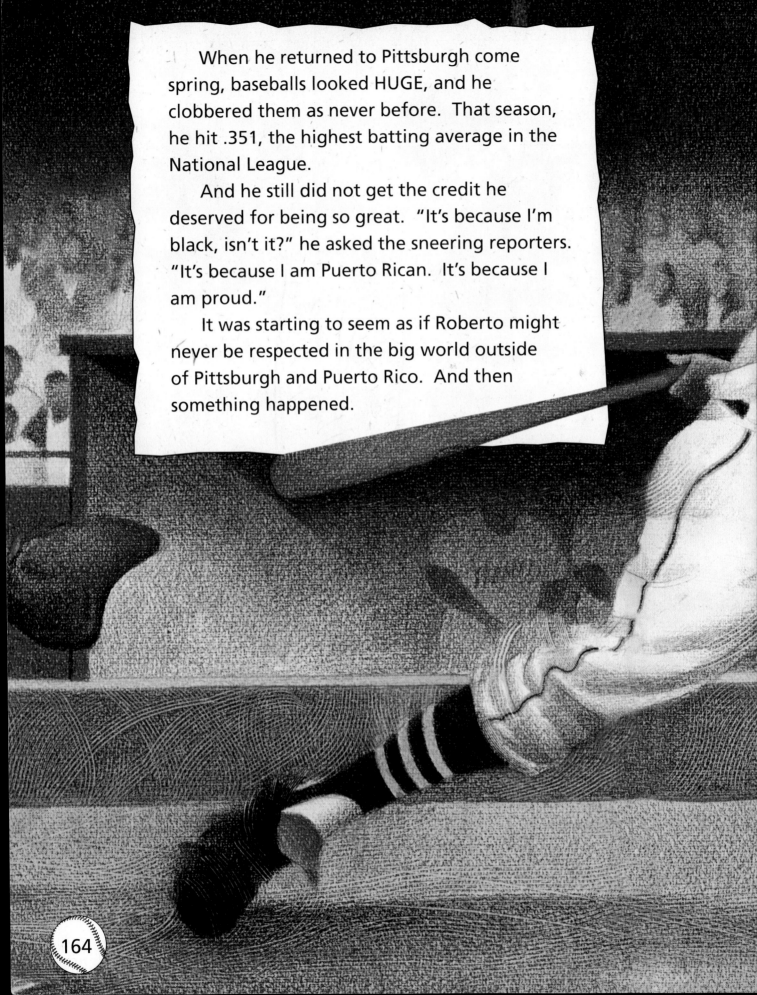

When he returned to Pittsburgh come spring, baseballs looked HUGE, and he clobbered them as never before. That season, he hit .351, the highest batting average in the National League.

And he still did not get the credit he deserved for being so great. "It's because I'm black, isn't it?" he asked the sneering reporters. "It's because I am Puerto Rican. It's because I am proud."

It was starting to seem as if Roberto might never be respected in the big world outside of Pittsburgh and Puerto Rico. And then something happened.

165

The year was 1971. The Pirates were in the World Series again, playing against the Baltimore Orioles, who were favored to win.

All around America and Puerto Rico, people sat watching on TV . . . as Roberto put on a one-man show. Stealing bases, hitting home runs, playing right field with a *fire* most fans had never seen before.

Finally, *finally*, it could not be denied: Roberto was the greatest all-around baseball player of his time, maybe of all time.

The very next year, he did something few have ever done: During the last game of the season, Roberto walked to the plate, creaked his neck, dug in his stance, stuck his chin toward the pitcher, and walloped a line drive off the center-field wall—his *three thousandth* hit!

The crowd cheered, and they wouldn't stop cheering. For many minutes the players stopped playing and Roberto stood on second base, amazed. How far he had come.

 STOP AND THINK

Visualize What words help you visualize how it looks, feels, and sounds when Clemente is up at bat?

TEKS 3.10

169

And yet, when the season was over, the hero returned to the place where his story began, to the land of muddy fields and soup cans and bottle caps, to his homeland of Puerto Rico, where he was worshipped.

But did he sit around and polish his trophies? No. That rainy New Year's Eve, Roberto sat in the San Juan airport and waited for mechanics to fix the tired old airplane that would take him to Central America. There had been a terrible earthquake, and he wanted to help the victims. The plane would carry food and supplies that Roberto paid for.

Right before midnight, he boarded. The rain was really coming down. One of the propellers buzzed loudly. As the plane took off, the engines failed and the plane fell into the ocean.

Just like that, it was over. Roberto was gone. How could his story end this way, so suddenly, and with such sadness?

The story doesn't end here. When someone like Roberto dies, his spirit lives on in the hearts of all he touched.

And Roberto's spirit is still growing. It grows
in the bats and gloves and arms and legs of all the
Latino baseball players who have flooded into the
major leagues. His spirit grows in the charities he
started for poor people in Puerto Rico. And his spirit
is still growing in Pittsburgh, where people who saw
him play tell their children and grandchildren of how
he used to sparkle—running, diving, firing game-
saving throws from deep right field all the way to
home plate—SMACK—right into the catcher's glove.

Your Turn

1. The word <u>slammed</u> on page 159 means —

   ◯ jumped

   ◯ touched

   ◯ banged

   ◯ covered

2. ✔ **TARGET SKILL** **Cause and Effect**

   Use a chart like this to describe two of Clemente's experiences in Puerto Rico. Tell how those events affected his life as a baseball player. **TEKS** 3.13C; **ELPS** 4K

   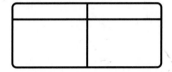

3. ✔ **TARGET STRATEGY** **Visualize**

   Visualize the Pittsburgh fans when Clemente bats on page 157, then on page 168. Describe what you picture.

4. **Oral Language** With a partner, take turns asking and responding to questions about events that take place in *Roberto Clemente*. Look back at the story as needed.

   TEKS 3.2B; **ELPS** 4G

 TEKS 3.2B ask questions/clarify/locate facts/details/use text evidence; 3.13C identify cause and effect relationships; **ELPS** 4G demonstrate comprehension through shared reading/retelling/responding/note-taking; 4K employ analytical skills to demonstrate comprehension

Poetry

✓ **TARGET VOCABULARY**

stands	slammed
fans	polish
score	style
league	pronounced

GENRE

Poetry uses the sound and rhythm of words to show images and express feelings. Which parts of the poem *Homer* best show readers how the experience feels and what it means to the batter?

TEXT FOCUS

Rhyme is words with the same ending sound. Read Jack Prelutsky's poem aloud to a partner, stressing the rhyming words. Discuss the pattern of rhymes and beats.

 TEKS 3.6 describe forms of poetry/how they create imagery

BASEBALL POEMS

What did most kids do for fun before television, computers, and video games were invented? They played baseball! For years, it was the most widely played sport in the United States. That's how baseball started being called "America's Pastime."

The ball game is over,
And here is the score —
They got ninety-seven,
We got ninety-four.
Baseball is fun,
But it gives me the blues
To score ninety-four
And still manage to lose.

by Jack Prelutsky

HOMER

Summer words, like *raspberry ice*,
beach, and *barbecue*, are all gone now.
But I find another warm word,
shaped like a bat. HOMER.
I wrap my fingers tightly round it
and swing.

by Nikki Grimes

Radio Days

When kids weren't playing baseball, they were listening to it. Major League Baseball games were heard on the radio starting in 1921. Announcers described the action in detail. They pronounced each word clearly so that fans didn't miss a thing.

Sounds gave clues about the action. The crack of a bat meant someone had slammed the ball out of the park. Boos from the stands meant the umpire had made a bad call. Cheering meant someone had been able to score.

If you used your imagination, listening to a game on the radio was almost as good as being in the ballpark!

Write a Baseball Poem

Write a baseball poem of your own. You might want to write about a game you have watched or about a favorite player. Try to use the words polish and style in your poem.

176

Making Connections

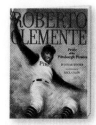

Text to Self

Sports Sense Imagine being at a baseball or other sports game. What might you see, hear, smell, touch, and taste? Write about how you would experience the game through each of your senses.

Text to Text

ELPS 5G

Connect to Art Study the pictures in *Roberto Clemente* and *Baseball Poems*. Write a short paragraph comparing and contrasting them. Then choose part of the story or one of the baseball poems and draw your own picture for it.

Text to World

TEKS 3.26A(iii)

Make a Map Roberto Clemente was born and raised in Puerto Rico. He moved to Pittsburgh, Pennsylvania, to play baseball. Find both places on a map. Learn how many miles apart they are. Then draw your own map, showing both Pittsburgh, Pennsylvania, and Puerto Rico.

 TEKS **3.26A(iii)** collect information from visual sources; **ELPS** 5G narrate/describe/explain in writing

177

Grammar

Plural Nouns with -s and -es A noun that names only one person, place, or thing is a **singular noun**. A noun that names more than one person, place, or thing is a **plural noun**. Add -s to form the plural of most singular nouns. Add -es to form the plural of a singular noun that ends with s, sh, ch, or x.

Academic Language

singular noun
plural noun

Singular Nouns	Plural Nouns
Julie has a baseball.	Julie has two baseballs.
She is better than her brother.	She is better than her brothers.
They play after class.	They play between classes.
She is an inch taller than Joe.	She is four inches taller than Joe.

 **Write the plural of each underlined noun.**

1 A <u>boy</u> walked to the park.

2 He met his <u>friend</u>.

3 They opened a <u>box</u> with a new baseball.

4 Their <u>game</u> lasted all afternoon.

5 He missed the <u>bus</u> home.

178

Conventions When you edit your writing, it is important to always check your spelling.   Using the correct spelling of plural nouns will make your writing clearer and easier to understand.

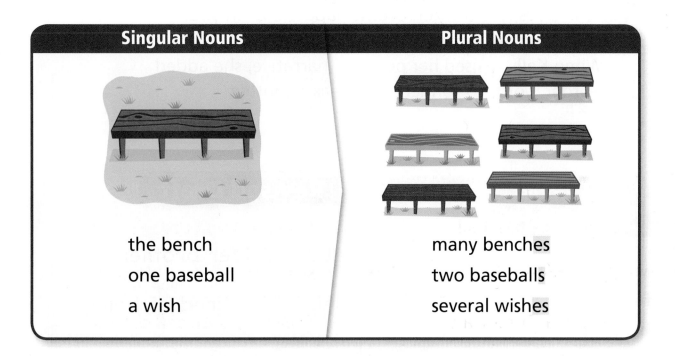

Singular Nouns	Plural Nouns
the bench	many benches
one baseball	two baseballs
a wish	several wishes

Singular: He swung the bat at the very first pitch.

Plural: He did not swing the bat at the first two pitches.

Connect Grammar to Writing

As you edit your personal narrative, be sure to write the correct form of all plural nouns.

Reading-Writing Workshop: Revise

Write to Narrate

✔ **Sentence Fluency** In *Roberto Clemente*, the author uses time-order words such as *first* and *then*. These are time clues to tell when events happened. In your **personal narrative**, use time-order words.

When Kelly revised her personal narrative, she added time-order words to connect her ideas smoothly.

Writing Process Checklist

Prewrite

Draft

▶ Revise

  ✔ Is my beginning interesting?

  ✔ Did I include important events and details?

  ✔ Are the events in order?

  ✔ Did I include time-order words?

  ✔ Did I share my thoughts and feelings?

Edit

Publish and Share

Revised Draft

I begged my older brother Cal for help. "I'm tired of being scared," I whispered. "Can you give me some lessons?" He took me to the pool when there weren't many other people around. First w̌We practiced strokes. Then ȟHe taught me how to tread water and float on my back.

Summer Splash!

by Kelly Belson

I used to hide whenever anyone said, "We're going to the deep end!" That was before everything changed.

Last summer, I was at the city pool when my friends played volleyball in the deep end. Of course, I sat out, for the millionth time. I could hear them laughing and cheering. I was so jealous!

I begged my older brother Cal for help. "I'm tired of being scared," I whispered. "Can you give me some lessons?" He took me to the pool when there weren't many other people around. First, we practiced strokes. Then he taught me how to tread water and float on my back.

In my final paper, I used time clues to connect ideas. I also made sure to use commas correctly.

Reading as a Writer

What words did Kelly use to show *when* events happened? Where could you add time clues in your own personal narrative?

181

Read the selection. Then read each question that follows the selection. Decide which is the best answer to each question.

Dinner at Binh's House

1   "Good-bye, Mom," I called before I shut our front door. I walked to the house next door. My best friend, Binh, lives there. I was going to have dinner with Binh and his family. When I knocked on the door, Binh welcomed me in.

2   Binh and I are the same age. He and his family are from Vietnam. They came to Texas to start a new life. They have lived next door to me for three years. Last month they became United States citizens.

3   I like eating meals with Binh's family. Sometimes we eat American foods, such as pizza or barbecue. Other times, Binh's mother and father make foods that people in Vietnam usually eat.

4   We started dinner with a beef and noodle soup called Bun Bo Hue. It had some bizarre ingredients in it. They were so strange that I didn't think I would like it. But it was delicious! It was pretty spicy, too. That's one way Vietnamese food is like Texan food! Binh reminded me how to use the chopsticks. It can be a challenge when you are used to eating with a spoon or fork.

5   Then Binh's mother filled my bowl with rice and fish. The first time I ate at Binh's house, I was surprised to see the fish still had scales. Now I know it tastes great that way.

6   We talked about school and work during dinner. We talked about our weekend plans, too. Sometimes Binh's family spoke to each other in Vietnamese. That is the language spoken by people from Vietnam. Mostly, though, they spoke English, because I was there. They understand that English is the only language I know.

7   I remembered the first time that I went to Binh's house. I thought that Binh's father was <u>impolite</u>. He didn't speak to me. Later, Binh explained that his father wasn't trying to be rude. Binh said his family usually speaks Vietnamese at home. His father understood English, but it was hard for him to speak it. Now Binh's father always speaks to me.

8   Binh told me that the English and Vietnamese languages are very different. For example, the Vietnamese word *ma* has six meanings. The meaning changes with the tone of voice you use to say the word! I'm amazed that Binh has learned how to speak English so quickly. I'm trying to learn some Vietnamese, but it's going slowly for me. All the different tones are <u>perplexing</u>!

9   I thanked Binh's family for the delicious dinner. Then I invited Binh to come over to my house for dinner the following night. I'm glad to have Binh as a best friend!

GO ON

1 Which sentence from the story shows that the narrator thinks Binh is smart?

⊂⊃ *I'm amazed that Binh has learned how to speak English so quickly.*

⊂⊃ *Binh reminded me how to use chopsticks.*

⊂⊃ *The first time I ate at Binh's house, I was surprised to see the fish still had scales.*

⊂⊃ *Sometimes Binh's family spoke to each other in Vietnamese.*

2 In paragraph 4, which word helps the reader know what the word bizarre means?

⊂⊃ *spicy*

⊂⊃ *strange*

⊂⊃ *challenge*

⊂⊃ *delicious*

3 Why does Binh's family speak English when the narrator is in their home?

⊂⊃ The narrator asks them not to speak Vietnamese.

⊂⊃ Binh's family always speaks English at home.

⊂⊃ The children in Binh's family do not speak Vietnamese.

⊂⊃ Binh's family wants to make the narrator feel included.

4 Which word from paragraph 7 means the same as impolite?

⊂⊃ *hard*

⊂⊃ *rude*

⊂⊃ *talk*

⊂⊃ *trouble*

5 What does the word perplexing mean in paragraph 8?

⊂⊃ simple

⊂⊃ confusing

⊂⊃ sensible

⊂⊃ exciting

STOP

Changes, Changes Everywhere

Unit 2

Big Idea

We communicate
in many ways.

Paired Selections

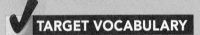

Poems
that Slither,
Walk, and Fly

✔ TARGET VOCABULARY

collect

scrambled

sorted

orders

ragged

rapidly

continued

darted

Vocabulary
Reader

Context
Cards

 TEKS 3.4B use context to determine
word meaning; **ELPS 4D** use
prereading supports to comprehend texts

Vocabulary in Context

1 collect

Some people collect, or gather, stamps from all over the world.

2 scrambled

These children scrambled, or mixed up, all of their baseball cards.

3 sorted

Rock collections may be sorted, or put into groups, by type, color, and size.

4 orders

This collector enjoys putting his cards in new orders, or arrangements.

- **Study each Context Card.**
- **Make up a new context sentence that uses two Vocabulary words.**

5 ragged

Some people collect old books. The pages can become worn and **ragged**.

6 rapidly

Seashells must be collected **rapidly** before the waves cover them up.

7 continued

This woman has **continued** to collect snow globes for many years.

8 darted

The students **darted** to school with their collections for show and tell. They ran!

Background

✓ TARGET VOCABULARY **Building a Collection** Has your room continued to fill up rapidly with baseball cards that you love to collect? Have you ever darted to a shop to buy a new stamp the day it arrives? Perhaps you have sorted and scrambled your comic books until they are ragged. If so, you are a collector!

Some collectors keep their special items safe in boxes. Others display them proudly on shelves, sometimes rearranging them in different orders. Collectors all have one thing in common, though. They love to collect!

Things People Can Collect

Coins	
Stamps	
Music	
Comic Books	
Sea Shells	
Baseball Cards	

TEKS 3.8A sequence/summarize main events/influence on future events; **3.2B** ask questions/clarify/locate facts/details/use text evidence; **ELPS 4I** employ reading skills to demonstrate comprehension

Comprehension

✓ TARGET SKILL Sequence of Events

The story events in *Max's Words* follow a certain sequence, or time order. Signal words such as *soon*, *afterwards*, and *finally* can help you figure out when things happen in the story. Use a chart like the one below to list the sequence of events.

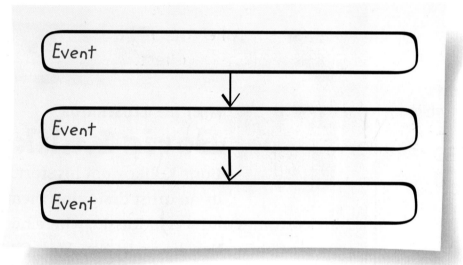

✓ TARGET STRATEGY Question

To think more carefully about the story events and their sequence, ask yourself questions as you read. Why is Max interested in words? Do words create a problem for Max, or do they help him solve one?

✔ **TARGET SKILL**

Sequence of Events
Tell the time order in which events happen.

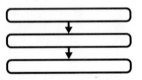

✔ **TARGET STRATEGY**

Question Ask questions before you read, while you read, and after you read.

GENRE

Humorous fiction is a story that is written to entertain the reader.
Use what you know about the genre to set a purpose for reading.

TEKS 3.2C establish reading purpose/ monitor comprehension

MEET THE AUTHOR
Kate Banks
In the fan letters Kate Banks receives, children want to know how old she is, what color car she drives, and whether she likes spaghetti. Mostly they ask how she comes up with her story ideas. She replies that many of her books are inspired by her sons, Peter and Max.

MEET THE ILLUSTRATOR
Boris Kulikov
Boris Kulikov got his start as an artist designing theater costumes and sets in Russia, where he was born. Now living in New York City, Kulikov illustrates children's books and, like Kate Banks, has a son named Max.

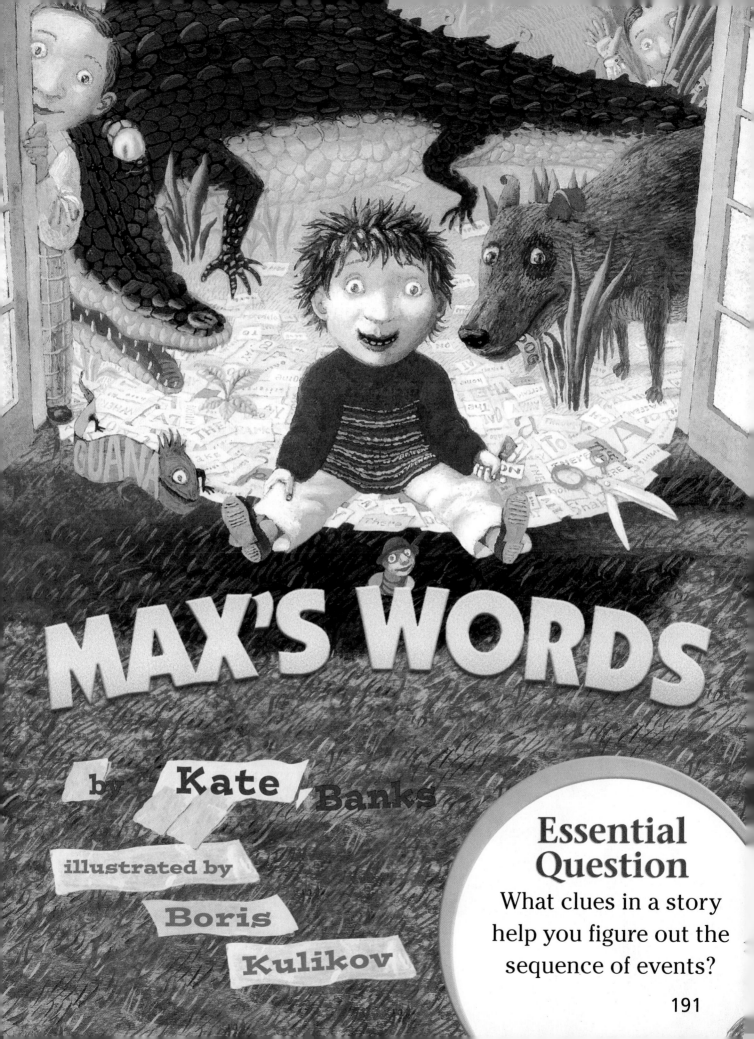

MAX'S WORDS

by Kate Banks

illustrated by Boris Kulikov

Essential Question

What clues in a story help you figure out the sequence of events?

191

Max's brother Benjamin collected stamps. He had stamps of many colors and sizes. They had ragged edges and sticky backs. Some had famous people on them. Others had places or buildings, or flowers or trees.

Benjamin spread his stamp collection across his desk. He showed it to his friends and family. Everyone admired it.

Max said, "Can I have a stamp?"

"No," said Benjamin.

Max's other brother, Karl, collected coins. He had coins of many sizes and values. They came from different countries. Some were silver-colored with rough edges. Others were copper-colored with smooth edges. They were all shiny. They had people and buildings on them and the year in which they were made.

When Karl showed them around, everyone admired them, too.

Max said, "Can I have a coin?"

"No," said Karl.

Max wanted to collect something, but he wasn't sure what.

He gave it some thought. Finally, he said, "I'm going to collect words."

"Words?" said Benjamin. He laughed.

"Very funny, Max," said Karl.

✔ **STOP AND THINK**

Sequence of Events Using your own words, summarize the events that made Max decide to start a word collection.

TEKS 3.8A **ELPS** 4I

Max began collecting small words.

a, *the*, **ITS**, an, ate, who, *to*, and, **but,**
was, in, on, **out,** big, *see,* you, **day**

He cut them out of magazines and newspapers.
And he spread them across his desk.

Pretty soon Max found bigger words.

hungry, **asked, through,** alligator, crocodile, hissed

He cut them out and added them to the others.
Max's collection grew rapidly.

Max collected words that made him feel good.

park, **baseball,** **DOGS,** *hugs*

He collected words of things he liked to eat.

bananas, pancakes, ice cream

He collected words that were spoken to him.

good morning, **GOODBYE**, go away!

He collected his favorite colors.

green, *blue,* brown

Max opened the dictionary and found words he did not know. He copied these on small slips of paper.

slithered

iguana

"What are you doing, Max?" asked Benjamin.

"Let me see," said Karl.

Max's collection grew too big for his desk. So he spread out his words on the floor. He separated them into neat piles.

201

When Benjamin and Karl arranged their collections in different orders, it didn't make much difference. But when Max put his words in different orders, it made a big difference.

A **blue** crocodile **ATE** the **green** iguana.

The blue *iguana* **ate** *a* green **crocodile.**

Soon Max's collection of words spread into the hallway.

✔ **STOP AND THINK**

Question Why does it make a big difference when Max puts his words in different orders?

202

Sometimes Max gave away a word or two.

See you **later,** alligator.

Have **A** nice day.

When Benjamin put his stamps together, he had just a bunch of stamps. When Karl put his coins together, he had just a pile of money. But when Max put his words together, he had a thought.

Maybe I could **trade** a *word* for a STAMP OR A coin. *Please?*

"No," said Benjamin.

"No," said Karl.

"I've got one thousand stamps," said Benjamin.

"When I get a few more coins, I'll have nearly five hundred," said Karl.

"And when I have a few more words, I'll have a story," said Max.

"A story takes a lot of words," said Benjamin.

"I know," said Max.

"You don't have enough," said Karl.

"Let's see," said Max.

Max sorted through his words. He picked out a few and began arranging them on the floor.

ONCE There WAS
a little BROWN
worm
WHO wished TO BE
A BIG
green SNAKE.

Benjamin and Karl stopped what they were doing and came over to look. Max continued his story.

green SNAKE.

THE worm slithered Through the GRASS. it stuck out ITS tongue and hissed LOUDLY.

STOP AND THINK
Author's Craft The word *slithered* is an example of onomatopoeia. The sound and the meaning of the word are the same. Find another example of onomatopoeia.
TEKS 3.10

207

LOUDLY .

Max stopped to choose some more words.
Benjamin butted in.

Then
ALONG CAME
a BIG mean
GREEN
CROCODILE

Then it was Karl's turn.

"I'M HUNGRY," it said.

208

Benjamin grinned. He chose a few more words.

Karl scrambled for more words. He wanted the crocodile to eat the worm. But Max was quicker.

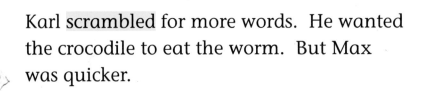

"Hey, I want another story," said Benjamin.

"So do I," said Karl.

"And I want a stamp and a coin," Max reminded them.

"Oh, all right," said Benjamin. He gave Max a stamp. Karl gave Max a coin. And Max gave them each some words.

And kept the rest for himself.

Once There WAS a BIG BROWN DOG

Your Turn

1. Which word from the story *Max's Words* means the opposite of <u>stopped</u>?

   ⬭ *scrambled*

   ⬭ *sorted*

   ⬭ *continued*

   ⬭ *rapidly*

   TEKS 3.4C

2. ✔ **TARGET SKILL** **Sequence of Events**

   Use a chart like this one to explain what happens when Max decides to use his words to make up a story. **TEKS** 3.8A

   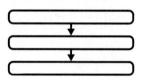

3. ✔ **TARGET STRATEGY** **Question**

   What questions would you like to ask the author about Max and his word collection?

4. **Oral Language** Work in groups of three. Pretend to be Max, Benjamin, and Karl. Use the Retelling Cards to tell the story from each brother's point of view. **ELPS** 4G

   Retelling Cards

 TEKS 3.4C identify/use antonyms; **3.8A** sequence/summarize main events/influence on future events; **ELPS 4G** demonstrate comprehension through shared reading/ retelling/ summarizing/ responding/ note-taking

Poems
that Slither,
Walk, and Fly

✓ **TARGET VOCABULARY**

collect	ragged
scrambled	rapidly
sorted	continued
orders	darted

GENRE

Poetry uses the sound and rhythm of words to show images and express feelings.

TEXT FOCUS

A **concrete poem** is a type of poem in which the words are arranged in the shape of its subject. Discuss how these poets arrange words in their poems to create pictures for readers. Tell how reading the poems would be different if the lines in each poem were arranged in straight rows.

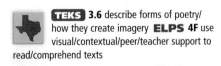

TEKS 3.6 describe forms of poetry/ how they create imagery **ELPS** 4F use visual/contextual/peer/teacher support to read/comprehend texts

Poems
that Slither, Walk, and Fly

"The Python" is a concrete poem. The words are arranged in the shape of a coiled snake!

The Python

by Douglas Florian

With thirty feet to squeeze your prey, Python, you take my breath away!

Giraffe

by J. Patrick Lewis

Tree-tall
giraffe
up
to his
neck

in brown and yellow
patchwork quilts, turns tail
and hobbles away
on wooden
stilts stilts stilts stilts

Have you ever watched a firefly as it darted about rapidly in the dark? Look at the poem "Firefly." The ragged margins form the shape of a firefly. If you have trouble seeing the firefly shape, use your finger to trace the outline of the poem.

Firefly
by Joan Bransfield

firefly,
flit
high
THEN LOW
do you
know
what
makes
you

G
L
O
W
?

Write a Concrete Poem

Write your own concrete poem. First, pick a topic. Then collect words that describe your topic. When you write your poem, arrange the words in orders that show what your poem is about. Try to use the words scrambled, sorted, and continued in your poem.

Making Connections

 Text to Self

Your Favorite Words Flip through a magazine or dictionary and write down at least five interesting words. Then try to use all the words in a short paragraph that tells a story. Share it with the class.

Text to Text

Make Words "Concrete" Choose three words from *Max's Words*. Draw each word so that it is "concrete," or written in a way to show its meaning. Reread "Poems that Slither, Walk, and Fly" for reminders about concrete poems.

Text to World

Connect to Language Arts Max wrote a story with animal characters. Research and read a traditional tale that includes an animal. In a journal, write the story in your own words.

 TEKS 3.11 read independently/paraphrase; **RC-3(A)** establish reading purposes **ELPS 1C** use strategic learning techniques to acquire vocabulary; **1E** internalize new basic/academic language; **5B** write using new basic/content-based vocabulary

Grammar

What Is a Verb? An action **verb** is a word that tells what people or things do. The verb is the main word in the predicate.

Academic Language

verb

predicate

Action Verb	
Dillon collects model boats.	The family bought Dillon a model boat for his birthday.
His brothers collect boats, too.	He put it on a special shelf.

Forms of the word *be* do not show action. They tell what something is or was.

Maria is a doll collector.
She was at a doll store yesterday.

 **Work with a partner. Read each sentence aloud. Identify the verb in each sentence.**

1. Carmine owns a stamp collection.

2. His stamp collection is huge.

3. Large notebooks hold the stamps.

4. Many people trade stamps with Carmine.

5. They love the stamps.

6. Maria and Whitney are stamp collectors, too.

Sentence Fluency Combining sentences can make your writing clearer. When two sentences have the same subject, you can put the sentences together. Join the predicates and put the word *and* between them to form a compound predicate.

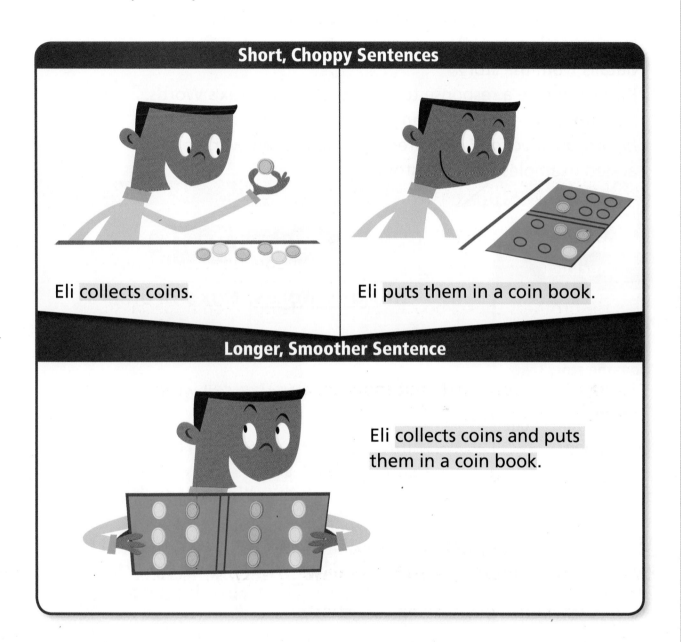

Short, Choppy Sentences

Eli collects coins.

Eli puts them in a coin book.

Longer, Smoother Sentence

Eli collects coins and puts them in a coin book.

Connect Grammar to Writing

As you revise your response paragraph, try to use compound predicates to join short sentences. Join the predicates with the conjunction *and*.

Write to Respond

☑ **Ideas** When you write a **response** paragraph for a story question, explain your answer by giving examples or details from the story.

Kareem wrote a response to this question: *In Max's Words, how do Max's brothers change in the way they feel about his word collection?* As Kareem revised his answer, he added examples from the story.

Writing Traits Checklist

☑ **Ideas**
Did I use examples from the story?

☑ **Organization**
Did I use words from the question?

☑ **Word Choice**
Did I put quotation marks around the author's words?

☑ **Voice**
Did I use formal language to address my audience?

☑ **Sentence Fluency**
Did I combine short, choppy sentences?

☑ **Conventions**
Did I use a computer to find and check correct spellings?

Revised Draft

In <u>Max's Words</u>, Max's brothers change from not liking his word collection to liking it. At first, they think the idea is silly. They laugh~~,~~ and Karl says, "Very funny, Max." ~~They~~ tease him. When Max has a lot of words, they start to get a little They ask Max what he is doing. interested. Then Max begins using his words to write a story.

220

From Silly to Great
by Kareem Mahmood

In <u>Max's Words</u>, Max's brothers change from not liking his word collection to liking it. At first, they think the idea is silly. They laugh and tease him. Karl says, "Very funny, Max." When Max has a lot of words, they start to get a little interested. They ask Max what he is doing. Then Max begins using his words to write a story. Suddenly, Karl and Benjamin get very interested. They take turns adding sentences. When the story is finished, they want another one. Now they think Max's collection is really great. They even trade a coin and a stamp for some words.

> I added more examples from the story. I also combined sentences that had the same subject.

Reading as a Writer

What examples did Kareem use to explain his answer? Where can you add story details or examples in your paper?

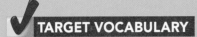
TARGET VOCABULARY

imagine

tools

illustrate

scribbles

sketches

tracing

research

textures

Vocabulary
Reader

Context
Cards

 ELPS 4D use prereading supports to comprehend texts

Vocabulary in Context

1 imagine

Some artists paint real things. Other artists paint things that they imagine.

2 tools

Artists use tools such as brushes, pencils, and markers to make art.

3 illustrate

This artist has started to illustrate, or draw, pictures for a storybook.

4 scribbles

Most children make messy scribbles before they learn to draw well.

- Study each Context Card.

- Discuss one picture. Use a different Vocabulary word from the one in the card.

5 sketches

Painters often make sketches, or rough drawings, before they begin to paint.

6 tracing

Using see-through tracing paper lets you make an exact copy of something.

7 research

Sometimes artists need to do research to find out what things look like.

8 textures

Paper can have different textures. It can look and feel smooth or rough.

Background

✔ **TARGET VOCABULARY** **Becoming an Artist**

Do your drawings look like scribbles? You might imagine this means you have no talent. However, research proves this is not true. Sure, some artists illustrate well as children. Their sketches look like those made by adults. Their paintings are full of rich colors and textures. Yet other famous artists drew poorly as children. Some could not even draw with the help of fancy drawing tools and tracing paper. So, keep on drawing. Winslow Homer did!

Winslow Homer drew this sketch at age ten. Compare it to the painting shown below. He made this painting as an adult.

Comprehension

✔ **TARGET SKILL** **Text and Graphic Features**

As you read *What Do Illustrators Do?*, pay attention to the text and drawings the author uses to help make her ideas clearer. Use a chart like this one to list special features, and tell why you think the author uses them.

Text or Graphic Feature	Page Number	Purpose

✔ **TARGET STRATEGY** **Analyze/Evaluate**

Think carefully about the purpose of the text and graphic features in *What Do Illustrators Do?* Then evaluate, or judge, how well they help to explain the author's ideas.

What Do Illustrators Do?

Written and Illustrated by
Eileen Christelow

TARGET VOCABULARY

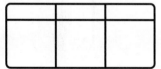

imagine	sketches
tools	tracing
illustrate	research
scribbles	textures

TARGET SKILL

Text and Graphic Features Tell how words and art work together.

TARGET STRATEGY

Analyze/Evaluate Think about what you read. Then form an opinion about it.

GENRE

Informational text gives factual information about a topic. Look at the title and flip through the selection. What do you predict you will learn?

 TEKS 3.13D use text features to locate information/make and verify predictions; **ELPS** 4D use prereading supports to comprehend texts

---

MEET THE AUTHOR AND ILLUSTRATOR

Eileen Christelow

Whenever Eileen Christelow speaks to students, they always ask, "What do you do?" To explain her job as both a writer and an illustrator, she created the books *What Do Authors Do?* and *What Do Illustrators Do?*

The funny cat in *What Do Illustrators Do?* is based on her daughter's cat, Leonard. Actually, the cat in the book is orange because Christelow wanted a more colorful cat. Leonard is mostly gray and tan.

What Do Illustrators Do?

written and illustrated by
Eileen Christelow

Essential Question

How do pictures help to tell a story?

What do illustrators do? They tell stories with pictures. This picture shows where two illustrators live and work.

Suppose those two illustrators each decided to illustrate *Jack and the Beanstalk*. Would they tell the story the same way? Would they draw the same kind of pictures?

I'm going to retell and illustrate JACK AND THE BEANSTALK. Go lie down, Scooter! I'll take you for a walk later.

I've been asked to illustrate JACK AND THE BEANSTALK. Go away, Leonard!

First, illustrators decide which scenes in the story they want to illustrate . . .

A *plan* shows which pictures go on which pages.

After illustrators make a plan for their book, they need to make a *dummy*. (A dummy is a model of the book.) First they decide what shape and size the book will be.

Then they make *sketches* of the pictures that will go on each page of the dummy. The first sketches are often rough scribbles on tracing paper.

As they are sketching, illustrators need to decide how things will look: the characters, their clothes, the setting. Illustrators can use their imaginations or they may have to do some research.

I'll make Jack look like me in fourth grade.

What is the shape of a beanstalk leaf?

I imagine Jack lives in a small country cottage surrounded by palm trees . . .

BEAN PLANT

✔ **STOP AND THINK**

Text and Graphic Features How do the graphic features on this page help you understand the text?

ELPS 4F

Some illustrators are also authors. They can change their story as they work on the sketches.

Each illustration has a different problem. For instance: From what *point of view* do you draw the magic bean being planted?

How do you draw a beanstalk so it looks like it's growing?

Raised eyebrows?
Eyes wide open?
Mouth open?

Jacqueline tiptoed across the table. "Hurry up!" whispered the hen. "She never sleeps for long!"

How would it feel to run across a table right under the nose of a sleeping GIANT?

Illustrators need to draw how their characters feel. Sometimes they make faces in a mirror to see how an expression would look. Other times illustrators need someone else to model for them.

Each illustrator has a different *style* of drawing, just as every person has a different style of handwriting.

Different styles for drawing Jack and Jacqueline

We're trying a new style.

STOP AND THINK

Author's Craft Why do you think the author uses both text and speech balloons to tell this story?

TEKS 3.16B

When illustrators have finished their dummies, they show them to the editor and the designer at the publishing company.

The editor decides whether the pictures tell the story. The designer makes suggestions about the design of the book. She chooses the typeface for the words and the cover.

I love your illustrations! But Jack looks too old at the end of the book. And on page 21 the giant doesn't look mean enough.

Okay, those things should be easy to fix.

If she loves his book, why does she want him to change it?

She's just suggesting ways to make it better!

Illustrators need to decide how they want to do the finished illustrations.

They can draw different kinds of lines and textures with different kinds of tools.

pencil

brush

pen with
flexible point

felt tip pen

They can color their illustrations with paint, pastels, pencils, or crayons. They can do an illustration without any black line at all!

watercolors

watercolor crayons

colored pencils

no black line

239

Sometimes illustrators throw away their pictures and start again. Sometimes they change the colors. Or they may change the composition. It can take months to finish all the illustrations for a picture book.

Before they are sent to the publisher, they need to be checked to make sure nothing is left out.

Illustrators often do the cover of the book last. The cover tells a lot about a story: What is it about? Does it look interesting?

The cover is a clue to how the illustrator will tell the story. Would these covers make you want to read the books?

✔ **STOP AND THINK**

Analyze/Evaluate Do you agree that book covers are clues to how illustrators tell the stories inside? Explain.

TEKS 3.16B, **ELPS** 3G

This illustration tells how the two illustrators celebrated when they finally finished all that work!

YourTurn

1. Which word means about the same thing as <u>study</u>?

   ⬭ dummy

   ⬭ scribble

   ⬭ setting

   ⬭ research

   TEKS 3.4C, **ELPS** 1C

2. ✔ **TARGET SKILL** **Text and Graphic Features**
   Pick three speech balloons from different parts of the story. On a chart like this one, list the details they give. Then explain why you think the author uses each one. **TEKS** 3.15B

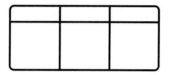

3. ✔ **TARGET STRATEGY** **Analyze/Evaluate**
   Think about the features this author uses. Which ones help you understand information? Why? **TEKS** 3.16B

4. **Oral Language** Use the Retelling Cards to tell a partner the steps it takes to make a book. Speak clearly so your partner understands the order of the steps. **TEKS** 3.15A, 3.30

Retelling Cards

 TEKS **3.4C** identify/use antonyms/synonyms/homographs/homophones; **3.15A** follow/explain written directions; **3.15B** locate/use graphic features of text; **3.16B** explain influence of media design techniques; **3.30** speak coherently/effectively about topics; **ELPS 1C** use strategic learning techniques to acquire vocabulary

245

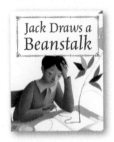
Jack Draws a Beanstalk

by Anne O'Brien

Jack loved to make up stories and illustrate them. He did research to find out what things looked like. He sketched his ideas over and over on tracing paper. He colored the pictures with different textures. When his pictures were just right, he could imagine that his stories were real.

One night, Jack drew a bean vine. "I wish I had a magic bean vine, just like in the fairy tale," Jack said. He worked on the sketches until he fell asleep.

When he woke up, there was the bean vine, growing out of his sketchbook. His scribbles were coming to life!

Jack grabbed his sketchbook and pencil and began to climb the beanstalk. He came to a huge castle in the clouds, just like the one in the fairy tale. And there was the giant's wife, who happily served Jack tea.

"But you must leave before my husband comes home," the giant's wife said. "He might try to eat you for dinner!"

Just then they heard a rumble like loud thunder. "He's home early!" cried the wife. She popped Jack into her apron pocket.

Jack heard the giant's voice yelling, "FEE FI FO FUM!"

"Oh, no," Jack said to himself. "This is too much like the fairy tale! The only tools I've got to help me escape are my sketchbook and pencil!"

Jack was shaking when he began to draw. He drew a
magic hen. The hen came to life and laid a golden egg, just
like in the fairy tale.

"Cluck, cluck!"

The wife reached into her pocket and pulled out the hen
and the golden egg. While the two giants exclaimed over the
hen, Jack escaped out of the castle and climbed down the vine.

When Jack got home, he opened his sketchbook.
He erased the bean vine as fast as he could. "From now
on, I'll be careful about what I wish for!" said Jack.

Making Connections

 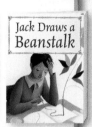

You Are an Illustrator! Choose a paragraph you like from *Jack Draws a Beanstalk*. Use what you learned in *What Do Illustrators Do?* to illustrate that part of the story.

Express Your Opinion In your library or online, find a copy of *Jack and the Beanstalk*, the story *Jack Draws a Beanstalk* is based on. In a small group, talk about how the two stories are alike and different. Give details about characters, setting, and plot. Express your opinion, telling which story you enjoyed more, and why.

Connect to Science Which inventions have changed the way stories are told? How? What new inventions might change the way stories are told in the future? Explain your ideas in a short paragraph.

TEKS **3.5B** compare/contrast settings of tales; **3.20A(i)** establish central idea in brief compositions; **3.20C** write responses to texts that demonstrate understanding; **3.31** participate in discussions/build on others' ideas; **RC-3(A)** establish reading purposes; **ELPS** **3G** express opinions/ideas/feelings; **4G** demonstrate comprehension through shared reading/retelling/responding/note-taking; **5G** narrate/describe/explain in writing

Grammar

Verb Tenses A verb tells when something happens. The **tense** of a verb lets you know whether something happens in the **present**, in the **past**, or in the **future**.

Academic Language

present tense
past tense
future tense

Present Tense	Past Tense	Future Tense
Now, the dog stays inside.	Yesterday, the dog stayed inside.	Tomorrow, the dog will stay inside.
The artist illustrates a book.	The artist illustrated a book.	The artist will illustrate a book.

Turn and Talk **Work with a partner. Tell whether the underlined verb is in the present tense, the past tense, or the future tense.**

❶ Andy <u>works</u> as an illustrator.

❷ He <u>painted</u> pictures in art class.

❸ The teachers <u>showed</u> him other paintings.

❹ A company <u>will publish</u> his new book next year.

❺ His friends <u>will get</u> a copy then.

Sentence Fluency When you write, make sure your verbs all tell about actions that happen in the same time. This will help make your writing clear.

Incorrect Paragraph

Yesterday, Mary looked at a book. Then she paints an elephant. Last, she will color a shady tree.

Correct Paragraph

Yesterday, Mary looked at a book. Then she painted an elephant. Last, she colored a shady tree.

Connect Grammar to Writing

As you revise your compare and contrast paragraph, make sure all the verbs are the same tense.

Write to Respond

☑ **Organization** One way to respond to literature is to write paragraphs that compare and contrast. One paragraph can tell how things are similar. The other can tell how they are different. Begin each paragraph with a topic sentence.

Emma wrote a response to this question: *How is the dummy for a picture book similar to and different from the final book?* Later, she added topic sentences.

Writing Traits Checklist

☑ **Ideas**
Did I use facts from the selection?

☑ **Organization**
Did I include topic sentences?

☑ **Word Choice**
Did I use words such as *both, alike, but,* and *different*?

☑ **Voice**
Did I use formal language to address my audience?

☑ **Sentence Fluency**
Did I change tense only if necessary?

☑ **Conventions**
Did I indent each paragraph?

Revised Draft

The dummy for a picture book is similar to the final book in many ways.

∧ They are both made by the same illustrator. They are also alike in size and shape, and they have the same number of pages. Another way they are similar is that they tell the same story.

252

Comparing the Dummy to the Final Book

by Emma Corcoran

The dummy for a picture book is similar to the final book in many ways. They are both made by the same illustrator. They are also alike in size and shape, and they have the same number pages. Another way they are similar is that they tell the same story.

However, there are big differences too. In the dummy, the pictures are sketches, but in the final book, they have colors and details. The final pictures may show more too. For example, a giant might look meaner in the book than in the dummy. All in all, the dummy is just a model, but the final book is the kind you buy in a store.

I added topic sentences in my final paper. I was also careful to use verb tenses correctly.

Reading as a Writer

How do Emma's topic sentences help her readers? What topic sentences would make your paragraphs easier to understand?

Lesson 8

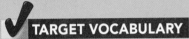

TARGET VOCABULARY

harvest

separate

ashamed

borders

advice

borrow

patch

serious

Vocabulary Reader

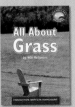

Context Cards

TEKS 3.4B use context to determine word meaning; **ELPS** 4D use prereading supports to comprehend texts

254

Vocabulary in Context

1 **harvest**
When there is a lot of corn to pick, it makes a good harvest.

2 **separate**
Separate, or divide, different kinds of seed before planting them.

3 **ashamed**
Don't feel ashamed, or guilty, if you forget to water a plant!

4 **borders**
This farm has a fence along its borders to keep the animals inside.

- Study each Context Card.

- Make up a new context sentence using two Vocabulary words.

5 advice

Adults often give good **advice**. They have ideas about solving problems.

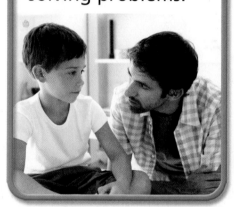

6 borrow

If you do not have gardening tools, you could **borrow** some from a friend.

7 patch

You can use a fairly small **patch**, or area, of land, to grow vegetables.

8 serious

If you are **serious** about something, you are not joking or fooling around.

Background

✓ **TARGET VOCABULARY** **How Does Your Garden Grow?** If you are serious about growing vegetables, you must start with a plan. Draw a map of your patch of land. Separate the garden into different areas for different plants. Mark the borders of your garden. If needed, borrow gardening tools from a friend or a neighbor.

Don't be ashamed if your first harvest is not as good as you had hoped! Ask for advice at a local garden center. Look for tips in library books or on the Internet. Most importantly, don't give up.

> Try growing plants in a window box or a pot if you don't have room for a garden where you live.

TEKS TEKS 3.2B ask questions/clarify/locate facts/details/use text evidence; 3.5A paraphrase themes/details of tales ELPS 4I employ reading skills to demonstrate comprehension

Comprehension

✔ TARGET SKILL Conclusions

As you read *The Harvest Birds*, tie story details together to figure out ideas the author does not state directly. Ask yourself, *What does the author mean here?* Use a chart like this one to describe your conclusions and the details that helped you to draw them.

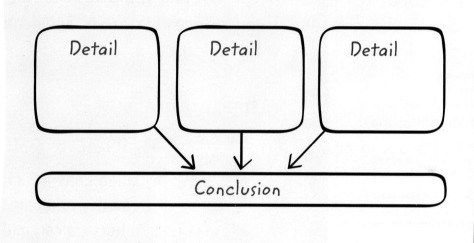

✔ TARGET STRATEGY Infer/Predict

Use your conclusions to figure out the theme, or the important message running through this story. Use your own words to tell what the author wants to teach readers.

JOURNEYS DIGITAL **Powered by** DESTINATIONReading®
Comprehension Activities: Lesson 8

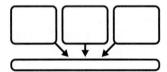

THE HARVEST BIRDS

✔ TARGET VOCABULARY

harvest	advice
separate	borrow
ashamed	patch
borders	serious

✔ TARGET SKILL

Conclusions Use details to figure out ideas that the author doesn't state.

✔ TARGET STRATEGY

Infer/Predict Use clues to figure out more about the selection.

GENRE

A **traditional tale** is a story that people have told for many years. Why does the author say she wrote this story, *The Harvest Birds*?

TEKS 3.12 identify topic/author's purpose

MEET THE AUTHOR

Blanca López de Mariscal

Blanca López de Mariscal teaches at a university in Mexico. She writes and gives speeches about Mexican art, history, and literature. *The Harvest Birds* is her first children's book. She says she wrote this story because it was important to her to introduce children to Mexican storytelling.

MEET THE ILLUSTRATOR

Linda Cane

Linda Cane lives in the country. She has two dogs, a horse, a cat, and two peacocks! Linda Cane loves outdoor activities, such as hiking, skiing, and horseback riding. She has traveled to many places in the United States and all over the world.

THE HARVEST BIRDS

by Blanca López de Mariscal
illustrated by Linda Cane

Essential Question

How can readers figure out the message in a story?

259

In a little town where everyone knew everyone, there lived a young man called Juan Zanate (sah NAH tay). He was given this name because he was always seen with one or two zanate birds.

Juan used to sit under his favorite tree, dreaming and planning his life. He had wanted to have his own land, as his father and grandfather had. However, when his father died and the land was divided, there was enough for only his two older brothers. Because of this, Juan had to go to work in the shops of the town.

"If only I had my own land, my life would be different," Juan thought. He went to see Don Tobias, the richest man in town, and asked to borrow a little piece of his land.

> ✔️ **STOP AND THINK**
>
> **Conclusions** Why do you think Juan's brothers got to keep their father's land, and Juan didn't? Do you think this is fair? Explain your answer.
>
> **TEKS** 3.2B

Don Tobias burst out laughing, and his wife laughed with him. "Why should I let you use my land?" he asked. "You don't know anything about making things grow."

Sad and ashamed, Juan returned to sit under his tree. It was the only place where he felt really happy. In its huge branches lived a flock of zanate birds who were so used to him that they thought of him as their friend.

There was one bird who cared very much for Juan and wanted him to find his way in life. This bird was always around Juan, resting on his shoulder or riding on his hat. Juan named him Grajo (GRAH hoh), or Crow, because zanates have black feathers.

263

After sitting and thinking for a long time, Juan decided to visit the oldest man of the town. "Old people know many things because they've lived longer," Juan thought. "He'll give me some advice, and maybe he'll even help me."

Juan greeted the old man, whom everyone called Grandpa Chon, with respect. The old man seemed to be in a good mood, so Juan dared to ask him for a piece of land. "Let me prove to you that I can be a good farmer and make things grow," he begged.

Grandpa Chon became serious. "I will help you," he said. "I will let you use some land. If you fail, however, you must work for me for free for as many days as you have used my land."

Juan ran into the town, shouting the good news. Instead of being happy for him, though, people laughed at him.

"Better you should straighten up my shop. Where you plant, not even weeds will grow," shouted the carpenter.

"Don't waste your time Juan. Come and work on this wheel," called the blacksmith.

"Help me with these sacks of flour and stop dreaming," added the baker.

Juan decided that nothing anyone said would stop him. "It's time to get to work," he told himself. He began to prepare his land for planting. It was a very tiny patch of land and didn't offer much promise of a big harvest. Still, Juan kept working, watched over by his good friends, the zanates.

"My head is small, like my garden patch, but it is big enough to hold many dreams," thought Juan.

He needed seeds to plant, but didn't have money to buy them, so he went to the shop and asked for some.

"Juan, sweep up the corn, bean, and squash seeds from my floor and take them to my pigs," the shop owner said. "Then if you wish, you can take some seeds for yourself."

268

Juan was happy, because now he had seeds to plant. He didn't scare away the zanates the way the other farmers did. Instead, he gave them some of his leftover seeds to eat so they wouldn't be hungry. After all, the zanates were his friends and he cared for them very much. Grajo was always with him, giving him advice as he worked.

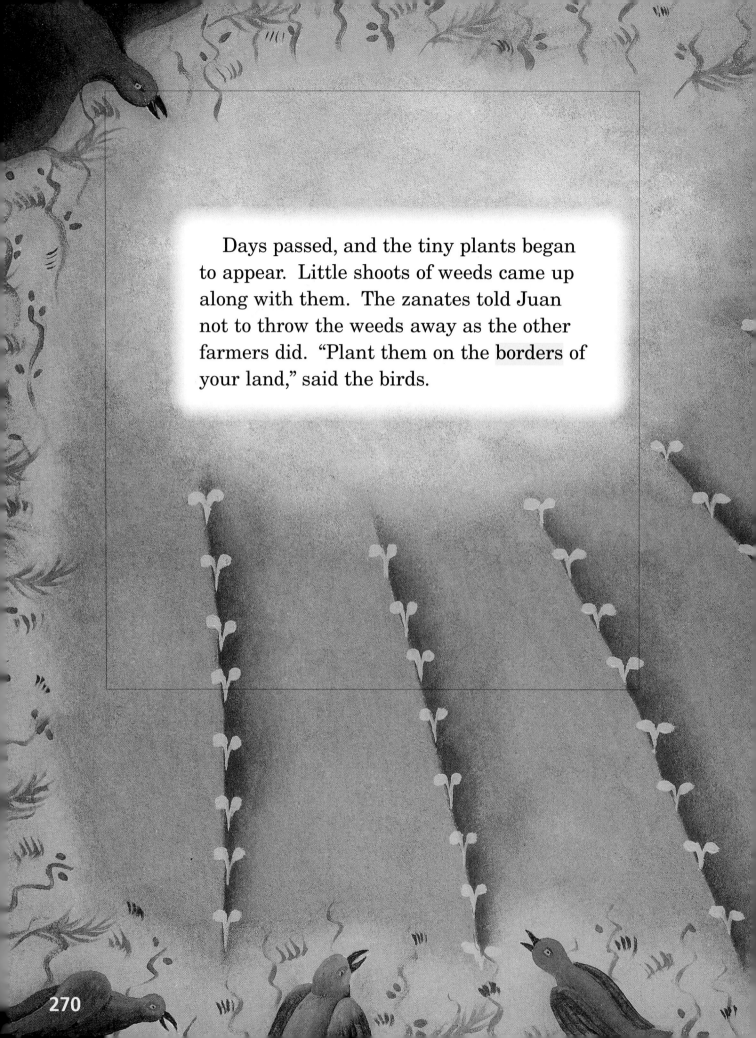

Days passed, and the tiny plants began to appear. Little shoots of weeds came up along with them. The zanates told Juan not to throw the weeds away as the other farmers did. "Plant them on the borders of your land," said the birds.

When the other farmers heard what Juan was doing, they laughed at him. "Imagine keeping weeds in your field!"

At harvest time, everyone was waiting to make fun of Juan once again. They were sure he would fail. When Juan arrived in town, everyone was amazed. He brought a wonderful harvest—huge ears of corn, brightly colored squashes, and tasty-looking beans.

273

"How did you do it?" they all wanted to know. Juan smiled and answered, "I did it with the help of my friends the zanates, the harvest birds. I learned to listen to the voice of nature!"

"Work for me, Juan!" everyone shouted. "Teach me your secrets!"

"No," answered the old man. "Juan works for no one now, because I am going to give him the land that he harvested."

STOP AND THINK

Author's Craft Where does the author use words that make nature seem like a person? What do these words really mean?

TEKS 3.2B

275

After selling the crop at an excellent price, Juan Zanate and Grandpa Chon returned to the little patch of land that was now Juan's. The old man asked Juan to tell him his secret.

"The zanates taught me that all plants are like brothers and sisters," replied Juan. "If you separate them, they become sad and won't grow. If you respect them and leave them together, they will grow happily and be content."

 **STOP AND THINK**

Infer/Predict Why was Juan successful? How do you think his life might change as a result of this experience?

TEKS 3.8A

Your Turn

1. What problem does Juan Zanate have in the beginning of this story?

   ⬭ He can't find a job.

   ⬭ He wants to have his own land.

   ⬭ The zanates want to eat his crops.

   ⬭ He has trouble growing vegetables.

   TEKS 3.2B

2. 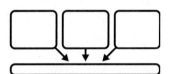 **TARGET SKILL** **Conclusions**

   In the beginning of the story, the townspeople draw a conclusion about Juan. Use a chart like this to show their conclusion and the details they used to draw it. **TEKS 3.8B**

3. **TARGET STRATEGY** **Infer/Predict**

   Make a prediction about how the townspeople will treat Juan in the future. Explain how you made your prediction. **TEKS 3.8A**

4. **Oral Language** Work with a partner. Use the Retelling Cards to tell the plot of *The Harvest Birds* in your own words. Tell events in order. Try not to say *uh*, *well*, and *um*. **TEKS 3.30, RC-3(E)**

   Retelling Cards

 TEKS **3.2B** ask questions/clarify/locate facts/details/use text evidence; **3.8A** sequence/summarize main events/influence on future events; **3.8B** describe characters' relationships/changes; **3.30** speak coherently/effectively about topics; **RC-3(E)** summarize information in text

Traditional Tales

The Farmer and the Dream

✓ TARGET VOCABULARY

harvest	advice
separate	borrow
ashamed	patch
borders	serious

GENRE

A **play**, such as this Readers' Theater, tells a story through the words of its characters.

TEXT FOCUS

Dialogue is the words spoken by the characters in a play. Discuss the characters in this play and what they are like. Say what the story problem is and how the characters deal with it.

TEKS 3.7 explain plot/character through dialogue in scripts; **ELPS** 4E read linguistically accommodated content area material

The Farmer and the Dream

by Kitty Colton

Cast of Characters
Narrator
Farmer
Neighbor
Rich Man
Farmer's Wife

Narrator: Long ago, a Texas farmer and his neighbor tended their harvest. The weary neighbor took a nap. He awoke with a cry.

Neighbor: I dreamed I found a pot filled with gold! The pot was hidden under a pecan tree near the house of the richest man in El Paso!

Farmer: My advice is to follow your dream. Dreams lead to wonderful things!

Neighbor: Hah! I'm not going all the way to El Paso to follow a foolish dream.

Farmer: Then may I borrow your dream?

Neighbor: You can't be serious.

Farmer: Well then, let me *buy* your dream!

Narrator: The neighbor shrugged and agreed. The farmer bought the dream. He raced across his patch of farmland to tell his wife. Then he left on his journey. He crossed the borders of town after town. Finally, he reached the richest man's house. He told the man about the dream.

Farmer: May I dig for the pot of gold under your tree? I will share what I find!

Rich man: Of course you may, but you are tired. Sleep first.

Narrator: While the farmer slept, the rich man sneaked out and dug up the pot. As he tried to separate the lid from the pot, he heard a loud WHOOSH. He looked inside.

Rich man: It's empty! What a fool that farmer is!

Narrator: The rich man buried the pot again. The next morning, the farmer dug up the pot. It was empty. The farmer was embarrassed and ashamed. He thanked the rich man for his help and started his trip home. When he arrived, his wife and children ran out, shouting.

Farmer's wife: Seven nights ago, we awoke to a loud WHOOSH. Hundreds of gold coins came flying into our house. Your dream came true!

Narrator: No one can explain how this happened, but I think the gold was meant to belong to the farmer. Only he dared to follow a dream with courage and a good heart.

Making Connections

 Text to Self

Give a Speech Imagine you are Juan at the end of the story. What would you say to Don Tobias about the way he treated you? Give a speech to a partner. Explain your feelings.

 Text to Text TEKS 3.5B ELPS 4K

Compare and Contrast How are the folktales *The Harvest Birds* and *The Farmer and the Dream* alike and different? Write a paragraph that compares and contrasts the two stories. Give details about characters, setting, and plot.

 Text to World TEKS 3.26A(ii)

Connect to Science In *The Harvest Birds*, the zanates tell Juan that plants like to grow like brothers and sisters. Research how to grow one kind of vegetable. Use reference books, look on the Internet, or interview a friend or a family member who knows about gardening. Explain your findings to classmates.

 TEKS **3.5B** compare/contrast settings of tales; **3.26A(ii)** collect information from experts/reference texts/online searches; **ELPS** **4K** employ analytical skills to demonstrate comprehension

Grammar

Commas in a Series A **comma** tells a reader where to pause. A comma also helps make the meaning of a sentence clear. When you list three or more words together in a sentence, the list is called a **series**. Use commas to separate the words in a series.

Academic Language

comma

series

Nouns in a Series
Mark saw gulls, pelicans, and terns near his home.
Verbs in a Series
They dove, swooped, and soared through the sky.

 **Write each sentence. Put commas where they are needed.**

1 Mike Jen and John worked at the school garden.

2 They raked planted and watered.

3 The garden had tomatoes cucumbers and lettuce.

4 The kids picked washed and ate the vegetables.

Sentence Fluency Good writers combine short, choppy sentences into longer, smoother sentences. One way of combining short, choppy sentences is to join single words in a series. Remember to add *and* after the last comma.

Short, Choppy Sentences		
Carlos harvested beans.	Carlos harvested corn.	Carlos harvested squash.

Longer, Smoother Sentence

 Carlos harvested beans, corn, and squash.

Connect Grammar to Writing

As you revise your summary paragraph, look for ways to combine choppy sentences. You may be able to join single nouns or verbs in a series.

Write to Respond

☑ **Word Choice** In a **summary** paragraph, tell the author's ideas in your own words. In *The Harvest Birds*, the author says, "In a little town where everyone knew everyone. . . ." In a summary, you could say, "In a small, friendly town. . . ."

Ben wrote a summary paragraph about part of *The Harvest Birds*. Later, he changed some words he had accidentally copied.

Writing Traits Checklist

☑ **Ideas**
Did I include important events and a concluding statement?

☑ **Organization**
Did I use time-order words?

☑ **Word Choice**
Did I use my own words?

☑ **Voice**
Did I make the story sound exciting?

☑ **Sentence Fluency**
Did I write complete sentences?

☑ **Conventions**
Did I use a dictionary to check correct spellings?

Revised Draft

Juan Zanate lived in a small, friendly town. He wanted to become a farmer, but he didn't
~~He had to get a job in town.~~
have any land. ⌃ ~~Because of this,~~

~~he had to go work in the shops~~
After a while,
~~of the town.~~ ⌃ Juan decided to

ask a rich man if he could use

some of his land.

A Summary of The Harvest Birds

by Ben Hughes

Juan Zanate lived in a small, friendly town. He wanted to become a farmer, but he didn't have any land. He had to get a job in town. After a while, Juan decided to ask a rich man if he could use some of his land. The rich man said no because Juan didn't know how to grow things. Juan was very disappointed. Then Juan decided to ask an old man for some land. The old man said yes. Juan told everyone his great news! The people in his town laughed, shouted, and insulted him.

I used my own words. I was careful to write complete sentences.

Reading as a Writer

In what other ways could you say "Juan was happy"? In your own paper, change any copied parts to your own words.

KAMISHIBAI MAN
ALLEN SAY

The True Story of
Kamishibai

✓ **TARGET VOCABULARY**

familiar

applause

vacant

rickety

blurry

blasted

jerky

rude

Vocabulary
Reader

Puppets,
puppets,
Puppets

Context
Cards

familiar

familiar

 ELPS 4D use prereading supports to comprehend texts

Vocabulary in Context

1 familiar

This illustration is from a familiar, or well-known, story. It is from Cinderella.

2 applause

At first, the applause was soft. Then the clapping grew louder.

3 vacant

This old movie theater is vacant. Nobody comes here anymore.

4 rickety

Some puppet theaters are rickety, not sturdy, and can easily collapse.

- Study each Context Card.
- Use two Vocabulary words to tell about an experience you had.

---

5 **blurry**

When a sad movie makes you cry, everything looks blurry, or fuzzy.

---

6 **blasted**

Horns blasted loudly during this school concert.

---

7 **jerky**

This dance uses quick, jerky motions that stop and start back up again.

---

8 **rude**

It is very rude, or impolite, to talk during a movie or a play.

Background

✔ **TARGET VOCABULARY** **Storytelling** Everyone loves a good story. How is a story best told? Some tales, like familiar bedtime stories, are spoken aloud. Others are told with puppets on a rickety stage. Adventure stories are often shown in movies, with sound effects blasted from speakers and action so fast it looks blurry or jerky. Even a vacant room can become a stage for acting out a play. No matter how a story is told, every storyteller hopes to hear applause and never the rude sounds of booing.

Speaking Tips
- Don't talk too fast or too slowly.
- Talk loudly enough to be heard.
- Speak with expression.

Other Tips
- Make eye contact.
- Use props.
- Use facial expressions and hand motions.

Tell a favorite story to a friend. Use these tips.

Stories can be told in many different ways. These people are acting out a story on stage.

288

Comprehension

✔ TARGET SKILL Cause and Effect

When the main character in *Kamishibai Man* decides to try storytelling again, some events cause other events to happen. The first event is the cause, or *why* something happens. The second event is the effect. Make a chart like this one to list some causes and effects from the story.

Cause	Effect

✔ TARGET STRATEGY Monitor/Clarify

As you read, check to be sure you understand the causes and effects of important story events. This can help you be clear about why the man feels as he does in different parts of *Kamishibai Man*.

✓ **TARGET VOCABULARY**

familiar	blurry
applause	blasted
vacant	jerky
rickety	rude

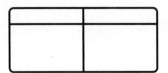

✓ **TARGET SKILL**

Cause and Effect Tell how one event makes another happen and why.

✓ **TARGET STRATEGY**

Monitor/Clarify As you read, find a way to clear up what doesn't make sense.

GENRE

Realistic fiction is a story with events that could happen in real life.

MEET THE AUTHOR AND ILLUSTRATOR

Allen Say

If you were to drop in on Allen Say in his art studio, you might find him lying on the floor. That's how he does his best thinking. He doesn't own a TV and never listens to music when he works because he likes to work in complete silence.

When he's creating a book, Say first paints all the pictures in order. Then he writes the words. His book *Grandfather's Journey* was awarded the Caldecott Medal for best illustrations.

KAMISHIBAI MAN

by Allen Say

Not so long ago in Japan, in a small house on a hillside, there lived an old man and his wife. Even though they never had children of their own, they called each other "Jiichan" (jee chan) and "Baachan" (bah chan). Jiichan is Grandpa, and Baachan is Grandma.

One day, Baachan said, "Jiichan, you haven't said a word in three days."

"Umm, I've been thinking how much I miss going on my rounds," he said.

Baachan stared. "How many years has it been?" she asked.

"Umm, yes, quite a while . . . but my legs are good. And I've kept the bicycle in good order."

". . . I don't know. But one day won't hurt, I suppose. Should I make some candies?"

"That would be very nice," Jiichan said.

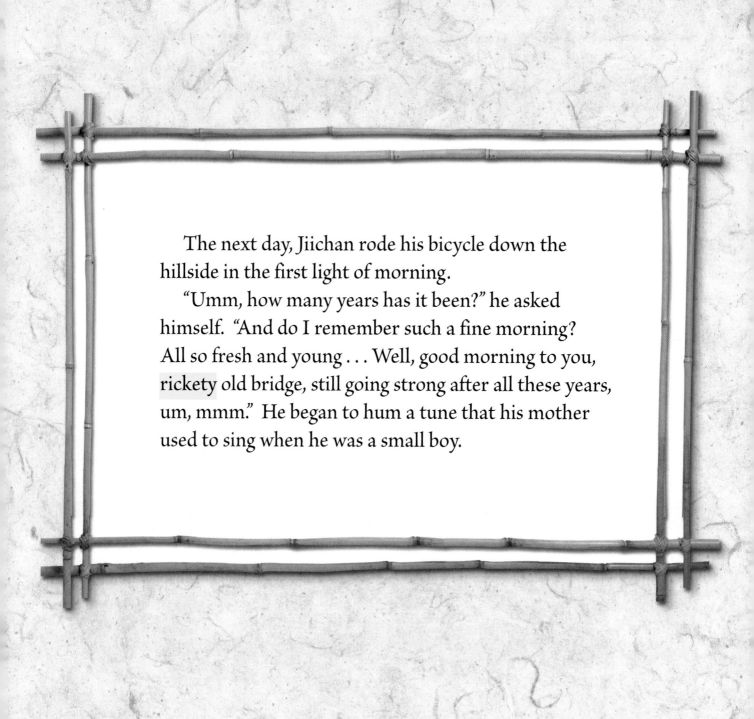

The next day, Jiichan rode his bicycle down the hillside in the first light of morning.

"Umm, how many years has it been?" he asked himself. "And do I remember such a fine morning? All so fresh and young . . . Well, good morning to you, rickety old bridge, still going strong after all these years, um, mmm." He began to hum a tune that his mother used to sing when he was a small boy.

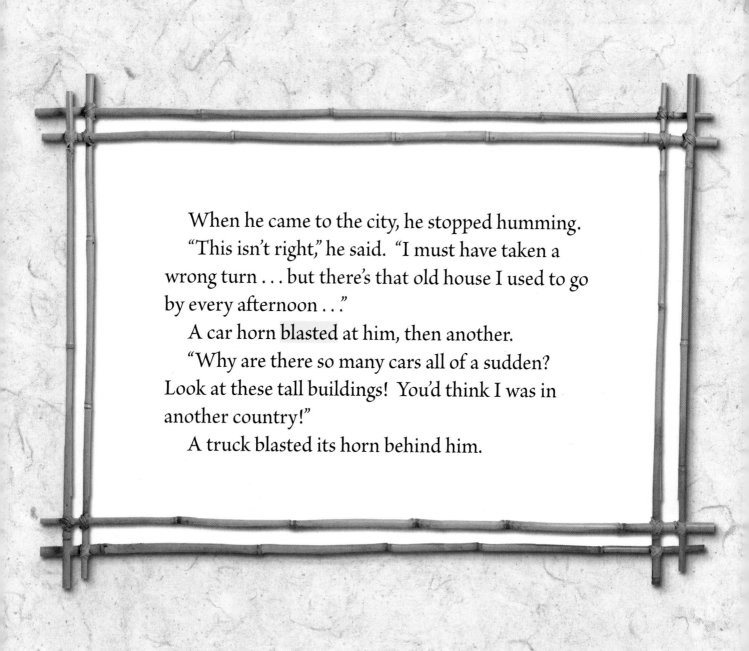

When he came to the city, he stopped humming.

"This isn't right," he said. "I must have taken a wrong turn . . . but there's that old house I used to go by every afternoon . . ."

A car horn blasted at him, then another.

"Why are there so many cars all of a sudden? Look at these tall buildings! You'd think I was in another country!"

A truck blasted its horn behind him.

297

He pulled into a vacant lot and panted. "Can't a man ride his bicycle in peace? Don't remember such rude drivers." Catching his breath, he looked across the street and gaped.

"Can this be? There's that old noodle shop . . . used to be the only building here—that and a nice park all around. Now look at all these shops and restaurants. They chopped down all those beautiful trees for them. Who needs to buy so many things and eat so many different foods?"

 STOP AND THINK

Cause and Effect The city has grown, causing more traffic. What is another result, or effect, of the city growing larger and busier?
TEKS 3.2B **ELPS** 4I

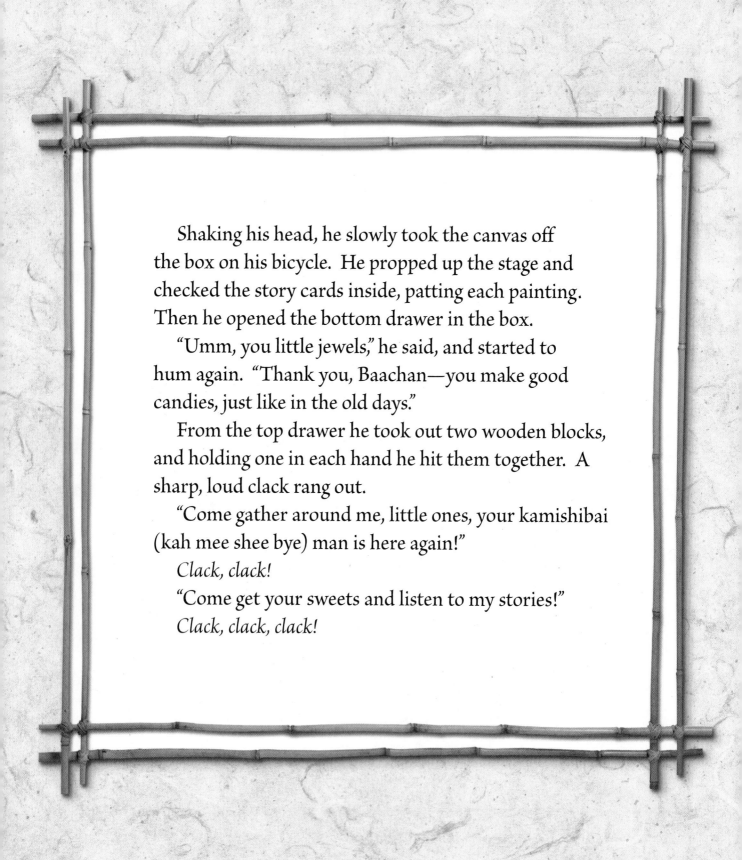

Shaking his head, he slowly took the canvas off the box on his bicycle. He propped up the stage and checked the story cards inside, patting each painting. Then he opened the bottom drawer in the box.

"Umm, you little jewels," he said, and started to hum again. "Thank you, Baachan—you make good candies, just like in the old days."

From the top drawer he took out two wooden blocks, and holding one in each hand he hit them together. A sharp, loud clack rang out.

"Come gather around me, little ones, your kamishibai (kah mee shee bye) man is here again!"

Clack, clack!

"Come get your sweets and listen to my stories!"

Clack, clack, clack!

"Ah, yes, I can see you now, all your bright faces, clasping coins in your little hands, so happy to hear my clappers, so happy to see your kamishibai man!

"Patience, everyone! You'll get your sweets, each and every one of you; I have all your favorites—red ones and green ones and the soft ones on sticks. And here comes that boy, the one who never has any money . . . umm, I'll get to him later.

"So, which story will it be today? The mighty 'Peach Boy'! Born from a giant peach! But wait, let's start at the beginning, umm . . . Long, long ago, there once lived an old man and his wife who had no children . . .

 STOP AND THINK

Monitor/Clarify How is this picture different from the others? What does this tell you about when events on this page took place?
TEKS 3.2C **ELPS** 4J

303

"After 'The Peach Boy,' 'The Bamboo Princess' was a nice change, a gentle story. Then my favorite, 'The Old Man Who Made Cherry Trees Bloom.' And when I was finished, you all went home happy, except for that poor boy. 'Would you like a candy?' I asked once. He said, 'I don't like candies!' and ran away.

"Then one night I was going home and saw a crowd of people gathered in front of a shop. They were staring at something called television. I was curious too, but not for long. It showed moving pictures; they were all jerky and blurry and had no colors at all.

"It wasn't long after that when television antennas started to sprout from the rooftops like weeds in the springtime. And the more they grew, the fewer boys and girls came out to listen to my stories.

"How can they like those blurry pictures better than my beautiful paintings? I asked. But there was nothing to be done. As I went around the familiar neighborhoods, the children started to act as though they didn't know me anymore.

"Even so, I went on clacking my clappers, and one day a little girl poked her head out the window and shushed me. Imagine, a little girl shushing me. The kamishibai man was making too much noise!

"I sat on a park bench and ate a candy for lunch. How could the world change so quickly? Was I a bad storyteller? Then that boy came, the boy who didn't like candies. 'Why aren't you watching television?' I asked. 'I don't like television!' he said. 'But you like my stories,' I said, and he nodded his little head.

"I got up and set the stage. 'What's your favorite story?' I asked. 'Little One Inch,' he answered. So I told him the story of a brave little boy who was only one inch tall. And as I told the story, the boy never looked at the picture cards in the stage. He was looking at me the whole time, with his mouth wide open. He even smiled now and then.

"When I finished the story, I started to take out some sweets to give him, but he was already running away. 'Wait!' I shouted, but he kept running and never turned his head. That was the last time I saw that boy. That was the last day I was a kamishibai man . . ."

"I was that boy!" a loud voice cried out.

Startled, the kamishibai man looked up and saw that a large crowd had gathered before him.

"We grew up with your stories!" someone else shouted.

"Tell us 'Little One Inch' again!"

"And 'The Bamboo Princess'!"

"'The Peach Boy'!"

He started to say something, and people began to clap their hands. He took a deep bow, and the applause got louder.

A young man with a movie camera struggled up to him. They bowed to each other, and as the old man gave him a candy, a roar went up.

"Look, he has all the same old sweets!"

"Just like the old days!"

And the office clerks and shopkeepers, bankers and waitresses, housewives and deliverymen, all lined up in a big circle around the kamishibai man.

STOP AND THINK

Author's Craft What clues help you know the author has finished telling about past events and is now talking about the present?

TEKS 3.2C **ELPS** 4K

It was dark when he got home. Baachan was watching the evening news. The kamishibai man was the featured story.

"I see you had a busy day," she said.

"It was a good day." Jiichan nodded.

"Will you be going out tomorrow?"

"Umm, yes. And the day after."

"Then you need more sweets."

"That would be very nice. Umm, could you make it twice the usual amount?"

"I'll see if I have enough sugar," she said, and shut the television off.

Your Turn

1. Which word from the story *Kamishibai Man* means the opposite of <u>steady</u>?

   ⬭ *rickety*

   ⬭ *noisy*

   ⬭ *dirty*

   ⬭ *crowded*

   TEKS 3.4C

2. ✔ **TARGET SKILL** **Cause and Effect**

   What events occur when the kamishibai man visits the city? Use a chart like this one to list three causes and three effects that help you understand how he feels and why. **TEKS** 3.2B

   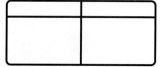

3. ✔ **TARGET STRATEGY** **Monitor/Clarify**

   How do the kamishibai man's memories on pages 305–307 help you figure out why he decides to stop telling stories? **TEKS** 3.2C; **ELPS** 4J

4. **Oral Language** Tell your favorite part of the kamishibai man's story to the class. Use the Retelling Cards. Speak so that everyone in the room can hear you. **TEKS** 3.30

   Retelling Cards

 TEKS 3.2B ask questions/clarify/locate facts/details/use text evidence; **3.2C** establish reading purpose/monitor comprehension; **3.4C** identify/use antonyms/synonyms/homographs/homophones; **3.30** speak coherently/effectively about topics; **ELPS** 4J employ inferential skills to demonstrate comprehension

The True Story of Kamishibai

by Elizabeth Manning

Clacking Sticks

Long ago in Japan, kamishibai men rode around on bicycles with wooden boxes on the back. Each man parked his rickety bike in his own special part of town. At the sound of two wooden sticks clacking together, children came running. They bought the candy the man kept in a drawer in the wooden box. Then they waited.

Kamishibai artist Hikaru Otsuki performs at a park in Tokyo, Japan.

Stories in the Street

The kamishibai man put a picture card in the frame at the top of the box. He began to tell a familiar story. One by one, he slipped the pictures in and out. His movements were smooth, not jerky. In case his memory was blurry, parts of the story were on the back of each picture. The kamishibai storytellers always stopped at an exciting part. The children came back another day to hear what happened next. They greeted the end of the story with applause.

What Happened Next?

In the 1960s, something changed. Children stayed indoors after school, leaving the streets vacant. Paper pictures were no match for stories shown on a new invention called television. The noise of televisions blasted from homes. The sound of two wooden sticks clacking together was now a rude interruption. Were the days of kamishibai over?

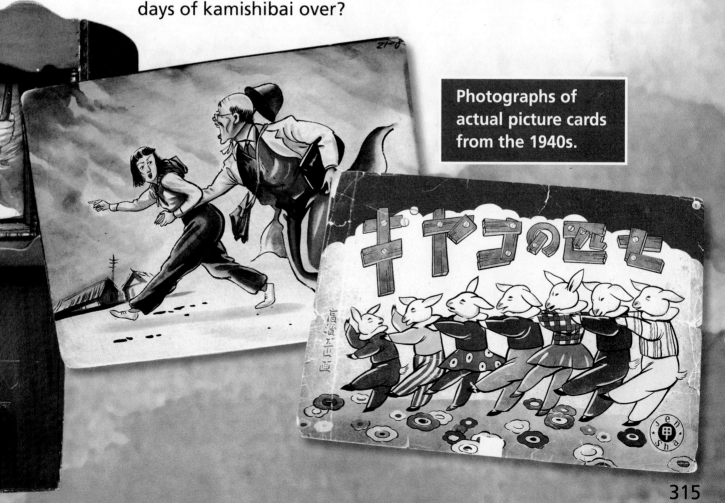

Photographs of actual picture cards from the 1940s.

315

A New Chapter

Some kamishibai artists found work making other kinds of pictures. They drew for the new Japanese comics, called *manga*. Some of their comics were made into cartoon movies, called *anime*. Today people create and read manga and anime all over the world.

Children can still listen to the old paper-theater stories. Storytellers have brought kamishibai to schools and libraries in Japan and the United States. This paper theater doesn't arrive on the back of a bicycle, but the stories and pictures are still wonderful!

Making Connections

 Text to Self

Tell a Story Choose one of your favorite stories or fairy tales. Tell it in the kamishibai style to a small group of students in your class. Make pictures to use while you tell the story.

 Text to Text

Interview a Kamishibai Man One student can play a kamishibai man and another a reporter. Take turns asking and answering questions about life as a kamishibai man.

 Text to World

Connect to Language Arts In *Kamishibai Man*, the man told stories, such as "Little One Inch," "The Peach Boy," and more. Read one of these stories on the Internet. Then write it in your own words in a journal.

 TEKS **3.11** read independently/paraphrase; **3.26A(ii)** collect information from experts/reference texts/online searches; **3.31** participate in discussions/build on others' ideas **ELPS** **3H** narrate/describe/explain with detail; **4G** demonstrate comprehension through shared reading/retelling/responding/note-taking

Grammar

Simple Subjects and Simple Predicates
The **simple subject** is the main word in the
subject. It tells exactly whom or what the
sentence is about. The **simple predicate**
is the main word in the predicate. It tells
exactly what the subject does or is.

Academic Language

simple subject
simple predicate

Simple Subject	Simple Predicate
The man	rode to town.
The busy city	looked different.
His favorite shop	is a clothing store now.

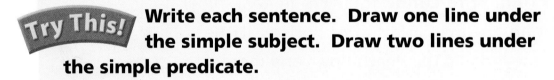 **Write each sentence. Draw one line under
the simple subject. Draw two lines under
the simple predicate.**

❶ I visit my grandparents.

❷ My grandparents make candy on an old stove.

❸ The chipped pot bubbles with melted sugar.

❹ Each batch takes about four hours.

❺ We eat the most delicious candy!

Ideas You can make a sentence clearer by adding a noun that tells more about the subject. Put the noun and any words that go with it right after the subject. Use a comma before and after the words you add about the subject.

Unclear	Clear
The bicycle still worked.	The bicycle, an old model, still worked.

Unclear: The woman made candy.
Clear: The woman, a fine cook, made candy.

Connect Grammar to Writing

As you revise your response to literature next week, think of nouns that will tell more about each subject. Use some of those nouns to make your sentences clearer.

Reading-Writing Workshop: Prewriting

Write to Respond

☑ **Organization** Plan your **response to literature** by first thinking about the question and the story. Write your opinion and the reasons for it. Then put them in a chart, adding details to support your reasons.

Hector wrote notes to answer this question: *Why do you think people stopped watching the kamishibai man's show?* Then he organized his ideas in a chart.

Writing Process Checklist

▶ **Prewriting**

☑ Did I understand the question?

☑ Did I think of strong reasons for my opinion?

☑ Did I find examples in the story to support my reasons?

☑ Did I put my ideas in an order than makes sense?

Drafting

Revising

Proofreading

Publishing

Exploring a Topic

My Opinion

stopped watching kamishibai man
  because of TV

Reasons

TV was new, exciting

lots of people got TVs

people home watching TV—liked
  TV better than Jiichan's shows

I think people stopped watching the kamishibai man's shows because of television.

Reason: The people in Jiichan's town were excited by this new invention.

Details: Crowds gathered around to look at a television in a shop window.

Reason: More and more people in the town got their own television sets.

Details: Jiichan saw antennas appearing on people's roofs.

Reason: People watched television instead of the kamishibai man's shows.

Details: A girl told him to be quiet.

> When I organized my response essay, I added details to support my reasons.

Reading as a Writer

What other story details could Hector have added in his chart? Where could you add details and examples in your own chart?

Young Thomas Edison

Moving Pictures

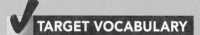
✔ **TARGET VOCABULARY**

invention

experiment

laboratory

genius

gadget

electric

signal

occasional

Vocabulary
Reader

Everyday Inventions

Context
Cards

 **ELPS 4D** use prereading supports to comprehend texts

Vocabulary in Context

1 invention

The light bulb was an invention that helped people do things at night.

2 experiment

First, an inventor must perform an experiment to test an idea.

3 laboratory

Scientists may test their ideas in a laboratory, using special equipment.

4 genius

Albert Einstein was a genius. Even very smart people like to act silly!

- Study each Context Card.
- Ask a question that uses one of the Vocabulary words.

5 gadget

A small gadget with many parts, such as a watch, can be hard to repair.

6 electric

The invention of the electric fan helps us to stay cool in hot weather.

7 signal

A red light is a signal to stop. This invention helps to save lives.

8 occasional

A good invention has an occasional problem but should not fail regularly.

Background

✔ **TARGET VOCABULARY**   **Bright Ideas** In cartoons, a light bulb often appears over someone's head. It's a signal that the character has a bright idea. The first long-lasting electric light bulb was an invention by Thomas Edison. Look on the timeline below to see when it was invented.

You don't have to be a genius to be an inventor. First, think of a problem. Next, think of a gadget that might fix it. Test the gadget in an experiment in a laboratory. It's okay to expect occasional failure. To succeed, an inventor must have lots of patience.

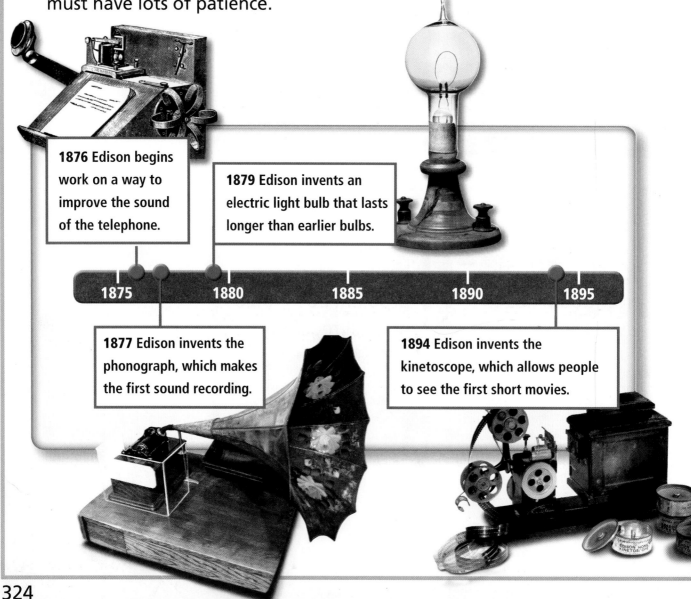

1876 Edison begins work on a way to improve the sound of the telephone.

1879 Edison invents an electric light bulb that lasts longer than earlier bulbs.

| 1875 | 1880 | 1885 | 1890 | 1895 |

1877 Edison invents the phonograph, which makes the first sound recording.

1894 Edison invents the kinetoscope, which allows people to see the first short movies.

Comprehension

✔ TARGET SKILL Main Ideas and Details

The author of *Young Thomas Edison* includes many main, or important, ideas about Edison as a boy. The supporting details, or facts and examples, tell more about each main idea. As you read *Young Thomas Edison*, use a chart like this to record details that support some main ideas about Edison.

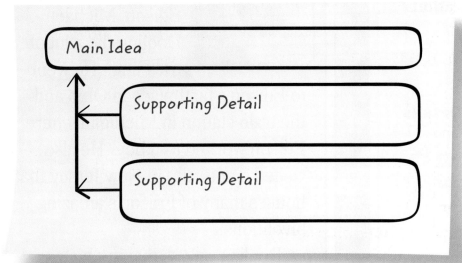

Main Idea

Supporting Detail

Supporting Detail

✔ TARGET STRATEGY Summarize

Sort out the main ideas from the supporting details in the selection. Then use the main ideas to summarize, or retell in your own words, the important events in Edison's life.

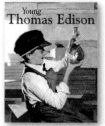

Young Thomas Edison

TARGET VOCABULARY

invention	gadget
experiment	electric
laboratory	signal
genius	occasional

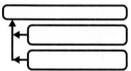

TARGET SKILL

Main Ideas and Details
Tell important ideas and details about a topic.

TARGET STRATEGY

Summarize Tell the important parts of the story in your own words.

GENRE

The author of a **biography** writes about another person's life. The author of an **autobiography** writes about his or her own life. Is *Young Thomas Edison* a biography or autobiography?

 TEKS **3.9** explain point of view in biography/autobiography;

MEET THE AUTHOR AND ILLUSTRATOR

Michael Dooling

When he was researching his book about Thomas Edison, Michael Dooling did a lot of traveling. He went to Edison's birthplace in Ohio and the train station in Michigan where Edison worked as a boy. He also visited a museum in New Jersey that houses many of Edison's amazing inventions.

Dooling enjoys making history come alive for students. If he ever visited your school, he would most likely show up dressed like Paul Revere.

Young Thomas Edison

by Michael Dooling

Essential Question

Why are details important in a biography?

Thomas Alva Edison was born in a little house in Milan, Ohio, on February 11, 1847, to Samuel and Nancy Edison. He was the youngest of seven children.

Thomas, who was called Young Al by his family, lived in an era very different from ours. There was no electric light, no telephone, no radio or CD player; not even a movie theater.

q ─ ─ . ─ .

$F = k \cdot \dfrac{Q_1 \cdot Q_2}{d^2}$

truths are easy to understand.

once they are discovered; the point is to discover them."
— Galileo

3.14159

9.6485×10^4

— electricity

$S =$

$c \quad \dfrac{dv \; at}{dt}$

$V = 0 \, m/s$

objects at rest stay at re

Ni = Nickel

P = Phospho

geolo

= Copr

Thomas loved to experiment. In 1856, at the age of nine, he turned his family's cellar into a laboratory complete with test tubes, beakers, and whatever chemicals he could buy. It was a mess—bottles were everywhere. Young Al would mix one chemical after another, sometimes following the experiments in his chemistry book—sometimes not. "A little of this and a little of that," he used to mumble.

His mother always encouraged him to ask questions, and he did. What is this? Why does that happen? How does it happen?

✔ **STOP AND THINK**

Main Ideas and Details Identify the main idea and supporting details in the first paragraph on this page.

TEKS 3.13A **ELPS** 4I

A bout of scarlet fever left Al hard of hearing, which made school difficult. While Al asked many questions at home, he did not ask any at school. Instead he spent his time there daydreaming about his next experiment.

Al's mother, a former teacher, took him out of school after only three months. From then on, she taught him at home. Mrs. Edison made sure he received an excellent education. He read Shakespeare, the Bible, history, and much more. Over the next few years he also studied the great inventors, such as Galileo.

At age twelve Young Al decided to look for a job.
He needed money to continue his experiments. So he
went into business as a paperboy on the train that
went from Port Huron, where the Edisons now lived, to
Detroit, Michigan. Every morning from 7 A.M. to
10 A.M. Al sold newspapers.

Then he spent all day at the Detroit library, reading and dreaming about his next experiment. He planned to read every book in the library, starting with the last book on the shelf and working back to the first. At night he took the train home and sold papers again.

✔️ **STOP AND THINK**

Summarize Using your own words, summarize how Al spent his days after getting his first job.
ELPS 4G

Eventually, with the permission of the conductor, Al set up a laboratory in the baggage car of the train. Soon the young scientist was experimenting with everything: chemicals, gadgets, test tubes, beakers, doohickeys, and thingamajigs.

Things were going well until one day when the train made a sudden lurch. Bottles, books, newspapers, candies, and fruits went flying—along with Al. A bottle of phosphorus burst into flames. Al scrambled to put out the flames, but they spread too fast. Soon a very upset conductor rushed in. At the next stop the conductor threw all of Al's things off the train—even him!

Al had never been so disappointed in his life. He went home and set up his laboratory again with the encouragement of his mother. He continued to experiment and tinker with every gadget he could get his hands on. Usually his experiments did not work—but he always kept trying.

Before long Al had another job. He was a "night wire"—a railroad telegraph operator—in Stratford Junction, Canada. There was a lot to learn. For weeks, he soaked up all the information he could about telegraphy.

Al learned Morse code and much more. He worked the 7 P.M. to 7 A.M. shift, often sleeping right in the station. He also set up his laboratory in the back room of the station so that he could experiment in his off-hours. Apart from the occasional explosion life was grand.

STOP AND THINK

Author's Craft Why does the author choose the words *soaked up* to describe Al's experience learning telegraphy?

TEKS 3.2B; **ELPS** 2C

One of Al's duties as the operator was to send the signal 6 every hour on the hour to show the dispatcher at the next station that he was awake. But the long hours sometimes caught up with him and he would fall asleep, so the scientist in him had an idea. Soon Al had invented a device that hooked the telegraphy key to a clock. When the hour struck, the minute hand of the clock sent the message 6 for him. It was a moment of pure genius, which quickly got him fired when his boss discovered he was sleeping on the job.

For the next five years, young Edison traveled all over the South and Midwest from one telegraph job to another. He continued to try to find ways to improve the telegraph. At age twenty-one he made his way to Boston, Massachusetts, and started using his first name, Thomas. He decided that he was going to be an inventor, and he set up his latest laboratory. He wanted to learn all he could about electrical forces. His first patented invention was the *Electrical Vote Recorder*. Unfortunately, Congress did not like his invention and he could not sell it.

Over the years, Thomas's hearing had grown worse. By now, he was nearly deaf. This did not hamper his creative abilities though. In fact, he thought it even helped him to concentrate because he was not distracted by noises. It created solitude where he could tune out the whole world and think.

In 1869 Thomas moved to New York City and then later established his laboratory in Newark, New Jersey. And then bad news came from home. His mother had died. Thomas, at twenty-four, was deeply saddened. For a long time he could not even speak of her. He would miss her letters—her advice and encouragement. He owed everything to his mother.

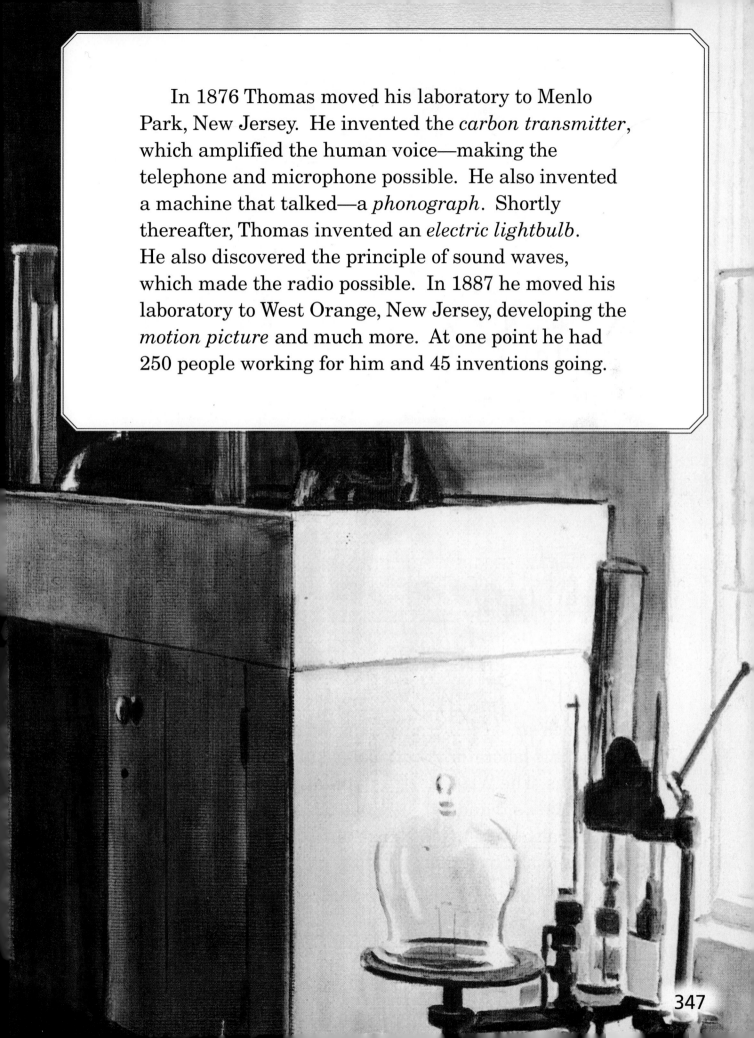

In 1876 Thomas moved his laboratory to Menlo Park, New Jersey. He invented the *carbon transmitter*, which amplified the human voice—making the telephone and microphone possible. He also invented a machine that talked—a *phonograph*. Shortly thereafter, Thomas invented an *electric lightbulb*. He also discovered the principle of sound waves, which made the radio possible. In 1887 he moved his laboratory to West Orange, New Jersey, developing the *motion picture* and much more. At one point he had 250 people working for him and 45 inventions going.

1847-1931

Such strange, incredible inventions were coming out of his laboratory that people started to call Thomas "The Wizard." He would live to be eighty-four years old and patent 1,093 inventions. Thomas would always remember his mother's encouraging words to ask questions. What is this? Why does that happen? How does it happen?

1. What happened right after Al recovered from scarlet fever?

  ⬭ He started to lose his hearing.

  ⬭ He dropped out of school.

  ⬭ He took a job selling newspapers.

  ⬭ He ran his first experiment.

  TEKS 3.8A

2. ✔ **TARGET SKILL** **Main Ideas and Details**

Write one main idea to describe Edison's education. In a chart like this one, list the details that support it.
TEKS 3.13A, **ELPS** 4I

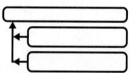

3. ✔ **TARGET STRATEGY** **Summarize**

Use the information in the chart above to summarize Thomas Edison's education. **TEKS** 3.2B, **ELPS** 4I

4. **Oral Language** Work with a partner. Take turns describing in detail the key events in Edison's life. Look at your partner as you speak. As you listen to your partner, make sure you understand all important events and details. **TEKS** 3.30; **ELPS** 2G, 3E

TEKS 3.2B ask questions/clarify/locate facts/details/use text evidence; **3.8A** sequence/summarize main events/influence on future events; **3.13A** identify details/facts that support main idea; **3.30** speak coherently/effectively about topics; **ELPS** 2G understand meaning/main points/details of spoken language; **4I** employ reading skills to demonstrate comprehension; **3E** share information in cooperative learning interactions

Moving Pictures

by Andrew Patterson

You can thank the genius Thomas Edison every time you watch a movie. His laboratory conducted one *moving picture* experiment after another. Workers took just an occasional break. One invention of theirs led to the development of movies. That gadget was the kinetoscope.

Thomas Edison's Kinetoscope, invented in the late 1800s.

The Kinetoscope

The kinetoscope was a wooden box with a peephole on top. Inside the box was a strip of film. It had photos of someone moving. Spools pulled the film along quickly. An electric lamp flashed on and off. The lamp lit up each photo so the person peering in could see it.

The viewer's eye sent a signal to the brain. It told the brain that the figure was moving, so the viewer thought the figure really *was* moving. This special effect, or trick, was a key part of making *moving pictures*, or movies.

Movie Magic!

By the early 1900s, Hollywood was becoming the world's movie capital. At the same time, westerns were becoming the most popular movies. Westerns often told stories about cowboys, horses, and the wide-open Texas plains. But in fact, many westerns were filmed in Hollywood studios!

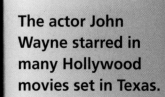

The actor John Wayne starred in many Hollywood movies set in Texas.

Special Effects

Filmmakers today use special effects, just as Edison did. Some special effects make events seem real. A blue screen is one way to make people look like they are flying!

How Superheroes Fly

1 Filmmakers film an actor hanging in front of a plain blue screen.

2 A film of city skyscrapers becomes the background.

3 Filmmakers make an empty space in the background. The space is the exact shape of the hanging actor.

4 Filmmakers fit the picture of the actor into the empty space to make a movie of a superhero flying above the city.

Making Connections

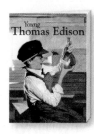 

 Text to Self

Make a Poster Thomas Edison's inventions changed the ways people lived and worked. Many of them are used today. Draw a poster to show all of the ways you use Edison's inventions in your life.

 Text to Text   **TEKS** 3.20B, 3.20C

Write a Letter Imagine you are Thomas Edison, writing a letter to your mother. Tell her about how you invented the kinetoscope, how it works, and what kinds of movies you'd like to make with it. Be sure to include a greeting and closing.

 Text to World   **TEKS** 3.31, RC-3(D); **ELPS** 3F

Connect to Science What do you think Edison would invent today if he were alive? Use what you know from *Young Thomas Edison* to support your ideas. Talk in a small group. Listen to each other and ask questions to come up with new ideas.

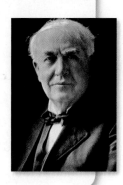

 TEKS **3.20B** write letters tailored to audience/purpose; **3.20C** write responses to texts that demonstrate understanding; **3.31** participate in discussions/build on others' ideas; **RC-3(D)** make inferences/use textual evidence; **ELPS** 3F ask/give information in various contexts

Grammar

Pronouns A **pronoun** can take the place of one or more nouns in a sentence. **Subject pronouns** take the place of a subject. The pronouns *I, you, he, she, it, we,* and *they* are subject pronouns. **Object pronouns** follow action verbs and words like *to, for, at, of,* and *with.* The pronouns *me, you, him, her, it, us,* and *them* are object pronouns.

Academic Language

pronoun

subject pronoun

object pronoun

Nouns	Pronouns
Ben is an inventor.	He is an inventor.
The lab is in Boston.	It is in Boston.
The workers have many ideas.	They have many ideas.
Ben lives with Aunt Joan.	Ben lives with her.
Luis meets Rob and Ben at the lab.	Luis meets them at the lab.
Ben brought a stopwatch.	Ben brought it.

Turn and Talk **With a partner, find the pronoun in each sentence. Classify it as a subject pronoun or an object pronoun. Explain your answer.**

➊ Ruth's mom told her about Thomas Edison.

➋ Do you know the story?

➌ She wanted a book to read.

➍ Dad drove us to the library.

Sentence Fluency Be careful not to repeat a noun too many times in your writing. You can use pronouns in place of nouns to keep your writing from being boring and choppy.

Repeated Nouns	Better Sentences
The inventor had a great idea. The inventor got a patent on the invention. The university gave the inventor an award.	The inventor had a great idea. He got a patent on the invention. The university gave him an award.

Connect Grammar to Writing

As you revise your response to literature, try to replace repeated nouns with pronouns.

Reading-Writing Workshop: Revise

Write to Respond

☑ **Sentence Fluency** Good writers don't say the same thing twice. They make sure each sentence says something new. In your **response to literature**, cross out any sentence that repeats what you have already said.

When Hector revised his response essay, he crossed out sentences that repeated ideas.

Writing Process Checklist

Prewrite

Draft

▶ **Revise**

☑ Did I answer the question?

☑ Did I use words from the question in my opening?

☑ Did I give details and examples from the story?

☑ Did I put my ideas in an order that makes sense?

☑ Did I sum up my reasons at the end?

Edit

Publish and Share

Revised Draft

I think people stopped watching the kamishibai man because of television. Television brought many big changes to Jiichan's town. ~~It made things different there.~~

When the kamishibai man first gave shows, television had not been invented. ~~There weren't any TV's.~~

Later, when people saw a TV in a shop, they ~~people~~ gathered around.

356

Television Was the Reason
by Hector Suarez

I think people stopped watching the kamishibai man because of television. Television brought many big changes to Jiichan's town.

When the kamishibai man first gave shows, television had not been invented. Later, when people saw a TV in a shop, they gathered around. They left Jiichan's show to go stare at the television screen. They were excited by the moving pictures.

Over time, more and more people in the kamishibai man's town bought televisions for their homes.

> I made sure each sentence states a new idea. I also used pronouns to avoid repeating nouns.

Reading as a Writer

Why is Hector's paper better without the two sentences that he crossed out? Cross out ideas in your paper that are repeated.

What Makes Bees So Busy?

1   Have you ever watched a honeybee fly back and forth? It might look as if the bee is just flying around for fun. In fact, the bee is hard at work.

2   Honeybees spend a lot of time <u>foraging</u> for food. They go buzzing from flower to flower, searching for nectar and pollen. Nectar is a sweet liquid. Pollen is a powder. They are both food for bees. When they find nectar and pollen, honeybees carry them home.

3   Bees live in homes called hives. Honeybees make their hives out of a special wax that comes from their bodies. Thousands of honeybees live and work together in a hive. Three kinds of bees live in the hive: a queen bee, drones, and worker bees. The queen and workers are female bees. The drones are male bees.

4   The queen is a very important bee in the hive. Only one queen bee lives in a hive at a time. She is longer than the other bees. She is the mother of all the bees that live in the hive. She lays all the eggs for her hive. One queen bee can lay more than a thousand eggs in a day. Young bees will hatch from these eggs and later grow into adults.

5   Worker bees do all the other jobs in the hive. They make and clean the hive. They guard the hive. They take care of the queen. They protect her. They even feed her because she cannot feed herself. They fly away from the hive to look for pollen and nectar. When they return, they use the pollen they have found to make a special food for the young bees to eat. They also make nectar into honey for the adult bees to eat.

 GO ON

6   Honeybees can communicate with one another. They do special dancing actions inside the hive. These actions send messages about food. Bees use different actions to give different kinds of information. They tell where food can be found and how far away food is from the hive. Bees can even tell each other how much food there is and how good the food is.

7   Bees are not the only fans of honey. People eat honey, too. Some people keep bees and collect honey to sell. They wear special clothes to protect themselves from bee stings.

8   Bees do another important job for people, too. When bees land on a plant, pollen clings to their fuzzy bodies. When bees fly to other plants, they leave bits of pollen behind. This can help certain plants grow.

9   Sometimes a group of bees leaves a hive to start a new hive. This usually happens when a new queen takes over a hive. When the new queen arrives, the older queen leaves the hive. Many worker bees and drones go with the older queen. The bees may cluster around a tree branch. The group waits in a huddle while some worker bees look for the right place to build a new hive. When the worker bees find a good spot, the bees all travel together to make a new hive.

10   The phrase "busy as a bee" makes sense! Bees are certainly interesting and hard-working insects.

GO ON

1   Look at the following diagram of information from the article.

The queen bee is very important.		
She is the only queen in the hive.	She is longer than the other bees.	

Which information belongs in the empty box?

◯ She cleans the hive.

◯ She lays all the eggs.

◯ She feeds the other bees.

◯ She makes the hive.

2   Which word from paragraph 2 means almost the same as <u>foraging</u>?

◯ *searching*

◯ *spending*

◯ *buzzing*

◯ *carrying*

3   What happens when a new queen takes over a hive?

◯ There is not enough pollen.

◯ The worker bees become drones.

◯ The older queen becomes a worker bee.

◯ The older queen leaves.

4   From the article, the reader can tell that —

◯ worker bees only work in the summer

◯ bees can be useful to people

◯ a hive can survive without worker bees

◯ all bees sting

STOP

LEARNING LESSONS

unit 3

Big Idea

Facing a challenge helps us to grow.

Paired Selections

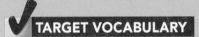

TARGET VOCABULARY

athlete

competitor

championship

professional

power

court

rooting

entire

Vocabulary Reader

Context Cards

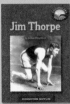

 TEKS **3.4B** use context to determine word meaning; **3.4E** alphabetize to third letter/use dictionary/glossary; **ELPS** **4D** use prereading supports to comprehend texts

Vocabulary in Context

1 athlete
Cycling is the favorite sport of this athlete. He raced in the Olympics.

2 competitor
Each competitor tries her best to help the team win the game.

3 championship
Each player got a medal for winning the championship, or competition.

4 professional
Professional basketball players are paid for their work.

- Study each Context Card.
- Place the Vocabulary words in alphabetical order.

5 power

This player uses all his power, or strength, to hit the ball out of the park.

6 court

Basketball, tennis, and volleyball are played on a court, not on a field.

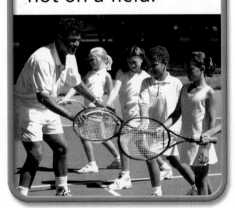

7 rooting

These students love rooting for their favorite team. They cheer loudly.

8 entire

The racer in front led the entire way, from start to finish.

Background

✓ **TARGET VOCABULARY** **Getting Paid to Play** Have you ever wondered what it takes to become a professional athlete? Michael Jordan was one of the best basketball players in the entire world. His power on the court helped his team win more than one championship. Fans everywhere were rooting for him! However, like many great athletes, Jordan was once just an ordinary kid with average skills. It takes years of hard work to become a fierce competitor, even for Michael Jordan.

Would you believe Michael Jordan didn't make the high school basketball team the first time he tried?

Comprehension

✔ TARGET SKILL Fact and Opinion

Identify facts and opinions about Michael Jordan and his family as you read *Jump!* Notice facts that can be proven and opinions that tell someone's thoughts or beliefs. Use a chart like this one to record the facts and opinions you find.

Fact	Opinion

✔ TARGET STRATEGY Question

As you read, keep track of how the facts and opinions on your chart answer questions you may have about Michael Jordan. Also use the chart to help you think of new questions you hope to answer.

JOURNEYS DIGITAL Powered by DESTINATIONReading®

Comprehension Activities: Lesson 11

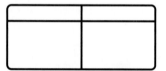
TARGET VOCABULARY

athlete	power
competitor	court
championship	rooting
professional	entire

TARGET SKILL

Fact and Opinion Tell if an idea can be proved true or is a person's belief.

TARGET STRATEGY

Question Ask questions before you read, while you read, and after you read.

GENRE

The author of a **biography** writes about another person's life. The author of an **autobiography** writes about his or her own life. Is *Jump!* a biography or an autobiography?

TEKS **3.2B** ask questions/clarify/locate facts/details/use text evidence; **3.9** explain point of view in biography/autobiography; **ELPS** **4I** employ reading skills to demonstrate comprehension

MEET THE AUTHOR AND ILLUSTRATOR
FLOYD COOPER

When Floyd Cooper makes school visits, students get to see exactly how he creates his artwork. He starts by holding up a blank canvas that he has painted completely brown. Then, using a large eraser, he begins erasing certain areas of the canvas. As his audience watches in amazement, an image like the face of a Native American chief begins to form.

Jump!

from the life of
Michael Jordan

BY
FLOYD
COOPER

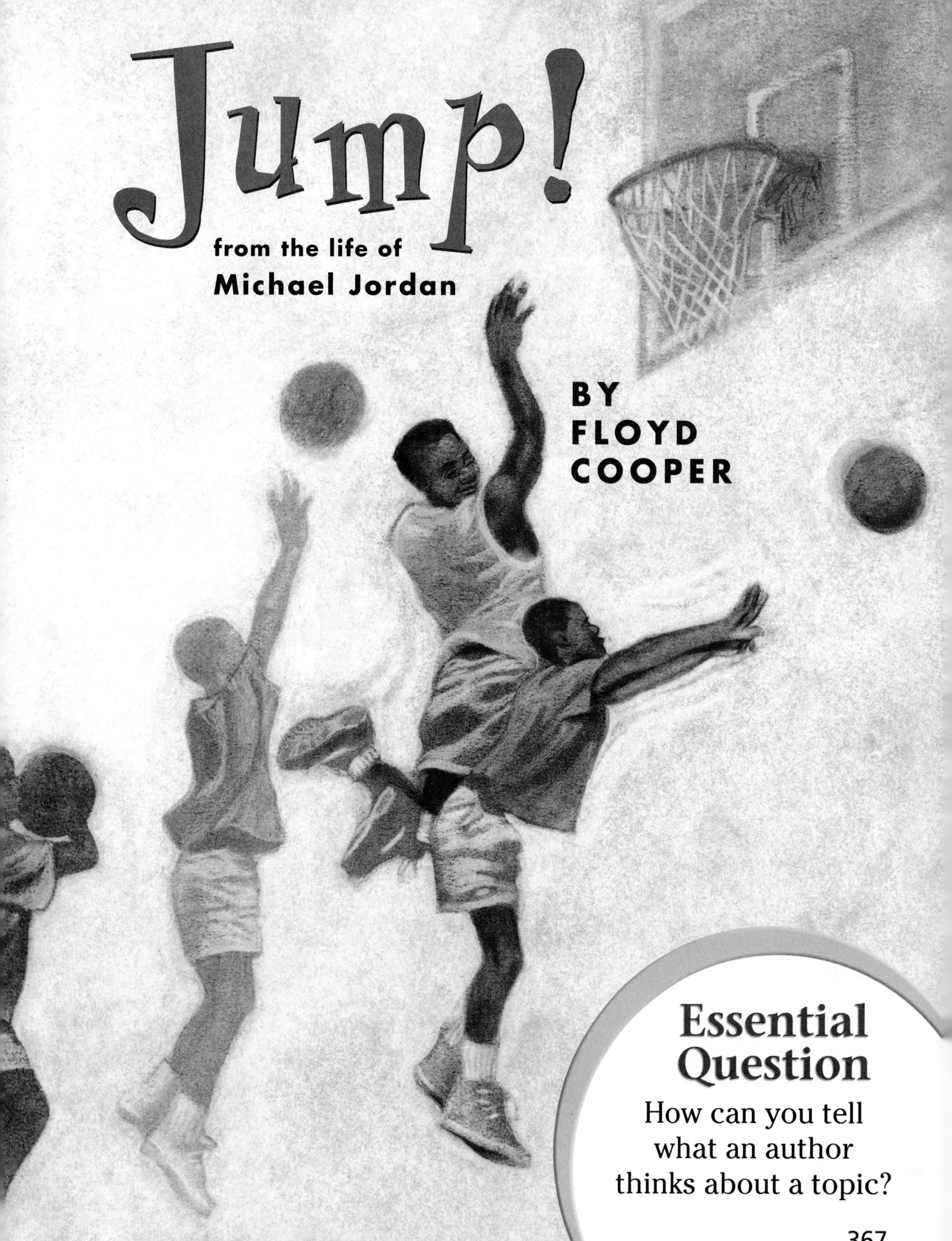

His name is Michael, and from the time he was a little boy, he always seemed to be in and out of mischief. His parents did their best to keep all of the Jordan kids busy at their home in Wallace, North Carolina. James Ronald and Deloris, Larry and Roslyn—those kids couldn't have been happier playing sports and games. But Michael? He just had a different kind of energy, and curiosity, too.

Along with sports, the Jordans gave all the children rules and chores to keep them plenty busy. But there just weren't enough rules or chores to match the boundless bustle of those Jordan kids. They bounced off the walls of their bungalow home. And young Michael was the bounciest.

STOP AND THINK

Author's Craft Find nearby words in the last paragraph that all start with the same sound. Why do you think the author uses this alliteration?

TEKS 3.4D

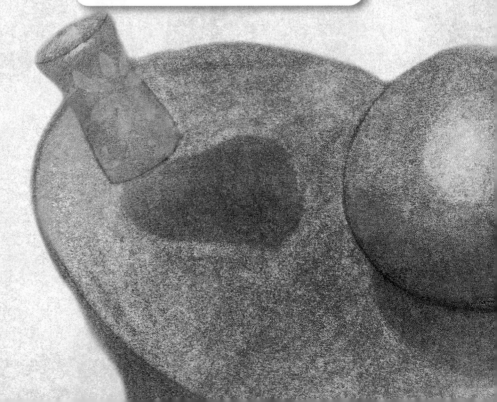

Maybe, the Jordans figured, if they moved to another house, with more room and space.

And that's what they did. When Michael was seven years old, the Jordans moved to suburban Wilmington, North Carolina. Michael's mom and dad even let the kids help build the house so they could learn how working together as a team was the way to get things done—and so they could get rid of some of that energy.

At the new house, Michael ran and played with his new friends. Mostly, though, Michael tried to keep up with his older brother Larry. Trouble was, no matter how Michael tried, it seemed as if Larry was bigger, quicker and luckier.

Michael did not give up. No, no. The more Michael lost, the harder he tried, but the truth is, Larry was always one jump sooner in checkers, one stroke faster in swimming, one breath longer underwater. Larry dashed, Michael only ran. Larry sang, Michael croaked. Larry leaped, Michael only hopped. In fact, growing up, his family called Michael "Rabbit."

One of the first things that Michael's father had done at the new house was to put up a basketball hoop right in the backyard. Kids from all over would play on that hoop. But more and more—after the other kids had gone—the games ended up being a contest between Larry and Michael. They would play one-on-one so much that the grass underneath the hoop refused to grow from the pounding.

Michael wasn't growing much, either! So he started hanging by his arms from a swing set for hours each day, hoping to stretch himself taller. But it was no use. For all too many years, Michael was still only "Rabbit."

✔️ **STOP AND THINK**

Question Why was it no use for Michael to hang from a swing set, hoping to stretch himself taller?

TEKS 3.2B; **ELPS** 4K

Now, Michael knew there was only one way for him to play basketball better than Larry, and that was to play more. He looked to pick up games on the blacktop at school or in the park. Or after he'd lose to Larry, he'd play alone, pounding and sweating and working that poor little backyard court from daybreak to day's end.

And he wouldn't stop until he heard the screen door spring and his father's voice saying, "Come in now, son, time for bed."

Just when he discovered the game at Laney High School is hard to say. But the sun seemed hotter there, the moves seemed quicker on the full blacktop court there, the hoops seemed higher—and the game seemed better to eleven-year-old Michael. The raw power of the springy older players as they shot the ball in the hot, salty breeze, now that was something to see. What did he want? Why, he wanted to be asked to play.

But for what seemed like a long time, he did little more than wish.

Time helps. And it helped Michael. By the time he was in junior high, he was turning out to be a fair baseball player. In fact, when he was twelve, he led his baseball team to the state championship!

He grew smarter, too, persuading his friends to do some of his dreaded chores, like mowing the lawn, and leaving him to do only the ones he enjoyed, like ironing his own shirts. And he began to grow taller, taller than anyone in his family.

Hanging on the swing set must have helped.

✔ **STOP AND THINK**

Fact and Opinion Find at least one fact and one opinion on pages 374–375.

TEKS 3.2B **ELPS** 4I

Despite all the baseball, by the time he was in high school, Michael started to live and breathe basketball. He loved everything about it—the smell of the ball, the swoosh of the net. Soon it was all he wanted to play. He even gave up baseball. He saw less and less of Larry these days because Larry was becoming a true sports star. He was too busy to play with his little brother. More and more Michael hung out at the blacktop by the high school.

One day, the blacktop kids asked him to play. There was a crowd gathered by the fence, boys and girls, but this was Michael's chance!

Suddenly Michael had the ball. He dribbled it down the court, taking the ball hard to the hole, and just as he reached the rim—bam! A huge body slammed into Michael. From the hot tack tar, he looked up at the ball as it bounced off the rim. Michael had blown the layup.

From the side a voice broke the slow-motion silence in a teasing, mocking whine. "Hey, Ears, open your eyes." Michael gritted himself back into the game, but the taunts began to spread from the onlookers.

With each dribble, he was scoffed at for his "little boy" haircut and the way his ears stuck out. With every layup he was jeered about the way his tongue hung out of his mouth when he shot the ball. And right in front of the girls!

None of it stopped Michael. He came back and played the next day, and the next, and the next. And the truth is, he got better and better. Finally one day, he and his buddy Leroy decided to try out for the Laney High School varsity basketball team. Surely he would make it—Larry had.

But at the end of the week, when the list of players was put up, there was no "Michael Jordan" on it. Even Leroy had made the team.

But Coach Herring had seen something he liked in the plucky kid. He put him on the junior varsity team and offered to coach Michael one-to-one if Michael would meet him before school every morning at 6:00 A.M. Michael not only came, he worked hard, dribbling, passing, shooting. Dribbling, passing, shooting. Shooting, shooting. And Michael began to get not just okay, but good.

He got so good, in fact, that the varsity players started coming to all the junior varsity games to watch Michael play.

We don't know exactly when Michael turned the tables on Larry for the first time, but it may very well have happened the summer that Michael shot up four inches and went to basketball camp. One afternoon, the two started going at it again on the backyard hoop.

At first, it seemed just like old times. Family and friends gathered around the hot, sticky court to watch the two brothers. But something was different. When Larry dashed across the court—Michael was there. Larry leaped for the hoop—Michael was there, too.

Soon the brothers were in the thick of the game, a tangle of
arms and legs flashing around the orange ball. Could Michael
actually win? Larry wasn't worried; he was ahead of Michael by
one point. Larry grinned. It was the usual end to the usual game.

Then Michael had the ball. They both knew what usual
meant: Michael would leap to dunk and Larry would jump
higher, grab it and dunk it for the win. Well, Michael leaped, just
like always. And Larry leaped, just like always. But Michael kept
going and going, past the wide span of Larry's hands!

It seemed as if Michael just hung there for a moment. As if
waiting. Was it possible he had outjumped the master?

He had, and he dunked the ball in the hoop for the win.

Michael smiled. He had beaten his brother, the best, at his
own game.

The laughing and hand-slapping that followed that magical game followed Michael Jordan—Rabbit—through his entire career. From basketball camps to college teams, and finally into the professional world of basketball, the NBA.

And Larry was there, too, always an athlete in his own right, but rooting for his best competitor. Brothers, friends: whatever Michael Jordan became had started at their backyard hoop, with Larry, with games that went on past dark, that pushed Michael Jordan to become more than he was. And more than any basketball player has ever been in all time.

Your Turn

1. Which word on page 374 means about the same as <u>strength</u>?

   ⬭ *better*

   ⬭ *springy*

   ⬭ *wish*

   ⬭ *power*

   TEKS 3.4C

2. 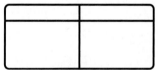 **Fact and Opinion**

   Identify one fact and one opinion about Michael Jordan or Larry Jordan. Use a chart like this to record what you find. **TEKS** 3.2B

3. ✔ **TARGET STRATEGY** **Question**

   Look at your chart. What questions did you ask yourself to help you decide whether what you found was a fact or an opinion? **TEKS** 3.2B

4. **Oral Language** Use the Retelling Cards to describe how Michael works to improve his basketball skills. Speak loudly enough to be heard by your classmates. **TEKS** 3.30 **ELPS** 4G

Retelling Cards

 TEKS **3.2B** ask questions/clarify/locate facts/details/use text evidence; **3.4C** identify/use antonyms/synonyms/homographs/homophones; **3.30** speak coherently/effectively about topics; **ELPS** **4G** demonstrate comprehension through shared reading/retelling/ responding/note-taking

385

Science
for Sports Fans

by Alice Cary

Think about science the next time you are rooting for your favorite team. Science is at work every time an athlete hits a home run or slam-dunks a basketball.

How high professional basketball players jump depends on how much force, or power, they use to push off the court. They jump higher when they push harder. As a result, they fly through the air longer. Scientists say that a player who jumps four feet to slam-dunk hangs in the air for one full second.

WHERE IS THE SWEET SPOT?

Do you want to win a baseball championship? You can send the ball flying if you hit it with the bat's *sweet spot*. To find it, get a wooden baseball bat and a hammer. Then follow these steps.

1 Hold the bat between your thumb and index finger, just below the knob.

2 Have a friend use the hammer to tap the bat, starting at the bottom and moving up inch-by-inch.

3 The entire bat should vibrate with each tap, but you won't feel a thing when your friend taps the sweet spot.

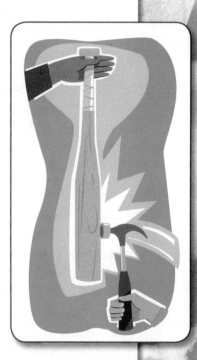

▶ What's Happening?

The bat hardly vibrates when you hit the ball at the sweet spot. Instead, more energy goes into the baseball, sending it farther.

Mastering the *Ollie*

Every skateboard competitor knows how to do an *ollie*. This trick allows skaters to jump over things. When airborne, the board seems glued to their feet.

This trick isn't magic. It's science. A skater pushes down with one foot on the back of the board when he or she jumps. This force raises the front of the board.

Next, the skater pushes the front of the board down. As the skateboard levels, the skater seems to fly through the air without losing contact with the board.

Making Connections

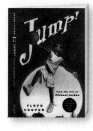

Text to Self   TEKS 3.19, 3.20A(i)

Write about Challenges Larry Jordan challenged Michael to help him learn. Who has challenged you to do better? How did you meet that challenge? Write a paragraph about the experience. Include a sentence that summarizes how the challenge helped you learn.

 Text to Text   TEKS 3.4E; ELPS 1E

Make a Dictionary List sports jargon from *Jump!* and "Science for Sports Fans." Use a dictionary to find out the meaning and the pronunciation of terms that are unfamiliar. Arrange the words in alphabetical order. Then write a short definition and simple sentence for each. Consider expanding your dictionary by adding other sports terms you may know or by adding illustrations.

 Text to World   TEKS RC-3(F)

Connect to Science Michael Jordan jumped high enough to slam-dunk a basketball. You read that jumping uses force from muscles. Find out about leg muscles. Then make a diagram to show and label these muscles.

 TEKS **3.4E** alphabetize to third letter/use dictionary/glossary; **3.19** write about personal experiences; **3.20A(i)** establish central idea in brief compositions; **RC-3(F)** make connections between texts; **ELPS 1E** internalize new basic/academic language

Grammar

More Plural Nouns If a noun ends with a consonant and *y*, change *y* to *i*, and add *-es*.

Singular: Marta picked a berry.

Plural: Marta picked berries.

Academic Language

plural noun

Sometimes the spelling of a **plural noun** changes in a special way.

Singular	Plural
woman	women
child	children
mouse	mice
tooth	teeth
foot	feet

 **Change each singular noun to a plural noun. Write your answer.**

❶ city   ❹ body

❷ foot   ❺ tooth

❸ child   ❻ man

Conventions Good writers pay attention to the spellings of plural nouns. Your writing will be clearer if you spell plural nouns correctly. Remember that not every noun is made plural by adding -*s* or -*es*.

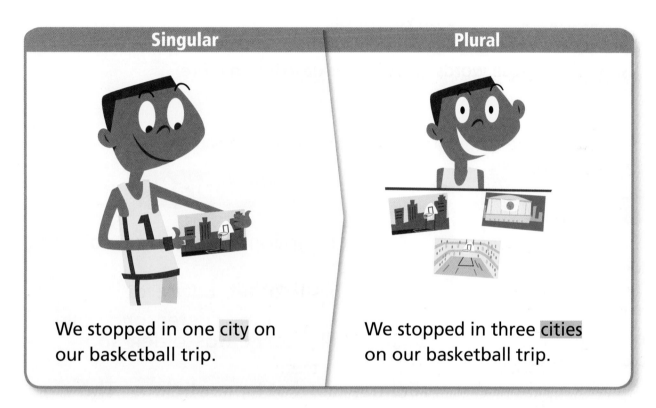

Singular	Plural
We stopped in one city on our basketball trip.	We stopped in three cities on our basketball trip.

Singular: The player stood on one foot to take her foul shot.

Plural: The player stood on two feet to take her foul shot.

Connect Grammar to Writing

As you edit your descriptive paragraph, check that you have spelled all plural nouns correctly.

Write to Narrate

☑ **Word Choice** In *Jump!*, the author uses the sense words *hot* and *sticky* to tell how the court felt. When you write a **description,** use sense words, too.

Jessica wrote a description of Michael Jordan. Later, she added sense words to make her description more interesting.

Writing Traits Checklist

☑ **Ideas**
Did I use details for at least two senses?

☑ **Organization**
Did I begin with a clear topic sentence? Are my details in order?

☑ **Word Choice**
Did I use sense words?

☑ **Voice**
Did I let my feelings come through?

☑ **Sentence Fluency**
Do my sentences flow smoothly?

☑ **Conventions**
Did I edit my work for correct grammar and punctuation?

Revised Draft

Michael Jordan always wanted

to beat his brother, Larry, at

bigger, faster, and taller,
basketball. Larry was ~~older,~~ so
                              ∧

Michael just kept practicing. The

clanged every day from his shots
backyard basketball hoop ~~got a lot~~
                          ∧

~~of use.~~ Michael shot baskets in the

morning, in the afternoon, and into

cool, dark
the ∧ night.

392

Practice Makes Perfect
by Jessica Olsen

Michael Jordan always wanted to beat his brother, Larry, at basketball. Larry was bigger, faster, and taller, so Michael just kept practicing. The backyard basketball hoop clanged every day from his shots. Michael shot baskets in the morning, in the afternoon, and into the cool, dark night. His arms ached at the end of the day. His sweaty clothes stuck to him. After school, he always said "yes" to a game in the park. During the summer, he watched older players move, push, bounce, and shoot on the hot, soft blacktop. Over time, the hard work paid off. Michael got better and better.

> I used sense words in my writing. I was also careful to write plural nouns correctly.

Reading as a Writer

What do Jessica's sense words help you see, smell, hear, taste, or feel? Where can you add sense words in your description?

393

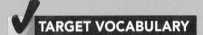

report

presentation

erupt

creative

educational

certificate

impressive

charts

Vocabulary
Reader

Context
Cards

TEKS 3.4B use context to determine word meaning; **ELPS 1E** internalize new basic/academic language

Vocabulary in Context

1 report

This student will report the results of her experiment to her class.

2 presentation

When you give a presentation, you show and tell your ideas about a topic.

3 erupt

To make a model volcano erupt, mix vinegar with baking soda.

4 creative

A creative person is good at creating things and thinking of original ideas.

- **Study each Context Card.**
- **Make up a new context sentence using two Vocabulary words.**

5 educational

When you do an educational activity, you learn something new.

6 certificate

A certificate is an official piece of paper. It is given for an achievement.

7 impressive

These are impressive models. They are well done and took skill to create.

8 charts

Charts, such as tables, diagrams, and graphs, show information.

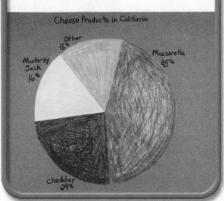

Background

✓ **TARGET VOCABULARY** **Science Fair Challenge** Have you ever thought about entering a science fair but didn't know where to start? First, pick a topic that interests you. Then think of science questions like these that your project will answer—*Why do volcanoes erupt? How does bread get moldy?* After you test your ideas, find a creative way to share the results. All models and charts should be clear and educational.

On the day of the fair, judges may come to your booth and expect you to make a presentation. Be prepared to report what you've learned and to answer any questions. If the judges think your project is impressive, you could win a prize or a certificate.

Comprehension

✔ TARGET SKILL   Story Structure

When a story is told in the first person, the narrator is a story character. This narrator can tell only what he or she sees, thinks, or feels. When a story is told in the third person, the narrator is not a story character. This narrator can tell what one or more characters see, think, and feel. A first-person narrator says *I*, while a third-person narrator says *he*, *she*, *it*, and *they*. As you read *The Science Fair*, use a story map like this to keep track of the characters, setting, and plot. Also identify the narrator.

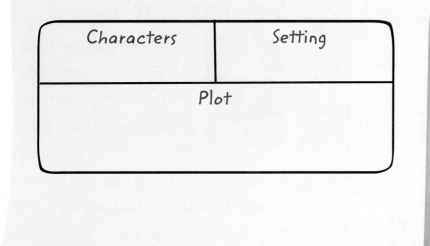

✔ TARGET STRATEGY   Visualize

Include details on your story map that help you picture how characters, story events, and the setting look, feel, and sound.

✔ TARGET VOCABULARY

report	educational
presentation	certificate
erupt	impressive
creative	charts

✔ TARGET SKILL

Story Structure
Name the setting, character, and plot in a story.

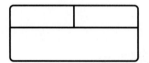

✔ TARGET STRATEGY

Visualize
As you read, use text details and what you already know about the topic to create a clear picture of what is happening in the story.

GENRE

Realistic fiction is a story with events that could happen in real life.

 TEKS RC-3(C) monitor/adjust comprehension; **ELPS 4F** use visual/contextual/ peer/teacher support to read/comprehend texts

---

MEET THE AUTHOR

Susan Wojciechowski

Susan Wojciechowski often writes while sitting in a big, squishy chair in her living room. Sometimes, an idea will come to her while she is doing the dishes. She thought of the character for Beany when she was in bed with the flu!

MEET THE ILLUSTRATOR

Susanna Natti

When she was only five years old, Susanna Natti liked to copy paintings from her parents' art books. By the time she was eight, she already knew she was going to be an illustrator. Susanna Natti likes to work with schools because she thinks that art is especially important there.

The Science Fair

by
Susan
Wojciechowski

illustrated by
Susanna
Natti

Essential Question

How do characters affect the plot of a story?

Ms. Babbitt's third grade class is having a science fair. Beany is a girl in that class who doesn't like science. Her partner, Kevin Gates, is good at science. He came up with two experiments to show that heat makes liquids and gases expand, or get bigger. Beany is proud of herself for figuring out how to show that solids also expand when they are heated.

But Beany is worried that their experiment will not get a good grade. Some of the other students are making glittery posters. Others are going to play music. Kevin insists that all they need is good science. How can they compete without fancy props?

On the day of the science fair, I woke up early, before the alarm went off. I lay in bed hugging Jingle Bell and worrying.

"What if our project is the worst one there? "I said to Jingle Bell. "What if I mess up when I do my part for the judges? What if the judges laugh when they walk away from our table? What if Ms. Babbitt told us that she liked our project just to be nice?" Ms. Babbitt would do something like that. Once I heard my dad tell my mom that Ms. Babbitt does a good job of building self-esteem. When I asked him what that meant, he said she works hard to make us kids feel good about ourselves.

Jingle Bell understood that there was a lot to worry about.

STOP AND THINK

Story Structure Say who is narrating, or telling, this story. Is it a story character? Is it a person from outside of the story? How can you tell?

TEKS 3.8C

On the bus that morning, I saw that Carol Ann and Stacy were dressed alike. Carol Ann and Stacy didn't seem worried. They were talking nonstop about how much fun the science fair was going to be.

"We're handing out rock candy to everyone who comes to see our project," Carol Ann said. "I bet we win first prize."

"Well, maybe second," said Stacy. "The volcano project sounds really good."

Nathaniel and Montrell's project was about how volcanoes erupt. They were going to build a volcano out of papier-mâché and put something inside that would make it all bubbly, like a volcano erupting.

Stacy said, "Your project is good, too," but I knew she was just doing self-esteem on me.

After lunch we went into the gym. There were three rows of tables with four tables in each row set up at the end of the gym.

"You have a half-hour to set up your projects," Ms. Babbitt said. "And have fun," she added. I felt like throwing up.

Gases, liquids, and solids get bigger when they're heated up. It is Not Magic! It is Science!

The Experiments

Heat makes things get bigger:

A. Gas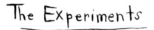

B. Liquid

C. Solid

A. Gas (air)

1.

2.

heat

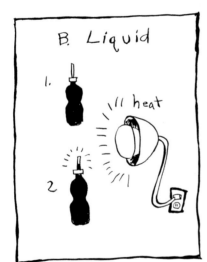

B. Liquid

1.

2.

heat

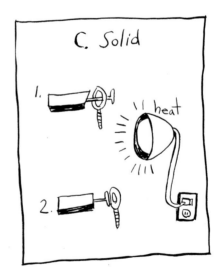

C. Solid

1.

2.

heat

Kevin and I covered our table with a white tablecloth that my mom let us use. It had a big gravy stain in the middle, but she said we could set something on top of the stain so it wouldn't show. We laid out our stuff and a sign. I taped my posters to the front of the table.

When we finished setting up, I walked around the gym to see what the other teams were doing. When I saw the volcano, I ran back to our table. "Kevin, you should see the volcano. It's huge. Why didn't we think of a volcano?"

Before Kevin could say anything, I ran off to look at other projects, then went back to report to Kevin. "Carol Ann and Stacy have streamers all around the edge of their table. Why didn't we think of that? Should I call my mom to ask if she'll run out and buy us some streamers? She'd do it. I know she would."

"We don't need streamers," said Kevin.

I left our table again, then went back with more news. "Manuel and Boomer are doing a planet project, and they have a black tablecloth with stars all over it. Why didn't we use a cool tablecloth instead of a dumb white one with a gravy stain on it?"

"You need to chill," said Kevin. "Forget about what other people are doing and just"—But before Kevin could finish, I ran off again. In a minute I was back.

"Linda and Elaine have bubbles for their project, big ones!" I said, out of breath. "Everybody loves bubbles. Why didn't we do bubbles?"

"Beany," he said, "could you go get some paper towels in case the red water comes up to the top of the straw and runs over?"

Then I noticed the crowd of kids around the table next to ours. I peeked over. It was Shaleeta and Jessica's project. They had a bunch of big balloons on their table and a plate sprinkled with black pepper. "Oh no," I said to Kevin. "Look at all those balloons! Balloons are better than bubbles! How come we only have one itsy-bitsy one in our project?"

Shaleeta rubbed a balloon on her arm and then held the balloon a few inches above the plate of pepper. The pepper jumped right off the plate onto the balloon.

"That happens because of static electricity," Shaleeta explained. Everyone said, "Wow." One kid even said, "That's a winner."

My stomach started to hurt. I told Kevin I had to go to Mrs. Facinelli's office to lie down. Mrs. Facinelli is the school nurse. She has *Ranger Rick* magazines we can look at while we try to feel better.

"If I'm not back by the time it's our turn, you go ahead without me," I said. I almost got away, but Kevin grabbed my arm.

"Paper towels," he said.

STOP AND THINK

Author's Craft Why does the author use dialogue on these two pages? What can you learn about Beany's relationship with other characters by reading peoples' exact words?

TEKS 3.8B

409

Parents started to come into the gym and walk from table to table. Teachers from our school brought their classes to see the projects, too. When I saw my mom and dad, I waved to them, and they came to wish us luck. Kevin said his mom was going to try to get off work early and come, but even though he kept looking toward the door and looking all around the gym, I don't think he saw her.

Then the judges showed up and went from table to table. I started to bite my nails. When they got to the balloon table, I knew we were next. My knees got wobbly.

As the judges walked to our table, Kevin took one last look toward the gym door. He started waving. "She made it," he said. I looked toward the door and saw a woman coming into the gym. She looked out of breath, like she'd been running.

Mr. Shanner said, "Hi, Beany and Kevin. What do we have here?"

"We have a project to show that heat makes things expand, or get bigger," Kevin said.

Then he poked me with his elbow, and I said, "We will now show how heat makes gases expand." Then Kevin did the experiment with the balloon on the bottle and explained everything he was doing as he went along.

Next I said, "We will now show how heat makes liquids expand." Kevin did the bottle and straw experiment and explained it. We did not need paper towels. The red water didn't come up too high, just high enough.

Then it was Kevin's turn to talk. He said, "We will now show how heat makes solids expand." This time I did the experiment, the one with the nail and the eye. When we were finished, Mr. Shanner said, "Hmm." The judges wrote on clipboards and asked us a few questions. They shook our hands and moved on to the next table.

"Why weren't they smiling when they shook our hands?" I asked Kevin. "Why didn't they say *wow* when the water came up the straw? Why did Mr. Shanner say *hmm*? What were they writing on their clipboards?"

Kevin sat down and smiled. "We did a good job," he said.

While we were waiting for the judges to make their decisions, I went over to Carol Ann and Stacy's table and asked how their presentation went.

"Well," said Carol Ann, "I think the judges liked our outfits and necklaces, but they told us to turn off the music so they could hear us better. Plus, we were supposed to start growing the crystals a few days ago, only we forgot to read the instructions on the box. We didn't do it till this morning, so the crystals are kind of small."

I looked at the fishbowl of water on their table. It had a string going through the water and the crystals were supposed to be growing on the string, but all I could see was a little bit of pink grainy stuff on one part of the string.

"And," Stacy added, "Boomer's mom broke a tooth eating our rock candy."

"How did yours go?" Carol Ann asked me.

"Okay, I guess."

The judges came back into the gym. We all went back to our tables. I crossed my fingers. Ms. Kowalski said, "We were very impressed with the efforts of all the students. We hope they are as proud of themselves as we are of them."

Then Mr. Shanner said, "It was hard for us to choose the three best, but after much deliberation, we have chosen for third place the static electricity experiment. It was creative and educational." Shaleeta and Jessica screamed.

My only hope had been third place. I sighed. I uncrossed my fingers and clapped as they went to get their certificates and third-place ribbons.

Next, Ms. Kowalski gave the second-place award. It went to the volcano project. "Nathaniel and Montrell's volcano was impressive," she said, "but it was their charts and their explanation of what causes a volcano to erupt that we especially liked. Those were thorough and easy to understand."

After the clapping, Mr. Shanner coughed, then said, "Now, for the first-place project. We felt the winning project was a fine example of real science. It was organized, clear, and complete."

I knew we wouldn't get first place. I started reciting the seven times table in my head, just to keep myself from crying. But right at seven times four, Kevin started pushing me out from behind our table.

"Go," he said. "We won."

"We what?"

"We won."

I screamed and jumped up and down. I couldn't believe it!

 STOP AND THINK

Visualize Picture how Beany must have looked and sounded when she won first prize. Describe the picture you've created in your mind.

Kevin and I each got a certificate and a blue ribbon that had FIRST PLACE, SCIENCE FAIR stamped on it in gold letters. Ms. Babbitt hugged us. Then she whispered in my ear, "I knew you could make it work." My mom and dad came up and hugged us. So did Kevin's mom.

"Thanks for coming," I heard Kevin say to her.

"I wouldn't have missed it for anything. I'm just sorry I was late," she said. Then his mom pulled a camera out of her purse. "Say *cheeseburger*," she told Kevin and me.

"Aw, Mom, come on," Kevin said. But he smiled.

1. How is Kevin different from Beany?

   ☐ Kevin sets up the science project.

   ☐ Kevin works on the science project.

   ☐ Kevin is co_____ ect.

   ☐ Kevin talk_____

   TEKS 3.2B

2. ✔ **TARGET SKILL** _____

   Use a chart like _____ es from the
   beginning to th_____ ails that
   explain how st_____ d her to change.
   TEKS 3.8B, **ELPS** 4K

3. ✔ **TARGET STRATEGY** **Visualize**

   Beany grows nervous as she walks around the gym to see the
   other teams' projects. Find details and descriptions the author
   gives in the text that help you picture these projects. **TEKS** 3.10

4. **Oral Language** Work with a partner to summarize the plot
   of *The Science Fair*. Take turns telling events in order. Listen
   for any important events or details that your partner leaves
   out or that may be incorrect. **TEKS** 3.8A, 3.29A, RC-3(E); **ELPS** 2I

TEKS **3.2B** ask questions/clarify/locate facts/details/use text evidence; **3.8A** sequence/summarize main events/influence on future events; **3.8B** describe characters' relationships/changes; **3.10** identify sensory language; **3.29A** listen/ask questions/make comments; **RC-3(E)** summarize information in text; **ELPS 2I** demonstrate listening comprehension of spoken English; **4K** employ analytical skills to demonstrate comprehension

Poetry

Poems
About
Science

✔ **TARGET VOCABULARY**

report	educational
presentation	certificate
erupt	impressive
creative	charts

GENRE

Poetry uses the sound and rhythm of words to show images and express feelings. Discuss what the poets here have done to paint pictures for readers. Which parts of the poems are easy to picture, and why?

TEXT FOCUS

Free verse does not follow any one pattern. It sounds like speech. Which poem in this section is written in free verse? Explain how you knew this.

 TEKS **3.6** describe forms of poetry/how they create imagery; **ELPS** **1H** develop/expand learning strategies

Poems About Science

What is science? Is it charts and graphs that report on educational topics? Is it an amazing invention that wins a certificate or award? Well, yes, but science is so much more than that. Science is a butterfly fluttering by. It's a volcano about to erupt. Science is everywhere!

What Is Science?

by Rebecca Kai Dotlich

What is science?
So many things.

The study of stars—
Saturn's rings.
The study of rocks—
geodes and stones—
dinosaur fossils,
old-chipped bones.
The study of soil,
oil, and gas.
Of sea and sky,
of seed and grass.
Of wind
and hurricanes
that blow;
volcanoes,
tornadoes,
earthquakes,
snow.

What is science?
the study of trees.
Of butterflies
and killer bees.
Glaciers, geysers,
clay, and sand;
mighty mountains,
the rolling land.
The power of trains—
planes that soar.
Science is this
and so much more.
So into the earth
and into the sky;
we question
the how
the where
when
and
why.

Metamorphosis

When water turns ice does it remember
one time it was water?
    When ice turns back into water does it
remember it was ice?
    by Carl Sandburg

Write a Poem

Write your own poem about science. Will it be rhyming, or free verse? What will your topic be? Maybe you can write about another kind of metamorphosis, the kind that caterpillars do. Or maybe you can write about killer bees, or tornadoes, or trees. Try to use these words in your poem: creative, presentation, impressive.

Making Connections

 Text to Self

Oral Report Look at the posters Beany made for the science project. Explain the experiment aloud to a partner as if you were speaking to one of the project judges. Then switch roles.

 Text to Text

Word Sort List science words you find in *The Science Fair* and in the two science poems. Use a dictionary to look up any unfamiliar words. Then find different ways to sort the words into categories, such as part of speech, word meaning, or number of syllables.

Metamorphosis

Science

 Text to World

Connect to Science With a partner, think of an idea for your own science fair project. Research the idea. Write a list of questions your project could answer.

 3.4E alphabetize to third letter/use dictionary/glossary; **3.25A** generate/narrow topics/formulate questions; **3.30** speak coherently/ effectively about topics; **ELPS 1C** use strategic learning techniques to acquire vocabulary; **4G** demonstrate comprehension through shared reading/retelling/summarizing/responding/note taking

Grammar

More Proper Nouns There are many kinds of **proper nouns**. The names of particular people, pets, places, geographical names, and historical periods are all proper nouns. Proper nouns begin with a capital letter.

Academic Language

proper nouns

Proper Nouns	
Grandma, Dad, Mom (when used in place of a name)	Mr. Foster
my dog Freckles	Kathy and Pete
Meadows Elementary School	Austin, Texas
the Stone Age	the Great Depression

 **Which nouns should begin with a capital letter? Write each sentence correctly.**

❶ The science fair was held at fullmore high school.

❷ We studied the iron age in science class.

❸ John and caitlin are doing an experiment with magnets as part of their science project.

422

Sentence Fluency Good writers use pronouns carefully. Be sure your reader can tell to whom or what a pronoun refers. Changing a pronoun to a noun or a proper noun might help make your writing clearer.

Unclear Paragraph

HOOOOW!

HOOOOW!

Pokey is our puppy. He loves to pester our older dog, Pal. He thinks he is a wolf. He howls instead of barking. He is really different from Pal. He obeys us.

Clearer Paragraph

HOOOOW!

Pokey is our puppy. He loves to pester our older dog, Pal. Pokey thinks he is a wolf. He howls instead of barking. Pokey is really different from Pal. Pal obeys us.

Connect Grammar to Writing

As you revise your writing, look for pronouns that repeat or are unclear. Try replacing some pronouns with proper nouns to make your writing clearer.

Write to Narrate

☑️ **Word Choice** When you write your **funny poem**, use onomatopoeia. The sensory words *zip, sizzle, chirp,* and *pop* are examples of onomatopoeia. They sound like what they mean.

Ben wrote a funny poem about a bee. He used onomatopoeia to make his poem more lively and fun to read.

Writing Traits Checklist

☑️ **Ideas**
Did I keep my poem focused on the topic?

☑️ **Organization**
Did I tell who, what, when, and where?

☑️ **Word Choice**
Did I use exact words and onomatopoeia?

☑️ **Voice**
Did I write in a funny tone?

☑️ **Sentence Fluency**
Did I use pronouns to vary my sentences?

☑️ **Conventions**
Did I edit for correct punctuation?

Revised Draft

Buzz! Buzz!

buzzed
A bee ~~flew~~ into the classroom.

shouted
Ms. Brown ~~said,~~ "Eek!"

She
~~Ms. Brown~~ was so scared.

424

The Classroom Visitor

by Ben Hughes

Buzz! Buzz!

A bee buzzed into the classroom.

Ms. Brown shouted, "Eek!"

She was so scared.

Boom! Crash!

Mrs. Brown fell off her chair.

I used onomatopoeia. I also changed a proper noun to a pronoun so my sentences would be different.

Reading as a Writer

How does onomatopoeia make Ben's poem more fun to read? Where can you add onomatopoeia to your poem?

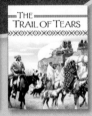

✓ **TARGET VOCABULARY**

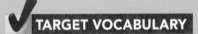

examined

peak

fondly

steep

rugged

mist

pausing

pleaded

Vocabulary
Reader

Context
Cards

ELPS 4D use prereading supports to comprehend texts

Vocabulary in Context

1 examined

The hiker examined the tree and saw claw marks left by bears.

2 peak

This goat lives near the peak, or top, of a mountain. It likes high rocky cliffs.

3 fondly

Wolf mothers treat their pups fondly. They are always kind and gentle.

4 steep

This mountain is steep. It reaches straight up into the sky!

- Study each Context Card.
- Make up a new context sentence that uses two Vocabulary words.

5 rugged

Riders on rugged trails go slowly to avoid bumps, rocks, and holes.

6 mist

Most animals enjoy a gentle mist but look for shelter in pouring rain.

7 pausing

The buffalo in this stream is pausing, or stopping briefly, to drink.

8 pleaded

This hungry eaglet pleaded with, or begged, its mother for food.

Background

✓ **TARGET VOCABULARY** **Cherokee History** The Cherokee people lived in what is now the southeastern United States for hundreds of years. They hunted and farmed around the steep, rugged Appalachian Mountains. Cherokee elders fondly taught their children traditional tales. Children examined the meaning of the stories to learn important lessons about their way of life.

In 1838, the Cherokee were forced to leave their lands, even though they pleaded to stay. They marched more than 1,000 miles west without pausing. Today, most Cherokee live in Oklahoma, but thousands still live in the Southeast.

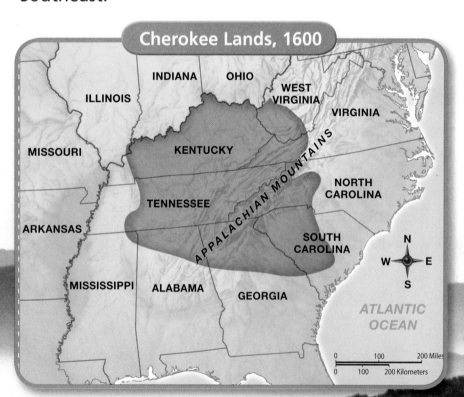

Cherokee Lands, 1600

INDIANA OHIO
ILLINOIS
WEST VIRGINIA
VIRGINIA
MISSOURI
KENTUCKY
APPALACHIAN MOUNTAINS
NORTH CAROLINA
TENNESSEE
ARKANSAS
SOUTH CAROLINA
N
W E
S
MISSISSIPPI ALABAMA
GEORGIA
ATLANTIC OCEAN

0   100   200 Miles
0 100 200 Kilometers

In the background photo of the Appalachian Mountains, peak after peak appear covered in mist. Find the mountains on the map. Which states do they stretch across?

Comprehension

✓ **TARGET SKILL** **Compare and Contrast**

When you read *Yonder Mountain*, figure out the main story problem. Pay attention to how the three young men in the story deal with the challenge they face. Use a chart like this one to record details that compare and contrast the three characters' experiences on the mountain.

Character 1	Character 2	Character 3

✓ **TARGET STRATEGY** **Analyze/Evaluate**

Use details from your chart to analyze what happens to the story characters and to evaluate how well you feel each character deals with the story problem.

Main Selection

 **TARGET VOCABULARY**

examined	rugged
peak	mist
fondly	pausing
steep	pleaded

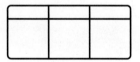 **TARGET SKILL**

Compare and Contrast
Tell how details or ideas are alike and different.

 **TARGET STRATEGY**

Analyze/Evaluate Think about what you read. Then form an opinion about it.

GENRE
A **legend** is a very old and popular story that may be true. After you read *Yonder Mountain*, tell in your own words the author's theme, or most important idea.

 TEKS **3.5A** paraphrase themes/details of tales **ELPS** **4K** employ analytical skills to demonstrate comprehension

MEET THE AUTHOR

Robert H. Bushyhead

Yonder Mountain is a story that was passed down in the Bushyhead family. Robert Bushyhead grew up speaking the Cherokee language, a language so beautiful that he once compared it to the sound of "a waterfall flowing." He worked to record the language so future generations could enjoy its beauty as much as he does.

 **MEET THE ILLUSTRATOR**

Kristina Rodanas

Kristina Rodanas uses watercolors, pastels, and colored pencils to create her illustrations. After reading one of Rodanas's books, a student once wrote her a letter, saying, "I can still see the pictures in my mind long after I closed the book."

Yonder Mountain
A Cherokee Legend

by Robert H. Bushyhead
illustrated by Kristina Rodanas

Chief Sky has grown too old too lead his people, and he's looking for someone to replace him. What is he looking for in a new chief? Find out by reading this Cherokee folktale.

Once in the land of the Cherokee people, there lived a beloved chief called Sky. Chief Sky had seen many summers and winters. He had led his people through long seasons of peace. He had seen their warriors go through great battles with enemies. But now his step was slow, and his hand trembled on the bow. He could no longer spot brother deer among the trees. He was no longer able to lead his people.

One day in the season of falling leaves, the chief called three young men to him and said, "One of you will take my place and become chief and lead our people. But first, I must put you to the test."

Chief Sky turned slowly, looking into the distance. "Do you see yonder mountain?"

STOP AND THINK

Compare and Contrast What is the same about Chief Sky long ago and today? What is different? Why does he think one of the young men should replace him?

434

The three young men followed the gaze of their chief and saw a great mountain rising out of the mist in the distance. "Yes," they answered. "We see the mountain."

Chief Sky pointed toward the highest peak. "I want you to go to the mountaintop. Bring back to me what you find there."

The first young man called Black Bear quickly started up the side of the mountain. After the sun reached the middle of the day, Black Bear came to a wide place in the trail where he stopped to rest. He leaned his head upon a rock, and his eyes grew heavy. Just as his eyes were closing, he caught sight of a thousand lights twinkling in the sun. Black Bear sat up straight and saw stones of great beauty lining each side of the trail. They sparkled and glowed in the sunlight. Black Bear examined a stone, carefully turning it over and over in his hand and watching the sun dance on each surface. "If my people had these stones, they would never be hungry again," he said. "We could trade them for food and our lives would be better."

Black Bear gathered many sparkling stones and ran down the mountain and back to his village. The people saw him coming and lined the path as he entered the village. The children pointed to the sparkling stones and said, "See the pretty stones Black Bear has found." Black Bear handed the stones to Chief Sky and said, "My chief, look what I have found—beautiful stones! We can trade them for food and will never go hungry. We will be safe through many winters."

The chief smiled fondly upon the young man and said, "You have done well, my son. You have done well. Let us now wait for the others."

The second young man called Gray Wolf climbed the mountain and went past the place of the sparkling stones. He climbed higher and higher. The trail became steep and rugged. Finally, he came to an open place where he rested beside the trail. He picked an herb, looking closely at its pointed leaves and long roots. "These are the healing plants of our medicine man," he said. "If my people have these herbs and roots, they will no longer be sick and suffer. We could be healed with these plants." Gray Wolf gathered one of each of the plants and hurried down the mountain.

The people saw him coming and lined the pathway. The children waved and the elders said, "See all the herbs Gray Wolf has found. We will never be sick again!"

Gray Wolf ran to his chief and spread the plants before him. "Look, my chief, what I have found. We no longer need to suffer. I have found all kinds of herbs, and we can be healed."

The old chief smiled fondly on Gray Wolf and said, "You have done well, my son. You have done well. Now let us wait for Soaring Eagle, our last young man."

✔ **STOP AND THINK**

Analyze/Evaluate Who do you think has done better so far, Gray Wolf or Black Bear? Which young man would you pick as chief? Why?
ELPS 4K

They waited. Days went by and Soaring Eagle did not return. Still the village waited. After six days, the people began to murmur. "Something must have happened to Soaring Eagle. Why wait any longer?" But Chief Sky said to his people, "We will wait one day longer." And so they waited.

On the seventh day, as the sun cast its long shadow over the village, the people saw Soaring Eagle coming. He stumbled with bleeding feet. His clothes were ripped and torn. He held nothing in his hands.

The people were quiet as Soaring Eagle fell at the feet of his chief. Soaring Eagle spoke softly to Chief Sky. "I went to the top of the mountain, my chief. But I bring back nothing in my hands. I passed a place where there were sparkling stones, but I remembered you said go to the top of the mountain. I passed a place where all sorts of herbs grew, but I remembered your words. The path was rough. There were great cliffs and sharp rocks. I have nothing in my hands to show you, but I bring back a story from the top of the mountain."

The old chief put his hand on the shoulder of the young man. "Tell us your story, my son."

Soaring Eagle began. "As I stood on yonder mountain and looked across the valley and beyond the farthest mountain, I saw a smoke signal. It was a signal calling for help. The signal said 'We are dying,' and then 'Come and help us.'"

Soaring Eagle rose to his feet. "Chief Sky," he pleaded. "We need to go to them quickly. They are in trouble."

Chief Sky stood straight before his people and the three young men. Pausing for a time, he lifted his eyes to the mountains and watched the mist settle on the peaks. He then turned to his people and spoke. "We need a leader who has climbed to the top of the mountain. We need one who has seen beyond the mountain to other people who are in need."

The people watched as Chief Sky carefully began to remove his robe. He turned to face Soaring Eagle. "You, my son, shall wear the chief's robe," the beloved old leader declared. Chief Sky placed the robe over the torn clothing of the chosen young man. "You shall be our next chief, Soaring Eagle. You will lead our people and help those in need. Yes, you will be our chief and help us climb yonder mountain."

STOP AND THINK

Author's Craft Why do you think Chief Sky gives the robe to Soaring Eagle? What does the robe stand for?

446

1. The word <u>pleaded</u> on page 444 means —

 ⬭ whispered

 ⬭ begged

 ⬭ ordered

 ⬭ yelled

 TEKS 3.4C; **ELPS** 1C, 4F

2. 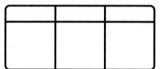 **Compare and Contrast**

 Black Bear, Gray Wolf, and Soaring Eagle each make a different discovery. Use a chart to record details that describe what each man found and why each of their discoveries is important. **TEKS** 3.2B

3. ✔ **TARGET STRATEGY** **Analyze/Evaluate**

 Do you agree with Chief Sky's decision to make Soaring Eagle the new chief? Use story details and your chart to support your opinion. **TEKS** 3.2B, RC-3(D)

4. **Oral Language** Work with the class to retell important parts of the legend in your own words. Use the Retelling Cards. Speak at a pace that is not too fast or too slow. **TEKS** 3.30 **ELPS** 4G

Retelling Cards

 TEKS 3.2B ask questions/clarify/locate facts/details/use text evidence; **3.4C** identify/use antonyms/synonyms/homographys/homophones; **RC-3(D)** make inferences/use textual evidence; **ELPS 1C** use strategic learning techniques to acquire vocabulary; **4F** use visual/contextual/ peer/teacher support to read/comprehend texts; **4G** demonstrate comprehension through shared reading/retelling/responding/note-taking

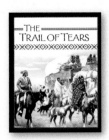

THE TRAIL OF TEARS

by Samuel Winters

The Cherokee Homeland

In 1830, the Cherokee lived in the southeast part of the United States. White settlers wanted Cherokee land. They wanted it to farm. They wanted to look for gold on it. Why? People had found gold in Georgia. Most of the gold was on Cherokee land.

Most Cherokee did not want to move west. The U.S. army examined them closely as they marched to make sure no Cherokee escaped.

Loss of Land

The U.S. government passed a law in 1830. It was the Indian Removal Act. The law let the President give land to Native Americans. The land was west of the Mississippi. In return, Native Americans would give up their land in the east. Then white settlers could have it.

In 1835, a small group of Cherokee signed a treaty. They sold their land to the U.S. government. They would move west. Most Cherokee did not want to give up their land, but the U.S. government said the treaty meant that all Cherokee had to move.

The Hard Journey

In 1838, the U.S. Army forced about sixteen thousand Cherokee from their homes. They left the farms they had tended fondly. They moved to what is now Oklahoma. Some went by boat. Most of them marched.

Parts of the trail were steep and rugged. Women carried their babies over each mountain peak. The weak and very young rode. Mist swirled around them. Rain and snow lashed at them. The Cherokee marched on, pausing only briefly for rest. Many people became ill. They had little food. Thousands died. The Cherokee pleaded with the soldiers to stop long enough to allow them to bury those who had died.

A survivor told what the sad journey was like. "Children cry and many men cry . . . . Many days pass and people die . . . ." The Cherokee reached Oklahoma in the winter. They called the hard journey *the Trail Where They Cried*.

The U.S. government created the *Trail of Tears National Historic Trail* in 1987 to honor the Cherokee. It stretches for 2,200 miles across nine states.

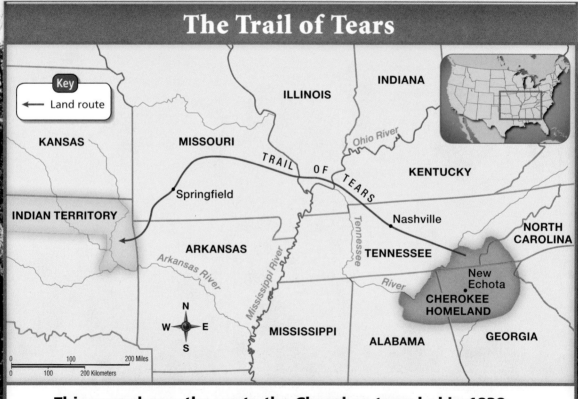

This map shows the route the Cherokee traveled in 1838. What made the journey so difficult?

Making Connections

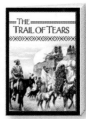

 ## Text to Self

TEKS 3.19, 3.20C; **ELPS** 5G

Write about Legends *Yonder Mountain* is a legend that teaches a lesson and also teaches about the Cherokee people. Think about a time when you learned a lesson. Write about it as a story so that it teaches the reader about you and about what you learned.

An Important Lesson About Helping Others

 ## Text to Text

TEKS 3.31; **ELPS** 3J

Compare and Contrast How were the journeys of the Cherokee men in *Yonder Mountain* similar to and different from the journey of the Cherokee you read about in "The Trail of Tears"? Discuss the reasons each had for leaving and the challenges they faced.

 ## Text to World

TEKS 3.26A(ii)

Connect to Social Studies Identify three historical details about the Cherokee people. Use *Yonder Mountain*, "The Trail of Tears," and your own research to find the information. Make a list to show the information and display it for the class.

 TEKS **3.19** write about personal experiences; **3.20C** write responses to texts that demonstrate understanding; **3.26A(ii)** collect information from experts/reference texts/online searches; **3.31** participate in discussions/build on others' ideas; **ELPS 3J** respond orally to information in media; **5G** narrate/describe/explain in writing

Grammar

Subject-Verb Agreement Verbs in the present tense have two forms. When the **subject** is singular, add *-s* or *-es* to the **verb**. When the subject is plural, do not add *-s* or *-es* to the verb.

Academic Language

subject

verb

subject-verb agreement

Singular	Plural
The boy climbs a mountain.	The boys climb a mountain.
The tribe waits below.	The tribes wait below.
Gray Wolf returns.	The scouts return.
He watches the boys.	They watch the boys.

Turn and Talk **Work with a partner. Read each sentence aloud. Choose the correct verb for each sentence.**

❶ The scouts (start, starts) their hike.

❷ A hill (rise, rises) sharply.

❸ They (struggle, struggles) over the rocks.

❹ The hot sun (beat, beats) down on them.

❺ Running Bear (get, gets) to the top first.

Conventions In your writing, pay attention to the endings of the verbs you use. The correct form to use depends on what the subject of the sentence is. Always check the spelling of each verb ending.

Singular Subject	Plural Subject
The <u>hiker</u> climbs the mountain.	The <u>hikers</u> climb the mountain.

Singular Subject: The <u>man</u> watches an eagle.
The <u>eagle</u> carries fish in its talons.

Plural Subject: The <u>men</u> watch an eagle.
<u>Eagles</u> carry fish in their talons.

Connect Grammar to Writing

As you edit your writing, look for incorrect spellings of verbs in the present tense. Change the verb form to make it go with the subject.

Write to Narrate

✓**Organization** A narrative poem is a poem that tells a story. Use rhyming couplets, or pairs of lines that rhyme, to make your **narrative poem** fun to read.

Chloe wrote a narrative poem about a challenge she faced. Later she revised it and added rhyming couplets.

Writing Traits Checklist

☑ **Ideas**
Did I write about a challenge I faced?

☑ **Organization**
Did I use rhyming couplets?

☑ **Word Choice**
Did I include details about people, places, and events?

☑ **Voice**
Did I tell how I felt when I faced my challenge?

☑ **Sentence Fluency**
Did I use only words that were necessary?

☑ **Conventions**
Do my sentences have the correct subject-verb agreement?

Revised Draft

I started third grade at a brand-new

school.

              not cool
Moving away was really ~~so sad~~!

Leaving old friends ~~that I've had forever~~

was hard enough,

             really tough!
but making new ones would be ~~too scary~~.

The First Day of School
by Chloe Williams

I started third grade at a brand-new school.

Moving away was really not cool!

Leaving old friends was hard enough,

but making new ones would be really tough!

My big sister Jan always calms my worst fears.

She tries to make sure I don't cry any tears.

Here is the new-kid advice that she gave.

Just be yourself: smart, friendly, and brave.

On the first day, I met my whole class.

I said "Hi!" so much that I ran out of gas.

It's not really hard to make friends, after all.

I made twenty new pals in one day last fall!

I used rhyming couplets in my poem. I also made sure I deleted any unnecessary words.

Reading as a Writer

Which rhyming couplets made the poem more fun to read? Where can you revise your poem to include rhyming couplets?

✔ **TARGET VOCABULARY**

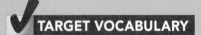

lying
loyal
partners
shift
quiver
patrol
ability
snap

Vocabulary Reader

Dog Helpers
by Kate-Jack Sullivan

Context Cards

TEKS 3.4B use context to determine word meaning; **ELPS 1E** internalize new basic/academic language

456

Vocabulary in Context

1 lying

This dog is lying down. It is stretched out on the floor.

2 loyal

Dogs are usually loyal pets. They stick by their human friends.

3 partners

Many police officers have partners they work with daily.

4 shift

A shift is a period of working time. A shift may be during the day or at night.

- Study each Context Card.

- Discuss one picture. Use a different Vocabulary word from the one in the card.

5 **quiver**

A dog has a strong sense of smell. Its nose may quiver, or twitch, when it sniffs.

6 **patrol**

When police officers patrol, they watch over an area to make sure it is safe.

7 **ability**

An ability is a special skill. Dogs have the ability to run fast.

8 **snap**

Never pet a strange dog without asking permission. It might snap at you.

Background

✔ **TARGET VOCABULARY** **A Partner and Pet** A police officer and a police dog make great partners. A police dog can help an officer patrol an area. A dog has the ability to run fast. It can smell things that humans can't. A police dog is also very loyal. It will snap at a criminal to protect its partner. This can make anyone quiver with fear and surrender!

At the end of a shift, a police dog goes home with its partner. It gets to take a break, do some lying around, and just be a pet.

TEKS 3.12 identify topic/author's purpose; 3.13A identify details/facts that support the main idea; RC-3(D) make inferences/use textual evidence; RC-3(E) summarize information in text ELPS 4I employ reading skills to demonstrate comprehension

Comprehension

✔ TARGET SKILL   Author's Purpose

As you read *Aero and Officer Mike,* identify the topic. Notice the details the author includes about this topic and the way she organizes her ideas. This will help you figure out the author's purpose for writing. Use a chart like this to figure out the author's purpose and the text details that helped you decide.

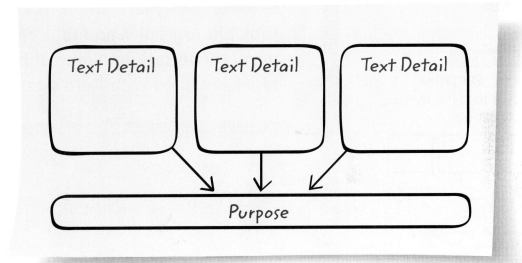

✔ TARGET STRATEGY   Summarize

Use the text details and author's purpose from your chart to summarize the author's main ideas about the topic.

Aero and Officer Mike
POLICE PARTNERS

by Joan Plummer Russell
Photographs by Kris Turner Sinnenberg

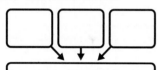

✔ TARGET VOCABULARY

lying	quiver
loyal	patrol
partners	ability
shift	snap

✔ TARGET SKILL

Author's Purpose Use text details to tell why an author writes a book.

✔ TARGET STRATEGY

Summarize Tell the important parts of the text in your own words.

GENRE

Informational text gives factual information about a topic. Skim the headings in this book before reading. Predict what you might learn about police dogs.

 TEKS 3.13D use text features to locate information/make and verify predictions; **ELPS** 4D use prereading supports to comprehend texts

MEET THE AUTHOR

Joan Plummer Russell

To prepare to write this book, Joan Plummer Russell rode along with Officer Mike and Aero twice a month for two years. She took notes, took photographs, and tape-recorded many conversations. Some of her tapes are filled with Aero's barking!

AERO AND OFFICER MIKE
POLICE PARTNERS

by
Joan Plummer Russell

photographs by
Kris Turner Sinnenberg

**Essential
Question**

Why do authors
write different
kinds of texts?

461

It is very early in the morning. Everyone in the house is still asleep. A large black-and-tan German shepherd is lying on the floor by Officer Mike's bed. The alarm rings. Officer Mike reaches down to pet his dog, Aero.

Aero is a police dog, also known as a K-9 officer. When Officer Mike puts on his uniform with a silver badge on his chest, Aero jumps up, ready to have his wide black leather collar with a police badge on it slipped over his head. He knows this will be a work day.

WORK AND PLAY

Officer Mike and Aero are partners. They work together. They practice together. They play together.

Aero, with his powerful nose, can do many things Officer Mike cannot. He can sniff and find lost children. He can sniff and find lost things.

Police dogs are very strong and well trained. They have to be ready to go anywhere they are needed. They can be very fierce when they are helping to catch criminals. They can run faster than any human being. But when police dogs are not working, they are gentle pets that like to have their tummies scratched.

Aero's most important jobs are to help and to protect his partner, Officer Mike. Together, Aero and Officer Mike patrol in all kinds of weather. Some weeks they patrol from early morning until dinnertime. Some weeks they sleep in the daytime and work all night.

STOP AND THINK

Author's Craft Use clues in the text or the photos to help you figure out the meaning of police **jargon,** or specialized language.
TEKS 3.2C

ON DUTY

Aero is always eager to jump into the back of the police car. Officer Mike's car is different from other police cars. There is no back seat. The floor is flat and covered with carpet for Aero to lie on. There is a water bowl built into the floor and a small fan keeps Aero cool in the summer. Screens cover the windows so no one can reach in and pet him.

When Aero is on duty, he's not allowed to play. Officer Mike sits in the driver's seat, but Aero will not let anyone else sit in the front until Officer Mike tells Aero it is OK.

Aero knows that one of his jobs is to protect the police car. When Officer Mike leaves the car, he either opens the front window for Aero to jump through or uses a remote control to open the back door when he needs Aero's help.

TIME FOR A BREAK

When Aero and Officer Mike have been in the police car for a few hours, Aero will need to take a break. Aero pushes his head against his partner's head to let him know. Officer Mike parks the cruiser as soon as he can and says to Aero, "Go be a dog!" Aero knows he'll also have time to explore a little and maybe chase a tennis ball while they are stopped.

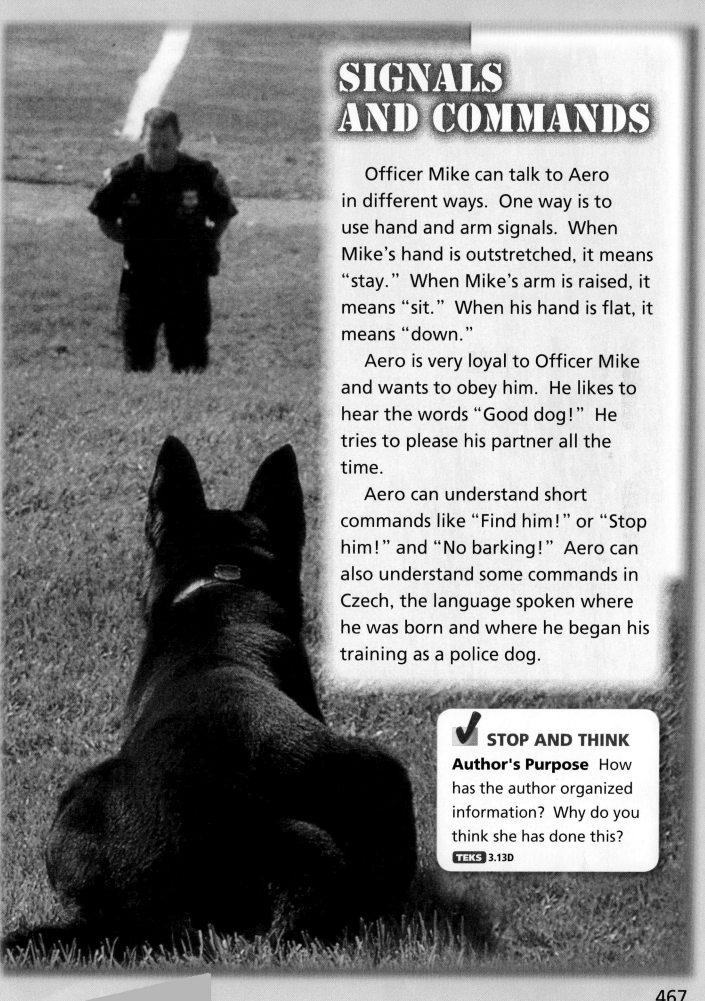

SIGNALS AND COMMANDS

Officer Mike can talk to Aero in different ways. One way is to use hand and arm signals. When Mike's hand is outstretched, it means "stay." When Mike's arm is raised, it means "sit." When his hand is flat, it means "down."

Aero is very loyal to Officer Mike and wants to obey him. He likes to hear the words "Good dog!" He tries to please his partner all the time.

Aero can understand short commands like "Find him!" or "Stop him!" and "No barking!" Aero can also understand some commands in Czech, the language spoken where he was born and where he began his training as a police dog.

✔ **STOP AND THINK**

Author's Purpose How has the author organized information? Why do you think she has done this?

TEKS 3.13D

K-9 TRAINING

Aero's training never ends. Several times a month Aero and Officer Mike train with other officers and their K-9 partners. One exercise the police dogs do is to run through an obstacle course. The dogs practice getting over, under, around, and through difficult spots.

Aero had to learn how to walk up and down very steep, open stairs. He also had to learn to walk over a large, open grating, the kind you often see on city streets. At first he spread his paws to help keep his balance. His legs began to quiver, and he whined a frightened cry. He had to practice over and over. Officer Mike kept saying, "Good boy, you can do it." Aero was brave and trusted his partner, but he still does not like open gratings or steep stairs.

 STOP AND THINK

Summarize Using your own words, briefly explain the steps involved in K-9 training.

TEKS 3.11, 3.15A

468

AERO'S SENSE OF SMELL

K-9s have very powerful noses—hundreds of times more powerful than human noses. That's why one of Aero's most helpful talents on the police force is his ability to find things by smell.

When children play hide-and-seek, they may think they are well hidden. Their dog can find them right away. The same is true when a child is lost or wanders away from home. Aero can find the child by using his sense of smell. Each person has scent that is different from everyone else's scent. Even twins do not smell the same. A person's unique smell comes from the food he or she eats, the soap and shampoo he or she uses, the clothes he or she wears, and the place he or she lives.

AT THE VET'S

Aero goes to Dr. Morse, a veterinarian, for regular checkups. Aero must lie still on a table while the doctor examines him. Once Aero had a small infection on his neck. Dr. Morse gave him some medicine so he would get better. Because a police dog works so hard and has such an important job, he needs to be healthy. At the end of the checkup, Dr. Morse lifts Aero to the floor, pets him, and says, "Good dog."

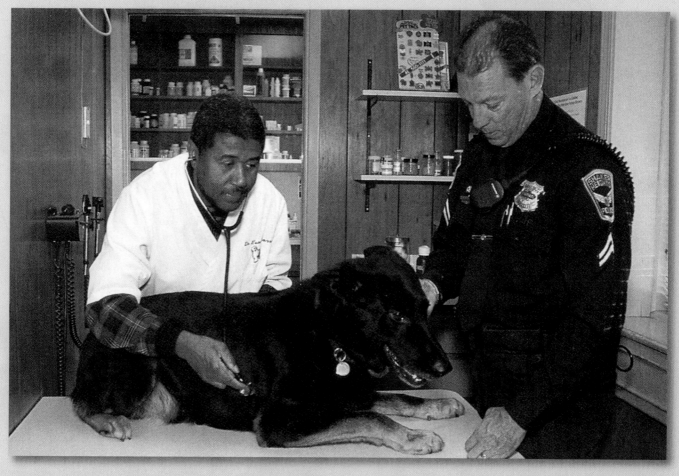

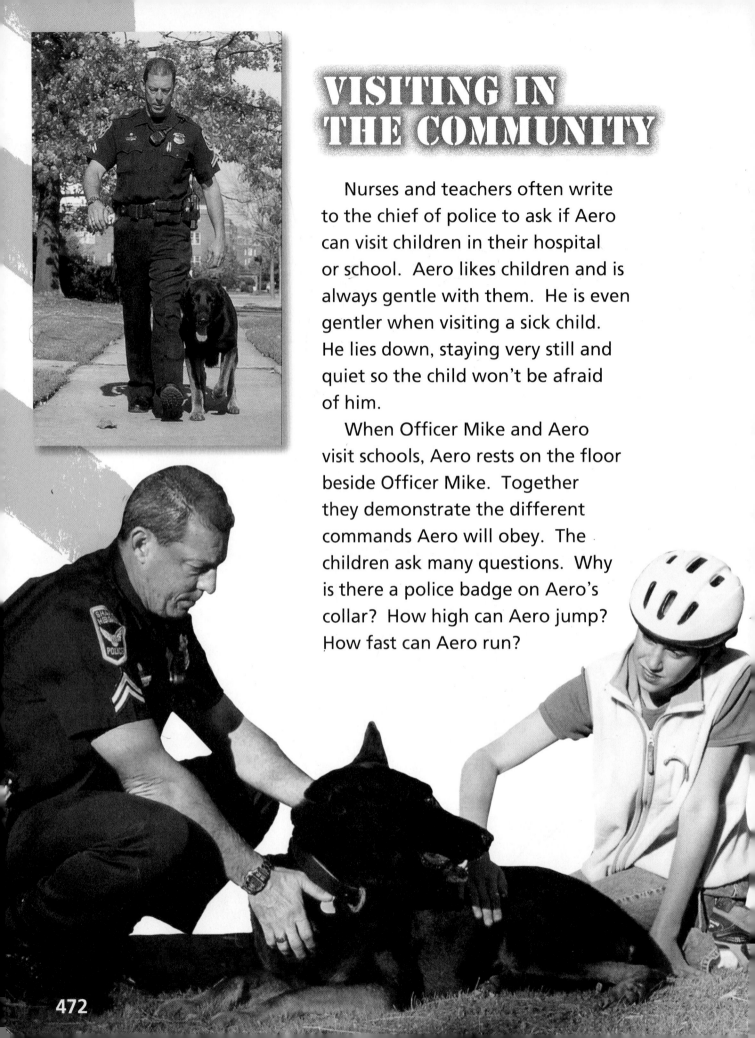

VISITING IN THE COMMUNITY

Nurses and teachers often write to the chief of police to ask if Aero can visit children in their hospital or school. Aero likes children and is always gentle with them. He is even gentler when visiting a sick child. He lies down, staying very still and quiet so the child won't be afraid of him.

When Officer Mike and Aero visit schools, Aero rests on the floor beside Officer Mike. Together they demonstrate the different commands Aero will obey. The children ask many questions. Why is there a police badge on Aero's collar? How high can Aero jump? How fast can Aero run?

Officer Mike carefully answers the questions. Aero's badge shows everyone that he is a working police dog. He can jump over an eight-foot wall when he is chasing a criminal. He can run very fast, about forty miles an hour. Even the fastest person can only run about twenty-four miles an hour.

PETTING AERO

Children often want to pet Aero. Officer Mike tells them the rules. Never try to pet a strange dog until you ask permission from the owner. Never come up behind Aero. He might get frightened and snap at you. Never ever hug a K-9 around the neck. Walk up to a police dog slowly from the front so he can see you. Let him sniff your hand. Pet his head and ears gently. Talk to him softly.

BACK AT THE STATION

At the end of a twelve-hour work shift, there is always a final job to be done at the police station. After talking with his friends on the force, Officer Mike sits down and writes a report for the police chief about the whole day or night. Aero lies down by Officer Mike's chair.

FELLOW OFFICERS

After the report is written, Officer Mike and Aero go home together. When Officer Mike goes to bed, Aero will plop down on the floor near the bed. He lays his head on his paws, and with a sigh goes to sleep near his best friend. Neither of them knows what surprises tomorrow's patrol will bring, but they are well prepared. They both love being police officers.

1. From the article, the reader can tell that police dogs —

   ⬭ live at the police station

   ⬭ work all the time

   ⬭ are only used to find people

   ⬭ have an important job

   TEKS 3.13B

2. ✔ **TARGET SKILL** **Author's Purpose**

   Look at the section "Visiting the Community." Why do you think the author wrote this section? Use a chart like this one to record the author's purpose and the text details that helped you decide. **TEKS** 3.13B

   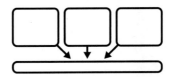

3. ✔ **TARGET STRATEGY** **Summarize**

   Show that you understood what you read by summarizing the section "Aero's Sense of Smell." Include only the main idea and the most important details. **TEKS** 3.13A, RC-3(E); **ELPS** 4G

4. **Oral Language** Work with a partner to retell facts about what Aero does as a police dog. **ELPS** 4G

 TEKS 3.13A identify details/facts that support the main idea; **3.13B** draw/support conclusions; **RC-3(E)** summarize information in text; **ELPS** 4G demonstrate comprehension through shared reading/retelling/summarizing/responding/note-taking

Social Studies

✓ **TARGET VOCABULARY**

lying	quiver
loyal	patrol
partners	ability
shift	snap

GENRE

Informational text gives factual information about a topic. This is a newsletter. Look at the title and the headings before you read. What do you think the topic will be? What might you learn about this topic?

TEXT FOCUS

An **advertisement** is a short message to get readers to do something. What does the author of the ad on page 480 want? Is the ad convincing? Why, or why not?

 TEKS 3.12 identify topic/author's purpose; **3.13D** use text features to locate information/make and verify predictions; **3.14** identify author's persuasion

Kids and Critters

A NATURE NEWSLETTER

What Is 4-H?

4-H is a program for boys and girls ages nine to nineteen. In a 4-H club, you'll make new friends and find new interests. You might care for animals, work with partners to plant a community garden, or patrol a park to pick up litter. You'll learn the 4-H motto, "To Make the Best Better."

All fifty states have 4-H programs. Look for a club near you.

A NATURE NEWSLETTER

Get the Rabbit Habit

4-H boys and girls in Bell County, Texas, have the rabbit habit. Each year they show their rabbits at 4-H fairs.

You don't need any special skill or ability to care for a rabbit. Just give your pet plenty of love, food, and water, and a clean, cozy place to live. Your rabbit will quiver its nose with delight!

This is how to pose a rabbit for a judge.

A City Nature Walk

There's so much to see on a city nature walk. Your 4-H leader can supervise the walk. Be attentive to what you see. You may spot a bird's nest, some squirrels, or even a coyote!

A NATURE NEWSLETTER

Use What You Learn!

In 4-H, you use what you learn to help your community. Maybe you can use what you learn about animals to work a shift in a local animal shelter.

Shelter animals can't spend all day lying in their cages. They need exercise and attention. By walking dogs or cuddling cats, a loyal volunteer can make a big difference. With your help, an animal that used to snap at strangers can become a friendly tail-wagger!

Summer Fair

August 10, at 1:00 P.M.
Juniper Park

Do not miss this exciting summer event!

- Groom your pet.
- Pick your biggest tomato.
- Choose something you've made.
- Show off your hard work!

Blue ribbons in these groups:

Animals
Vegetables
Handicrafts

A NATURE NEWSLETTER

Making Connections

 Text to Self TEKS 3.17E; ELPS 4G

Make an Advertisement Imagine that Officer Mike and Aero are going to visit students at your school. Make a poster advertising their visit. Include a picture and text about Mike and Aero that will make everyone excited to meet them.

 Text to Text TAKS 3.21; ELPS 5G

Write a Persuasive Essay Imagine that you would like to be a police officer working with a K-9 dog someday. Write a persuasive essay asking permission to join 4-H. Explain how joining would help you prepare for this job.

 Text to World TEKS 3.26A(ii)

Connect to Social Studies With a small group, find out different ways animals work to help people. Use reference books or the Internet, or interview someone. Make a poster that shows the animals and their jobs.

 TEKS **3.17E** publish writing for a specific audience; **3.21** write persuasive essays; **3.26A(ii)** collect information from experts/reference texts/online searches; **ELPS** **4G** demonstrate comprehension through shared reading/retelling/responding/note-taking; **5G** narrate/describe/explain in writing

Grammar

Pronouns and Verbs You know that a **pronoun** can be the **subject** of a sentence. Remember that **verbs** in the present have two forms. The correct form of the verb to use depends on the subject pronoun.

Academic Language

pronoun

subject

verb

- Add *-s* or *-es* to a verb in the present when the subject is *he, she,* or *it.*

    He places the collar on the dog.

    It fits the dog perfectly.

- Do not add *-s* or *-es* to a verb in the present when the subject is *I, you, we,* or *they.*

    I like the collar.

    They wear the collar proudly.

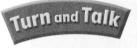 **Work with a partner. Read each sentence aloud. Decide which verb form completes each sentence.**

❶ They (train, trains) police dogs.

❷ She (watch, watches) them learn.

❸ We (like, likes) our police officers.

❹ They (keep, keeps) us safe.

Sentence Fluency Be careful not to repeat a noun too many times. When two sentences have the same nouns as the subject, you can put the sentences together. Change one noun to a pronoun. Then join the two subjects and use the word *and* between them.

Short, Choppy Sentences

Mack barks at birds.

Mack chases them.

Longer, Smoother Sentence

Mack barks at birds, and he chases them.

Connect Grammar to Writing

As you revise your autobiography, look for short, choppy sentences that repeat a noun. Try to replace one of the repeated nouns with a pronoun and combine the sentences.

Reading-Writing Workshop: Prewrite

Write to Narrate

✔ **Ideas** When you choose a topic for your **autobiography**, think about important events in your life. Choose an event that will be interesting to your audience.

Josephine made a list of events for her autobiography. She decided which event would be most interesting. Then she made a chart to put her ideas in order.

Writing Process Checklist

▶ **Prewrite**

☑ **Did I choose an important event in my life that my audience will enjoy?**

☑ **Did I include interesting details about the event?**

☑ **Did I put the details in the order they happened?**

☑ **Did I write in the first person?**

Draft

Revise

Edit

Publish and Share

Choosing a Topic

-having a lemonade stand

-swimming at day camp

-rafting down the Rio Grande with my family

-taking a big spelling test last week

Flow Chart

Event:	rafting down the Rio Grande with my family
Detail:	five years old
Detail:	nervous about rafting
Detail:	saw wildlife and cliffs

When I organized my autobiography, I added more details.

Reading as a Writer

Which of Josephine's details help you picture what is happening? What details can you add to your chart to help your audience picture the event?

✓ **TARGET VOCABULARY**

festive

ingredients

degrees

recommended

anxiously

cross

remarked

tense

Vocabulary
Reader

Context
Cards

 ELPS 4D use prereading supports to
comprehend texts

Vocabulary in Context

1 festive

Everybody felt happy and merry at the festive birthday dinner.

2 ingredients

The ingredients in this salad include tomatoes, lettuce, and cucumbers.

3 degrees

This snack was baked in a hot oven. It was set to 350 degrees.

4 recommended

It is recommended that pizza cool before you eat it. That is good advice.

- **Study each Context Card.**

- **Use two Vocabulary words to tell about an experience you had.**

5 anxiously

This boy anxiously measured the sugar. He was afraid of making a mistake.

6 cross

Children often feel cross, or angry, when asked to eat food they dislike.

7 remarked

The guest remarked, or said, that the meal was delicious.

8 tense

Relax when you frost a cake. If you're tense your hand will shake and ruin it.

Background

✔ **TARGET VOCABULARY** **Following Recipes** Do you **anxiously** examine your plate each night, only to find there's nothing on it that you like? Have friends and family **remarked** that you are a picky eater? Well, try cooking dinner yourself! That way, you can use only your own **recommended** **ingredients**. Remember, an oven as low as two hundred **degrees** can still burn, so always ask an adult for help. Get ready to leave those **tense**, **cross** feelings behind and enjoy your **festive** meal!

Read this cornbread recipe. Then explain it to a friend.

Cornbread Recipe

Ingredients:

- 1 cup yellow cornmeal
- $\frac{3}{4}$ cup flour
- $\frac{1}{4}$ cup sugar
- 1 tablespoon baking powder
- 1 teaspoon salt
- $1\frac{1}{4}$ cups milk
- $\frac{1}{3}$ cup vegetable oil
- 1 egg, lightly beaten

Directions:

1. Preheat oven to 400° F.
   Grease an 8-inch-square baking pan.
2. Combine cornmeal, flour, sugar, baking powder, and salt in large bowl.
3. Combine milk, oil, and egg in small bowl.
4. Add milk mixture to flour mixture.
   Stir until blended.
5. Pour into greased baking pan, and bake for 20 to 25 minutes.

Comprehension

✔ TARGET SKILL   **Understanding Characters**

In *The Extra-good Sunday*, the characters speak and act like real people. The characters' thoughts, actions, and words are clues about their feelings and traits, or what they're like. Use a chart like this to list details and your ideas about the traits of one character.

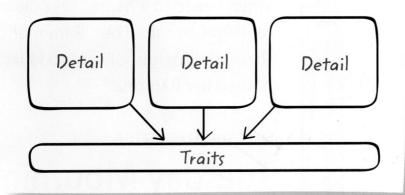

✔ TARGET STRATEGY   **Infer/Predict**

Use your understanding of the characters' traits and your chart to think more about why the characters think, speak, and act as they do. Also use story details to predict, or figure out, what the characters might do next.

festive	anxiously
ingredients	cross
degrees	remarked
recommended	tense

✔ **TARGET SKILL**

Understanding Characters Tell why characters act as they do.

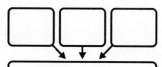

✔ **TARGET STRATEGY**

Infer/Predict Use clues to figure out more about the selection.

GENRE

Humorous fiction is a story that is written to entertain the reader.

Use what you know about the genre to set a purpose for reading.

 TEKS 3.2C establish reading purpose/ monitor comprehension

MEET THE AUTHOR

Beverly Cleary

 One day, while working on one of her first stories about Klickitat Street, Beverly Cleary couldn't come up with a name for the bothersome younger sister. "At the moment when I needed a name," says Cleary, "a neighbor called out 'Ramona!' to another neighbor, and so I just named her Ramona."

MEET THE ILLUSTRATOR

Tuesday Mourning

Like Ramona Quimby, Tuesday Mourning knows all about not getting along with her older sister. In fact, Mourning grew up with four sisters. Although they sometimes used to fight, today she calls them her "best friends."

THE EXTRA-GOOD SUNDAY

from Ramona Quimby, Age 8

by Beverly Cleary

selection illustrated by Tuesday Mourning

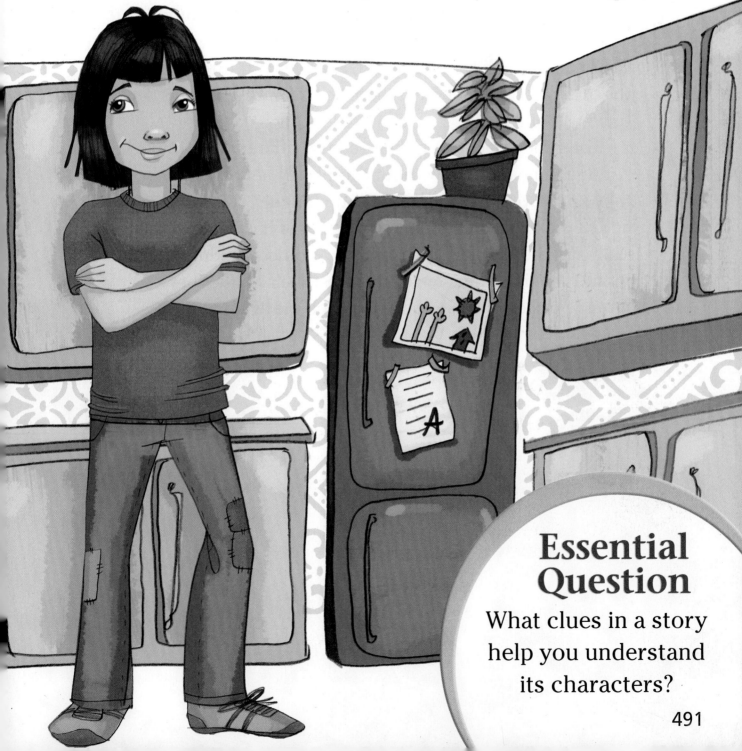

Essential Question

What clues in a story help you understand its characters?

After Beezus and Ramona refuse to eat tongue for dinner, Mr. Quimby suggests the girls cook dinner themselves the very next night. Can Beezus and Ramona make their parents forget this request by acting on their best behavior?

*S*unday morning Ramona and Beezus were still resolved to be perfect until dinnertime. They got up without being called, avoided arguing over who should read Dear Abby's advice first in the paper, complimented their mother on her French toast, and went off through the drizzly rain to Sunday school neat, combed, and bravely smiling.

Later they cleaned up their rooms without being told. At lunchtime they ate without complaint the sandwiches they knew were made of ground-up tongue. A little added pickle relish did not fool them, but it did help. They dried the dishes and carefully avoided looking in the direction of the refrigerator lest their mother be reminded they were supposed to cook the evening meal.

Mr. and Mrs. Quimby were good-humored. In fact, everyone was so unnaturally pleasant that Ramona almost wished someone would say something cross. By early afternoon the question was still hanging in the air. Would the girls really have to prepare dinner?

Why doesn't somebody say something? Ramona thought, weary of being so good.

"Well, back to the old foot," said Mr. Quimby, as he once more settled himself on the couch with the drawing pad and pencil and pulled off his shoe and sock.

The rain finally stopped. Ramona watched for dry spots to appear on the sidewalk and thought of her roller skates in the closet. She looked into Beezus's room and found her sister reading. The day dragged on.

When dry spots on the concrete in front of the
Quimbys' house widened until moisture remained only
in the cracks of the sidewalk, Ramona pulled her skates
out of her closet. To her father, who was holding
a drawing of his foot at arm's length to study it, she said,
"Well, I guess I'll go out and skate."

"Aren't you forgetting something?" he asked.

"What?" asked Ramona, knowing very well what.

"Dinner," he said.

The question that had hung
in the air all day was answered.
The matter was settled.

 STOP AND THINK

Infer/Predict Why does Ramona
pretend to forget about dinner?
What is she hoping will happen?

"We're stuck," Ramona told Beezus. "Now we can stop being so good."

The sisters went into the kitchen, shut the door, and opened the refrigerator.

"A package of chicken thighs," said Beezus with a groan. "And a package of frozen peas. And yogurt, one carton of plain and one of banana. There must have been a special on yogurt." She closed the refrigerator and reached for a cookbook.

"I could make place cards," said Ramona, as Beezus frantically flipped pages.

"We can't eat place cards," said Beezus. "Besides, corn bread is your job because you brought it up." Both girls spoke in whispers. There was no need to let their parents, their mean old parents, know what was going on in the kitchen.

In her mother's recipe file, Ramona found the card for corn bread written in Mr. Quimby's grandmother's shaky handwriting, which Ramona found difficult to read.

"I can't find a recipe for chicken thighs," said Beezus, "just whole chicken. All I know is that Mother bakes thighs in the flat glass dish with some kind of sauce."

"Mushroom soup mixed with something and with some kind of little specks stirred in." Ramona remembered that much from watching her mother.

Beezus opened the cupboard of canned goods. "But there isn't any mushroom soup," she said. "What are we going to do?"

"Mix up something wet," suggested Ramona. "It would serve them right if it tasted awful."

"Why don't we make something awful?" asked Beezus. "So they will know how we feel when we have to eat tongue."

"What tastes really awful?" Ramona was eager to go along with the suggestion, united with her sister against their enemy—for the moment, their parents.

Beezus, always practical, changed her mind. "It wouldn't work. We have to eat it too, and they're so mean we'll probably have to do the dishes besides. Anyway, I guess you might say our honor is at stake, because they think we can't cook a good meal."

Ramona was ready with another solution. "Throw everything in one dish."

Beezus opened the package of chicken thighs and stared at them with distaste. "I can't stand touching raw meat," she said, as she picked up a thigh between two forks.

"Do we have to eat the skin?" asked Ramona. "All those yucky little bumps."

Beezus found a pair of kitchen tongs. She tried holding down a thigh with a fork and pulling off the skin with the tongs.

"Here, let me hold it," said Ramona, who was not squeamish about touching such things as worms or raw meat. She took a firm hold on the thigh while Beezus grasped the skin with the tongs. Both pulled, and the skin peeled away. They played tug-of-war with each thigh, leaving a sad-looking heap of skins on the counter and a layer of chicken thighs in the glass dish.

"Can't you remember what little specks Mother uses?" asked Beezus. Ramona could not. The girls studied the spice shelf, unscrewed jar lids and sniffed. Nutmeg? No. Cloves? Terrible. Cinnamon? Uh-uh. Chili powder? Well. . . . Yes, that must be it. Ramona remembered that the specks were red. Beezus stirred half a teaspoon of the dark red powder into the yogurt, which she poured over the chicken. She slid the dish into the oven set at 350 degrees, the temperature for chicken recommended by the cookbook.

STOP AND THINK

Author's Craft What comparison does the author make to help you picture the sisters peeling skin off the chicken?

TEKS 3.10

From the living room came the sound of their parents' conversation, sometimes serious and sometimes highlighted by laughter. While we're slaving out here, thought Ramona, as she climbed up on the counter to reach a box of cornmeal. After she climbed down, she discovered she had to climb up again for baking powder and soda. She finally knelt on the counter to save time and asked Beezus to bring her an egg.

"It's a good thing Mother can't see you up there," remarked Beezus, as she handed Ramona an egg.

"How else am I supposed to reach things?" Ramona successfully broke the egg and tossed the shell onto the counter. "Now I need buttermilk."

Beezus broke the news. There was no buttermilk in the refrigerator. "What'll I do?" whispered Ramona in a panic.

"Here. Use this." Beezus thrust the carton of banana yogurt at her sister. "Yogurt is sort of sour, so it might work."

The kitchen door opened a crack. "What's going on in there?" inquired Mr. Quimby.

Beezus hurled herself against the door. "You stay out!" she ordered. "Dinner is going to be a—surprise!"

For a moment Ramona thought Beezus had been going to say a mess. She stirred egg and yogurt together, measured flour, spilling some on the floor, and then discovered she was short of cornmeal. More panic.

"My cooking teacher says you should always check to see if you have all the ingredients before you start to cook," said Beezus.

"Oh, shut up." Ramona reached for a package of hot breakfast cereal, because its grains were about the same size as cornmeal. She scattered only a little on the floor.

✔ **STOP AND THINK**

Understanding Characters Does Beezus answer truthfully when Mr. Quimby asks what's going on? Why is Beezus so determined to keep him out of the kitchen?
TEKS 3.8B; **ELPS** 4J

Something was needed to sop up the sauce with the little red specks when the chicken was served. Rice! The spilled cereal gritted underneath Beezus's feet as she measured rice and boiled water according to the directions on the package. When the rice was cooking, she slipped into the dining room to set the table and then remembered they had forgotten salad. Salad! Carrot sticks were quickest. Beezus began to scrape carrots into the sink.

"Yipe!" yelped Ramona from the counter. "The rice!" The lid of the pan was chittering. Beezus snatched a larger pan from the cupboard and transferred the rice.

"Do you girls need any help?" Mrs. Quimby called from the living room.

"No!" answered her daughters.

Another calamity. The corn bread should bake at 400 degrees, a higher temperature than that needed for the chicken. What was Ramona to do?

"Stick it in the oven anyway." Beezus's face was flushed.

In went the corn bread beside the chicken.

"Dessert!" whispered Beezus. All she could find was a can of boring pear halves. Back to the cookbook. "Heat with a little butter and serve with jelly in each half," she read. Jelly. Half a jar of apricot jam would have to do. The pears and butter went into the saucepan. Never mind the syrup spilled on the floor.

"Beezus!" Ramona held up the package of peas.

Beezus groaned. Out came the partially cooked chicken while she stirred the thawing peas into the yogurt and shoved the dish back into the oven.

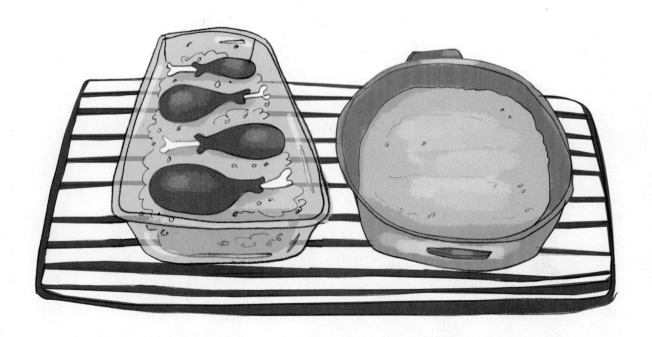

The rice! They had forgotten the rice, which was only beginning to stick to the pan. Quick! Take it off the burner. How did their mother manage to get everything cooked at the right time? Put the carrot sticks on a dish. Pour the milk. "Candles!" Beezus whispered. "Dinner might look better if we have candles."

Ramona found two candle holders and two partly melted candles of uneven length. Beezus struck the match to light them, because although Ramona was brave about touching raw meat, she was skittish about lighting matches.

Was the chicken done? The girls anxiously examined their main dish, bubbling and brown around the edges. Beezus stabbed a thigh with a fork, and when it did not bleed, she decided it must be done. A toothpick pricked into the corn bread came out clean. The corn bread was done—flat, but done.

Grit, grit, grit sounded the girls' feet. It was amazing how a tiny bit of spilled cereal could make the entire kitchen floor gritty. At last their dinner was served, the dining-room light turned off, dinner announced, and the cooks, tense with anxiety that was hidden by candlelight, fell into their chairs as their parents seated themselves. Was this dinner going to be edible?

"Candles!" exclaimed Mrs. Quimby. "What a festive meal!"

"Let's taste it before we decide," said Mr. Quimby with his most wicked grin.

The girls watched anxiously as their father took his first bite of chicken. He chewed thoughtfully and said with more surprise than necessary, "Why this is good!"

"It really is," agreed Mrs. Quimby, and took a bit of corn bread. "Very good, Ramona," she said.

Mr. Quimby tasted the corn bread. "Just like Grandmother used to make," he pronounced.

The girls exchanged suppressed smiles. They could not taste the banana yogurt, and by candlelight no one could tell that the corn bread was a little pale. The chicken, Ramona decided, was not as good as her parents thought—or pretended to think—but she could eat it without gagging.

Everyone relaxed, and Mrs. Quimby said chili powder was more interesting than paprika and asked which recipe they used for the chicken.

Ramona answered, "Our own," as she exchanged another look with Beezus. Paprika! Those little specks in the sauce should have been paprika.

"We wanted to be creative," said Beezus.

Conversation was more comfortable than it had been the previous evening. Mr. Quimby said he was finally satisfied with his drawing, which looked like a real foot. Beezus said her cooking class was studying the food groups everyone should eat every day. Ramona said there was this boy at school who called her Egghead. Mr. Quimby explained that Egghead was slang for a very smart person.

The meal was a success. If the chicken did not taste as good as the girls had hoped and the corn bread did not rise like their mother's, both were edible. Beezus and Ramona were silently grateful to their parents for enjoying—or pretending to enjoy—their cooking. The whole family cheered up.

When they had finished their pears with apricot jam, Ramona gave her mother a shy smile. Mrs. Quimby smiled back and patted Ramona's hand. Ramona felt much lighter.

"You cooks have worked so hard," said Mr. Quimby, "that I'm going to wash the dishes. I'll even finish clearing the table."

"I'll help," volunteered Mrs. Quimby.

The girls exchanged another secret smile as they excused themselves and skipped off to their rooms before their parents discovered the pile of chicken skins and the broken eggshell on the counter, the carrot scrapings in the sink, and the cereal, flour, and pear syrup on the floor.

1. Which word from page 506 helps the reader know what <u>festive</u> means?

   ⬭ *taste*

   ⬭ *meal*

   ⬭ *candles*

   ⬭ *wicked*

   ELPS 1C

2. ✔ **TARGET SKILL** **Understanding Characters**

   Beezus suggests making something awful. Ramona likes this idea. Why do the girls decide not to do this? Use a chart like this to record your answer. **TEKS** 3.8B

   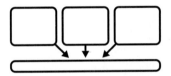

3. ✔ **TARGET STRATEGY** **Infer/Predict**

   What do the story details on your chart tell you about Beezus and Ramona? **TEKS** RC-3(D); **ELPS** 4J

4. **Oral Language** Work with a partner. Use the Retelling Cards to summarize what happens as the girls make dinner. Be sure to speak clearly. **TEKS** 3.30, RC-3(E)

   Retelling Cards

 TEKS 3.8B describe characters' relationships/changes; 3.30 speak coherently/effectively about topics; RC-3(D) make inferences/use textual evidence; RC-3(E) summarize information in text; **ELPS** 4J employ inferential skills to demonstrate comprehension

Connect to
Social Studies

Tía Luisa's
Fruit Salad

✓ TARGET VOCABULARY

festive	anxiously
ingredients	cross
degrees	remarked
recommended	tense

GENRE

Readers' Theater is text that has been written for readers to read aloud. As you read the dialogue, notice how characters and events are similar to and different from those in *The Extra-good Sunday*. Discuss your ideas with a partner after you read.

TEXT FOCUS

A **recipe** tells how to make something to eat or drink.

 TEKS 3.7 explain plot/character through dialogue in scripts; **RC-3(A)** establish reading purposes

---

Tía Luisa's Fruit Salad

by Liam Elder

Cast of Characters

Elisa
Marcos
Tía Luisa

Elisa: *Hola!* That means "hello" in Spanish. I am Elisa. This is my brother Marcos.

Marcos: Welcome to our cooking show, everybody!

Elisa: Today, we are going to make a tropical fruit salad. This is our Tía Luisa's recipe. *Tía* means "aunt" in Spanish. Here she is!

Tía Luisa: *Hola!* Are you ready to make my festive fruit salad?

Marcos: Of course!

Elisa: Here are the yummy ingredients. Look at the mangos, papayas, grapes, strawberries, and pineapple.

Tía Luisa: The best part of this recipe is that the oven stays at zero degrees. Adults don't need to be tense or worry anxiously that a child will be burned by a hot oven.

Marcos: What is the first step?

Elisa: Cut the fruit into pieces. Have an adult help you.

Marcos: Then, all the fruit goes into a bowl.

Tía Luisa: Adding a spoonful of honey is recommended.

Elisa: Next, stir it all together.

Marcos: Now it's time to make whipped cream for the top.

Elisa: Pour heavy cream into a bowl. Add sugar and vanilla. Then use an electric beater to whip the cream until it is fluffy.

Marcos: Now we are ready to spoon the whipped cream over the fruit.

Tía Luisa: Great job! This fruit salad looks *deliciosa*!

Elisa: *Deliciosa,* remarked our favorite aunt. That means *delicious* in English!

Marcos: Sorry we can't share our tropical salad with you. Don't be cross with us!

Elisa and Marcos: That's it for this week's show. *Adios, amigos!* Good-bye, friends!

Tía Luisa's Fruit Salad

Ingredients

Mixed fruits

Honey

1 cup heavy cream

1/4 cup sugar

1 teaspoon vanilla

1. Cut fruit into pieces. Put it in a large bowl. Add one spoonful of honey and stir.
2. Pour cream into a separate bowl. Add sugar and vanilla. Mix with electric mixer until fluffy.
3. Spoon whipped cream over fruit and enjoy!

Making Connections

Text to Self

ELPS 3H

Perform a Skit Perform a short skit that shows what happened when you made something in the kitchen. Tell about your ingredients, how you put them together, what went well, what went wrong, and how the food turned out.

Text to Text

TEKS 3.15A

Write a Recipe In *Tia Luisa's Fruit Salad*, Elisa explains how to make her aunt's fruit salad. Using this example, write the steps it would take to make the meal in *The Extra-Good Sunday*. Then explain the steps to a partner.

Text to World

TEKS 3.26A(i), 3.26A(ii)

Connect to Social Studies Use reference books or the Internet to research a dish that is popular in another country, or interview someone about it. Copy the ingredients and directions. Publish the recipe with your classmates' recipes in a cookbook.

TEKS 3.15A follow/explain written directions; **3.26A(i)** collect information from surveys/inspections/interviews; **3.26A(ii)** collect information from experts/reference texts/online searches; **ELPS 3H** narrate/describe/explain with detail

Grammar

Forming the Past Tense You can make most verbs show **past tense** just by adding -ed. However, the spelling of some verbs changes in other ways when you add -ed.

- Some verbs end with e. Drop the e and add -ed.

- Some verbs end with a consonant and y. Change the y to i and add -ed.

- Some verbs end with one vowel followed by one consonant. Double the consonant and add -ed.

Present	Past
smile	smiled
fry	fried
tap	tapped

Try This! **Write each verb in the past tense.**

1 smile

2 dry

3 drop

4 carry

5 chat

6 juggle

514

Word Choice Use exact verbs in your writing so that readers can picture the action you write about. Spell exact verbs correctly when you write about them in the past tense.

Less Exact Verb	More Exact Verbs		
walked	strolled	hiked	stepped
ran	charged	zipped	raced
looked	studied	gazed	peered
ate	gobbled	munched	feasted
fell	dropped	slipped	plunged
wanted	desired	fancied	craved

Connect Grammar to Writing

As you revise your autobiography, look for verbs that you could change to more exact verbs.

Reading-Writing Workshop: Revise

Write to Narrate

✓ **Voice** Good **autobiography** writers let their feelings come through. When you revise your autobiography, use words that will make your reader understand how you felt. Josephine drafted her autobiography. Later, she added details that told about her thoughts and feelings.

Writing Process Checklist

Prewrite

Draft

▶ **Revise**

☑ Are the details in order?

☑ Did I leave out unimportant events and details?

☑ Did I include details that show what I thought and felt?

☑ Did I include time-order words?

☑ Did I think about my audience and purpose?

Edit

Publish and Share

Revised Draft

When I was just five, my family and I went to Big Bend National Park. ~~Our dog had to stay home.~~

The best part was the river rafting. Before we started, I was nervous because I had never been rafting. Finally, the guides promised the water would not be too rough. First, the guides showed us how to steer. Next, they gave us life jackets. After that I was ready to go!

When I was just five, my family and I went to Big Bend National Park. The best part was the river rafting. Before we started, I was nervous because I had never been rafting. First, the guides showed us how to steer. Next, they gave us life jackets. Finally, the guides promised the water would not be too rough. After that I was ready to go!

We got in our raft. It carries six people, so we all fit! We headed down the Rio Grande. We traveled through beautiful canyons. I saw lots of wildlife and huge craggy cliffs. We stopped for a hike. Then we soaked in the natural hot springs. The water felt amazing. When we paddled to our last stop, we watched the sunset. This was one of the best days of my life.

In my final paper, I included details about what I thought and how I felt.

Reading as a Writer

Which words tell how Josephine feels? Where can you make changes in your autobiography to show how you felt about the event?

Read the selection. Then read each question that follows the selection. Decide which is the best answer to each question.

Science Kids

Volume 7, Issue 6

 # Kids Invent!

by Roberto Gutierrez

1   Suppose that you are eating a bowl of soup. As you slurp, some soup drips down your chin. What can you do? You could wipe your mouth on your sleeve. You would probably get in trouble for doing that, though.

2   Matthew had the same problem. He always wiped his mouth on his sleeve. He thought that a thick shirtsleeve worked better than a thin napkin. Matthew's parents didn't agree, so he went to work. He invented, or made up, a new kind of shirt. It held a paper napkin on one sleeve. After Matthew ate a meal, he threw away the napkin.

3   This may seem like a silly example, but many inventors get ideas in the same way that Matthew did. They have problems and need to find solutions. They make inventions to solve their problems or to make something better.

Making Something Better

4   The physical education teacher at Jessica's school taught the students how to play jump-rope games. Jessica learned that different games need different-size ropes. When the kids changed games, they had to change ropes. Jessica invented a new kind of jump rope that can be made into different lengths. It can also be worn as a belt.

GO ON

5   Jessica's first jump-rope belt did not work, but she did not give up. She just made some changes. Then she made a model of her jump-rope belt for a doll. The model worked, so Jessica made a new jump-rope belt for herself. It worked, too. Inventors almost always have to try several times before they succeed.

6   Like most kids, Larry had chores. One chore was watering the yard. When Larry watered the trees in his yard, he saw that much water was wasted.

7   So Larry invented a new kind of sprinkler. Shaped like a circle, the sprinkler has holes on the top and on the bottom. It fits around the <u>base</u> of a tree. Because water comes out of both the top and the bottom, more water soaks into the ground and reaches the tree roots. Thousands of people have bought Larry's sprinkler.

A New Idea

8   When Richie was ten years old, he went swimming with his dad in the ocean. He was amazed at the ocean life he saw. He wanted to talk to his dad about it, but it was <u>hopeless</u>. You can't talk underwater. This gave Richie an amazing idea!

9   When Richie got out of the water, he started making drawings. Richie came up with an invention for talking underwater. He tested his invention in the bathtub. He made changes until he was happy with it.

10   Richie and his parents started a company. They sold Richie's invention to toy stores around the world. Since that time, Richie has invented other water toys.

Be an Inventor

11   You can be an inventor, too! Follow these steps. First, make a list of problems. Next, make a list of <u>solutions</u>. Write down every idea you have. Then think about your ideas. Which one seems to work best? Which idea fixes the problem in the fastest, easiest way?

12   After you choose an idea, draw a picture of your invention. Label the picture to show how the invention will work. Next, you will need to build a model of the invention. Ask an adult to help you. When the model is ready, test it. Make any changes that you think should be made. Then share your invention with others.

GO ON

1 This article was most likely written to —

◯ tell a funny story

◯ show how to make a jump rope

◯ give information about inventing

◯ make people want to buy Richie's toys

2 Read the meanings below for the word base.

> base \bās\ noun
>
> 1. the lowest or bottom part
> 2. a main part or ingredient
> 3. a safe area in sports
> 4. a camp or headquarters

Which meaning best fits the way base is used in paragraph 7?

◯ Meaning 1

◯ Meaning 2

◯ Meaning 3

◯ Meaning 4

3 In paragraph 8, the word hopeless means —

◯ full of hope

◯ hope again

◯ without hope

◯ someone who hopes

4 Which word from paragraph 11 means the opposite of solutions?

◯ *steps*

◯ *fixes*

◯ *ideas*

◯ *problems*

5 Which sentence from the article is an opinion?

◯ *This gave Richie an amazing idea!*

◯ *Thousands of people have bought Larry's sprinkler.*

◯ *Richie and his parents started a company.*

◯ *Jessica's first jump-rope belt did not work, but she did not give up.*

STOP

520

POWER Practice

TEKS 3.4E alphabetize to third letter/use dictionary/glossary; **ELPS 3A** practice sounds/pronunciation of English words; **4A** learn English sound-letter relationships/decode; **4H** read silently with increasing ease/comprehension

Phonics

Decoding Unknown Words Read the article about sugar gliders. If you come across a word that is hard to read, try skipping the word and reading the rest of the sentence without it. Are there any clues that help you guess what the word might be? Look for familiar word parts in the unknown word, such as prefixes, suffixes, base words, or root words. Try breaking the word into smaller word parts you can pronounce.

Sugar Gliders

Have you ever heard of a sugar glider? A sugar glider is a small mammal that is found in the forests of Australia. This unusual animal is a member of a family called *marsupials*. Sugar gliders, kangaroos, opossums, wombats and Tasmanian devils are all marsupials. The females have pouches, in which they carry their babies.

The sugar glider got the first part of its name because it prefers sweet foods. The second part of its name comes from its ability to glide through the air like a flying squirrel.

- Next, take turns reading the paragraph aloud with a partner.

- List the words that were difficult for you to read.

- Compare your lists. Tell how you tried to decode each word.

- Use your dictionary to check the meaning and the pronunciation of the words on your list.

TEKS **3.16A** understand communication changes in media genres; **3.31** participate in discussions/build on others' ideas;
ELPS **3H** narrate/describe/explain with detail; **4G** demonstrate comprehension through shared reading/retelling/responding/note-taking

Media Literacy

Comparing Stories in Books and Movies Have you ever read a book that has been made into a movie? Below is a short list of examples. Can you think of any others?

- *Horton Hears a Who*
- *The Tale of Despereaux*
- *The Secret Garden*
- *Sarah, Plain and Tall*
- *James and the Giant Peach*

Books and movies communicate stories in different ways.

Reading a Book	Watching a Movie
Books use words to tell the story.	Movies use images, sounds, and motion to tell the story.
Readers use the books' descriptions to picture the characters and the setting.	The audience sees and hears the characters and the setting.
Readers can tell what characters are thinking or feeling by what the writer says about them.	Actors use facial expressions, gestures, and dialogue to show how characters think and feel.

- Work in a small group. Read and discuss the chart above. Describe stories you read that were made into movies. Tell how the stories and movies were alike and different. Say which you enjoyed more, and why.

TEKS 3.16A understand communication changes in media genres; **ELPS 5G** narrate/describe/explain in writing

Media Literacy

Make a Comparison   Copy the following chart onto a sheet of paper. Choose a book you read that was made into a movie. Make a list of things that are the same and things that are different. Focus on how information about the plot, the characters, and the setting was given in each version of the story.

Things That Are the Same	Things That Are Different

TEKS **3.16C** compare digital media written conventions; **ELPS** **4H** read silently with increasing ease/comprehension; **4K** employ analytical skills to demonstrate comprehension

Media Literacy

Conventions in Digital Media A news article on the Internet looks and sounds different than an e-mail to a friend does. Read the Internet article below about a heroic dog. Then turn the page and read the e-mail that describes the same experience. Notice how they are alike and how they are different.

| File | Edit | View | Favorites | Tools | Help |

Family Dog Saves Children from Fire

A brave dog saved two brothers from a fire in Fort Worth, Texas. The dog got her young owners out of their home after a fire broke out, shortly after 9:00. The children were sleeping upstairs.

Jason Brown, 9, tells it this way, "My dog came up and pulled on my pajama sleeve to wake us up because there was smoke everywhere."

The mother of the two children woke to the sound of Nellie's barking. She and the children got out safely and ran to a neighbor's house to call 911.

When firefighters arrived on the scene, the fire had spread throughout the house. The firefighters report that the building has serious damage.

TEKS 3.16C compare digital media written conventions; **ELPS 4K** employ analytical skills to demonstrate comprehension

Subject: | Dog Hero

Hi Sandy,
Did you hear about the dog that saved a family from a fire? Incredible! Two kids were in the house and could have been badly hurt. How scary! They were so lucky to have that dog. Of course, I'm lucky to have a dog too. I know Mason would try to save me if I were in trouble, for sure!

Venn diagram Copy the Venn diagram onto a separate sheet of paper. Write details that tell how the article and the e-mail are different in the outer circles. Write details that tell how they are alike where the circles overlap.

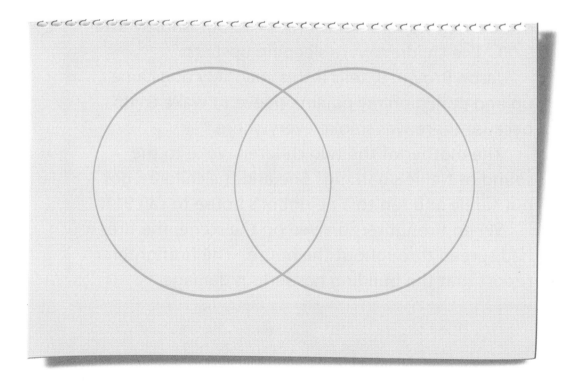

TEKS 3.4B use context to determine word meaning; **ELPS** 4K employ analytical skills to demonstrate comprehension; 4F use visual/ contextual/peer/teacher support to read/comprehend texts

Vocabulary Strategies

Multiple-Meaning Words   Some words have more than one meaning. For instance, the word *roll* may mean "a small, round piece of bread" or "to move along on wheels."

To figure out which meaning of a word is being used in a sentence, read the rest of the sentence and ask, *What part of speech is this word? Are there words in this sentence, or in nearby sentences, that give clues about its meaning?* If the meaning is still unclear, look up the word in a dictionary and find the definition that fits.

Work with a partner. Read the sentences in the box. Discuss what the word *fine* means in each. How many different definitions for the word *fine* are used?

1. It was warm and sunny at the lake. It was a <u>fine</u> day for a canoe trip!

2. The police officer gave the driver a <u>fine</u> for not stopping at the red light.

3. A spider's web is so <u>fine</u>, it can be difficult to see.

4. Yesterday I had a headache, but today I feel <u>fine</u>.

5. Use a <u>fine</u> spray to mist the tiny, new plants. Don't water them too heavily.

TEKS **3.4B** use context to determine word meaning; **ELPS 1C** use strategic learning techniques to acquire vocabulary

Vocabulary Strategies

Multiple-Meaning Words Read each sentence in the box. Decide which definition in ( ) is used in each sentence.

Choosing Correct Meaning

1. Mom said I could pick a <u>single</u> rose from the garden. (a hit in baseball that allows the runner to get to first base OR one and no more than one)

2. The <u>wave</u> was so big it knocked me over, and I got soaked. (to signal by moving your hand OR a moving ridge on the surface of the water)

3. Shelly likes to <u>skip</u> on the playground. (to move along in a bouncy way OR to avoid or pass over)

4. There is only one <u>drop</u> of vanilla left in the bottle. (a very small amount OR to fall from a higher to a lower place)

5. The sheep are kept in a <u>pen</u>, next to the barn. (a small fenced-in area OR a writing instrument)

TEKS 3.11 read independently/paraphrase; **ELPS** 4H read silently with increasing ease/comprehension; 5G narrate/describe/explain in writing

Independent Reading

Choosing a Book Ask yourself these questions to help you choose a book for independent reading.

- **Purpose**—What is my purpose, or reason, for reading? Do I want to be entertained? Do I want to get information about a topic?

- **Topic**—What topic or subject do I want to read about?

- **Genre**—Do I want to read fiction or nonfiction?

- **Difficulty**—Does this book look too easy, too difficult, or just right for me?

How to Paraphrase

Paraphrasing can help you better understand and remember what you've read. Once you have chosen a book, begin by reading the first chapter. At the end of the chapter, write an entry in a reading log or a journal paraphrasing what you've read. Follow these steps.

1. **Tell the topic. Use your own words to restate the author's most important ideas about this topic.**

2. **Explain what the reading was about in an order that makes sense.**

3. **Make sure you don't stray from the topic or change the author's meaning when you write. Do not include opinions.**

TEKS **3.3** read aloud with fluency/comprehension; **3.29A** listen/ask questions/make comments; **ELPS 3A** practice sounds/pronunciation of English words; **2A** distinguish sounds/intonation patterns of English

Fluency

Partner Reading   Work with a partner to select a few pages from this week's story, *The Trial of Cardigan Jones.*

1. Read the pages silently to yourself. Make sure you understand how to say all the words.

2. Read the pages aloud, alternating paragraphs with your partner.

3. As you read, use rate, expression, and phrasing to show the feelings of the author or characters.

4. As you listen, think about how your partner uses rate, expression, and phrasing.

5. Give your partner feedback. Then read the pages aloud again to improve your fluency.

TEKS 3.4C identify/use antonyms/synonyms/homographs/homophones; **ELPS 1E** internalize new basic/academic language

Vocabulary Strategies

Write an Antonym   Antonyms are words with opposite meanings. For instance, *new* is an antonym for *old*. Read these nonsense sentences. Think of antonyms for the underlined words that make each sentence make sense. Copy the new sentences on a separate sheet of paper.

new
old
down
up

1. The sign <u>below</u> the door said, "Frida's Fresh Fruit."

2. Some animals use their <u>short</u> tails to hang from tree branches.

3. The article "<u>Nothing</u> You Need to Know About Cats" is very helpful.

4. "I can't wait to get to the <u>beginning</u> of this book!" Keila exclaimed.

5. Raymond felt <u>happy</u> after he lost his favorite baseball cap.

6. The children's bookstore <u>opened</u> at 9:00 in the evening.

7. A <u>shallow</u> pool is not safe for children who cannot swim.

8. Because it was a special occasion, she wore her <u>ugliest</u> dress.

Opposites Attract

Copy this chart. Write one or more antonyms for each word listed. Try adding more words and antonyms.

Word	Antonyms
best	
tough	
stop	
huge	
thick	
easy	

TEKS 3.2C establish reading purpose/monitor comprehension; **RC-3(A)** establish reading purposes; **ELPS** 4A learn English sound-letter relationships/decode; **4H** read silently with increasing ease/comprehension

Phonics

Decoding Unknown Words Read the essay. If you come to unfamiliar words, stop and decode them. First, read the sentence without the word. What part of speech is the word? What word might make sense there? Next, examine the word. Are there any prefixes, suffixes, base words, or root words you recognize? Can you break the word into smaller word parts you can pronounce?

My Favorite Person Day

Today is a special day at Mountainside School. Jenna's class was told to dress up as their favorite person. Jenna thought she would dress as her favorite television star. She searched everywhere in her disorganized closet for the perfect outfit to wear but found nothing. Then she had an idea!

The clothes Jenna needed were in her mother's closet, not hers. She chose a silk scarf, a pearl necklace, and a lacy sweater. They were all her mother's favorites. Her mother smiled as Jenna explained, "Mom, you're my favorite person, so I'm going to wear all of your favorite things!"

Work with a Partner

- Take turns reading the paragraphs aloud with a partner.
- List words that were difficult. Compare your list with a partner's.
- Tell how you decoded each word. Then look each word up in a dictionary. Check the meanings and pronunciations.

TEKS **3.2C** establish reading purpose/monitor comprehension; **3.3** read aloud with fluency/comprehension; **ELPS** **2A** distinguish sounds/intonation patterns of English; **4G** demonstrate comprehension through shared reading/retelling/responding/note-taking

Fluency

Shared Reading   Work with your teacher and classmates. Together, decide on a passage from *Pop's Bridge* to read together. Follow these steps:

1. Join in on the reading with your teacher. Make sure you understand how to say all the words and what the passage is about.

2. As you read, use appropriate rate, expression, and phrasing to show the feelings of the author or the feelings of the characters.

3. After you have finished reading, make sure you understood the text. Retell your favorite part for your teacher and classmates.

TEKS **3.2C** establish reading purpose/monitor comprehension; **3.3** read aloud with fluency/comprehension; **ELPS 2A** distinguish sounds/intonation patterns of English; **4G** demonstrate comprehension through shared reading/retelling/responding/note-taking

Fluency

Partner Reading

Work with a partner. Take turns reading aloud paragraphs from this week's paired selection, "Bridges." Before you begin, look over the following tips for reading comprehension.

- **Set a purpose. Ask yourself what might be the purpose of reading a story called "Bridges." Do you think you will learn something new?**

- **As you read, think about what you are reading and make sure you understand it. You may have to reread a section of the text if it doesn't make sense.**

- **When you are finished reading, discuss the story with your partner. Did you learn something new about bridges? Tell what you think is the most interesting thing you learned.**

TEKS 3.22A(viii) use/understand transitions; **3.29B** follow/restate/give oral instructions involving sequence; **ELPS** 2G understand meaning/main points/details of spoken language; **2I** demonstrate listening comprehension of spoken English

Listening and Speaking

Listen Carefully! Instructions give steps to complete a task. You follow instructions every day in all parts of your life. When you listen to instructions, it is important to pay attention to time-order words, such as *first, second, third, next, then,* and *finally.*

Work with a partner. Take turns completing the activity below. As your partner reads the instructions, listen carefully to make sure you understand the important details in each step and the time-order context of the information.

- **First,** draw a large circle on your paper. **This will be the outline of a head and face.**

- **Second,** draw two eyes.

- **Third,** draw a nose.

- **Next,** draw a mouth.

- **Then** add some hair.

- **Last,** write your name at the bottom of the paper.

Susan

TEKS 3.22A(viii) use/understand transitions; **3.29B** follow/restate/give oral instructions involving sequence; **ELPS 2I** demonstrate listening comprehension of spoken English

Listening and Speaking

Follow the Sequence

Work with a partner to complete this sequence activity.

- Explain the sequence of activities you do each morning before school. Remember to use time-order words, such as *first*, *second*, *third*, *next*, *then*, and *finally*.

- When you are finished telling your sequence of activities, ask your partner to restate what you said you do each morning.

- Switch roles.

TEKS 3.22A(viii) use/understand transitions; 3.29B follow/restate/give oral instructions involving sequence; **ELPS** 2H understand implicit ideas/information in spoken language; 2I demonstrate listening comprehension of spoken English

Listening and Speaking

Simon Says In the game "Simon Says," you follow the leader's instructions only if they begin with the words *Simon says.* For example, if the leader says, "Simon says touch your toes," you touch your toes. However, if the instructions are only "Touch your toes," you should not obey.

Work with a partner. Take turns being the leader. To make the game more challenging, the leader should list three things in a row when he or she gives the instructions. For example, "Simon says pat your head, poke your stomach, and then wiggle your fingers." Listen closely and have fun!

How-To Instructions

In this activity, you and a partner will take turns giving and then restating instructions. Think of something you know how to do or make very well and can describe to someone else. Here are some examples: making a sandwich, making a bed, building a birdhouse. Remember to use time-order words, such as *first, second, third, next, then,* and *finally.*

- **Choose one person to go first. The first person gives instructions while the other person listens very carefully.**

- **Then the listener shows he or she understands the information by repeating the sequence of instructions. Give clues to help your partner remember the sequence, if he or she forgets.**

- **Switch roles.**

TEKS 3.1A(iv) decode using prefixes/suffixes; **3.4A** identify meanings of prefixes/suffixes; **ELPS 1E** internalize new basic/academic language; **4C** develop/comprehend basic English vocabulary and structures

Phonics and Vocabulary

Prefixes *mis-*, *re-*, and *non-* A prefix is a word part that is added to the beginning of a root word. Adding a prefix usually changes a word's meaning. Read the definitions and the examples below aloud. Identify each root word, and discuss how the prefix changes its meaning.

mis- means "badly or wrongly" *misread, misunderstand, misplace*

re- means "back or again" *redo, replay, repaint*

non- means "not" *nonfiction, nonstop, nonsense*

Copy the words below on a sheet of paper. Add one of the prefixes above to each word to make a new word. Read your list aloud to a partner.

1. **sense**   4. **appear**

2. **state**   5. **stop**

3. **lead**   6. **word**

What Does It Mean?

Copy the following chart. Fill in the second column with each word's meaning. Then write a sentence using each word.

Word	Meaning
misunderstand	
rearrange	
nonprofit	
refill	
nonfat	
misbehave	

TEKS 3.1A(iv) decode using prefixes/suffixes; 3.4A identify meanings of prefixes/suffixes; **ELPS 1E** internalize new basic/academic language; 4C develop/comprehend basic English vocabulary and structures

Phonics and Vocabulary

Making New Words   A suffix is a word part that is added to the end of a root word. Each suffix has its own meaning. When the suffix is added, a new word with a different meaning is made.

-ly

-er

-est

-ful

Read each example to a partner as if it were a math problem. For example, "*slow + –ly = slowly.*"

1. slow + *-ly* =

2. hope + *-ful* =

3. perfect + *-ly* =

4. small + *-er* =

5. fast + *-er* =

6. bright + *-est* =

7. care + *-ful* =

8. cold + *-est* =

Match Word Parts

Match each root word with a suffix from the box. Then write the new word on a separate sheet of paper. Some of the root words may work with more than one of the suffixes. Read your list aloud to a partner.

–ful	–er	–est

play	short	quick
big	smart	thank

After you have written the new words, discuss with a partner how the suffixes change the meanings of the root words.

TEKS 3.4D identify/apply playful language uses; **ELPS** 1E internalize new basic/academic language; **3A** practice sounds/pronunciation of English words

Vocabulary

Tongue Twisters   A tongue twister is a phrase, sentence, or rhyme that is difficult to say because it contains many similar sounds. *Sally sells seashells at the seashore,* for example. To get the full effect of a tongue twister, try to repeat it several times, as quickly as possible.

- **Read this tongue twister.**

  Big Ben the brown bear bites bananas.

- **Practice repeating the tongue twister as fast as you can three times.**

- **Work with a partner. Write a new tongue twister and ask your partner to read it three times fast! Then have your partner write one for you.**

Riddles   A riddle is a question that seems to make no sense but has a clever answer. For example: *I run but have no legs. What am I?* Answer: *a nose*

- **Work with a partner to come up with a few new riddles.**
- **Share the riddles with your classmates. Can they guess the answers?**

TEKS 3.4D identify/apply playful language uses; ELPS 1E internalize new basic/academic language; 4B recognize directionality of English reading

Vocabulary

Palindromes   A palindrome is a word or phrase that reads the same in both directions. Here are a few examples. Can you think of any others?

mom   pop   deed   radar   racecar

Look at the palindrome square on the left below. You can read a word in either direction in every row and column *(net, ten, eye)*. Now copy the other word square onto a separate sheet of paper. Can you fill in the blanks?

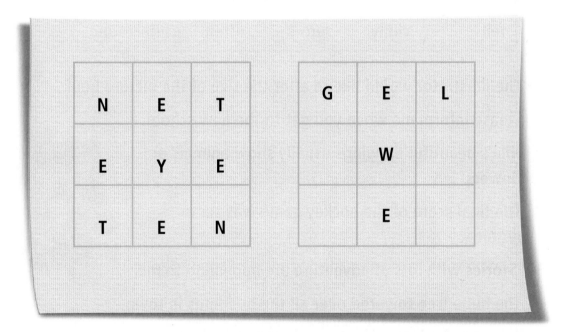

TEKS 3.4C identify/use antonyms/synonyms/homographs/homophones; **ELPS** 2C learn new language structures/expressions/vocabulary; **1E** internalize new basic/academic language; **1F** use accessible language to learn new language

Vocabulary Strategies

Identify the Synonym A synonym is a word that means the same thing, or almost the same thing, as another word. For instance, *wonderful* is a synonym for *great*.

Selecting Synonyms

Select a synonym from the box to replace the underlined word in each sentence. Write the new sentences on a separate sheet of paper.

| sketches | rough | change | giant | finished |
| tell | chilly | zero | often | interesting |

1. The illustrator would like to <u>alter</u> the size of the picture book.

2. Please <u>inform</u> me when you get to the new school.

3. Nila's beautiful <u>drawings</u> usually show animals or flowers.

4. The final score of the hockey game was six to <u>nothing</u>.

5. Stories with lots of adventure are <u>appealing</u> to me.

6. The <u>huge</u> tree towered over all the buildings in town.

7. The page had <u>jagged</u> edges where she had ripped it.

8. Mrs. Kendall's class <u>frequently</u> hangs art in the hall.

9. When it gets <u>cold</u> and damp outside, my cat likes to curl up by the fire.

10. Thomas shouted, "Hooray, I am finally <u>done</u> with my picture!"

TEKS **3.3** read aloud with fluency/comprehension; **ELPS** **3A** practice sounds/pronunciation of English words **4G** demonstrate comprehension through shared reading/retelling/responding/note-taking

Fluency

Timed Reading   Reading too slowly or too quickly will make it hard for listeners to understand what you read. Practice timed reading to improve your rate. Work with a partner.

1. Select a passage from this week's story, *The Harvest Birds*.

2. Read the passage aloud as your partner uses a watch or a wall clock to record your time. Focus on reading accurately and with appropriate rate, expression, and phrasing.

3. Write your time.

4. Read the passage again. Try to read the passage in less time.

5. Switch roles with your partner.

6. After you have both finished reading, discuss with your partner what you enjoyed most about *The Harvest Birds.* Did you learn anything new about the story while you were listening to your partner read?

Tips for Reading Well

- Accuracy—**Read all the words correctly.**

- Rate—**Read at an appropriate rate, or speed.**

- Expression—**Use your voice to show feeling.**

TEKS 3.4B use context to determine word meaning; **ELPS** 1C use strategic learning techniques to acquire vocabulary; 4C develop/comprehend basic English vocabulary and structures; 5B write using new basic/content-based vocabulary

Vocabulary Strategies

Multiple-Meaning Words Multiple-meaning words are words with more than one meaning. Read the sentences below. Then choose a word from the word box to complete each sentence. Each word will be used twice. Write your answers on a separate sheet of paper.

star	land	fall

1. The farmer had a beautiful crop of corn on his _____.

2. Leaves began to _____ from the huge tree.

3. Meghan danced perfectly and was the _____ of the show.

4. The sky was brightly lit by an amazing _____.

5. The birds liked to _____ on the top branch of the tree.

6. After a long, hot summer, the cool _____ nights are refreshing.

Write Sentences

Work with a partner. Choose a word from the box.

right	ball	change	band
play	trip	left	nail

- Write two sentences showing two different meanings of the word.
- Say the sentences to your partner.
- Switch roles.
- Continue choosing words and taking turns until you have used all the words in sentences.

TEKS 3.4E alphabetize to third letter/use dictionary/glossary; **ELPS 1C** use strategic learning techniques to acquire vocabulary;
4A learn English sound-letter relationships/decode

Vocabulary Strategies

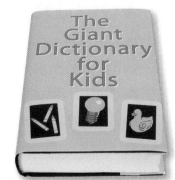

Using a Dictionary   A dictionary gives many kinds of information about words. You can use it to

- find how a word is spelled

- find what a word means

- see how a word is pronounced

Use a dictionary to complete the activity below.

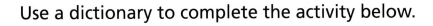

The following words are from this week's selection, *Kamishibai Man*. Copy the words onto a separate sheet of paper.

1. rickety	3. pant	5. bamboo
2. jerk	4. blur	6. sprout

Use your dictionary to find the meaning of each word. Some will have more than one meaning listed. You may need to look back at the story to see how the words were used. Then you can figure out which meaning is correct. Copy the correct definition.

When you are done, look through *Kamishibai Man* again. Can you find more words that are unfamiliar to you? Add them to your list and use your dictionary to find their meanings.

TEKS 3.4E alphabetize to third letter/use dictionary/glossary; **ELPS** 1H develop/expand learning strategies;
3A practice sounds/pronunciation of English words; **4A** learn English sound-letter relationships/decode

Vocabulary Strategies

Dividing Words into Syllables   How a word is divided into syllables makes a difference in how the word is pronounced. A dictionary shows how words are divided into syllables. For example, here is a dictionary entry for the word television:

tel·e·vi·sion (tel ə vizh ən)

Reread *Kamishibai Man* and pick out some words that have more than one syllable. Use your dictionary to look them up. On a piece of paper, write the words and show how they are divided into syllables. Read your list to a partner.

Correct Pronunciation   Pronunciation is the way a word is spoken. A dictionary shows how each sound in the word is pronounced. Here is an example:

bi·cy·cle (bī si k′l)

Work with a partner on this activity.

1. **Divide a blank sheet of paper into six squares.**

2. **Use a dictionary to find six words that are unfamiliar to you, and write a word in each square.**

3. **Swap papers with your partner. Use the dictionary to look up the words your partner listed. Write the correct pronunciation next to each word.**

4. **Read your words aloud to your partner.**

TEKS **3.3** read aloud with fluency/comprehension; **3.2C** establish reading purpose/monitor comprehension; **ELPS** **4G** demonstrate comprehension through shared reading/retelling/responding/note-taking; **4H** read silently with increasing ease/comprehension; **4I** employ reading skills to demonstrate comprehension

Independent Reading

Paraphrasing a Story   Paraphrasing is using your own words to tell or write about what you read. Paraphrasing helps you think about and remember what you read. Select and read a few pages from this week's story, *Young Thomas Edison*. On a separate sheet of paper, paraphrase what you read.

> **Tips for Paraphrasing**
>
> • **Explain events in the order in which they happen.**
>
> • **Include important vocabulary from the story.**
>
> • **Use your own words.**

Fluency

Shared Reading   Reading a text several times will help improve your comprehension and your fluency. Join in as your teacher reads with fluency.

1. **With classmates, decide on a few pages from *Young Thomas Edison*. Your teacher will guide you through the reading.**

2. **Take turns reading the pages aloud. As you read together, think about what's happening in the story. Also, focus on reading accurately and with appropriate rate, expression, and phrasing.**

3. **After you have finished reading, make sure you understood the text. Retell your favorite part for your teacher and classmates.**

ELPS **3A** practice sounds/pronunciation of English words; **4A** learn English sound-letter relationships/decode

Phonics

Decoding Unfamiliar Words Read the following article. Try to decode any unfamiliar words. First, read the rest of the sentence. Look for clues that help you guess what the word might be or the part of speech. Next, notice any familiar word parts, such as prefixes or suffixes. Last, break the word into syllables, or smaller word parts, you can pronounce.

Our Solar System

Our solar system is made up of Earth, its moon, the sun, and seven other planets and their moons. It also includes asteroids and comets. Scientists use telescopes to study the solar system.

Earth is extraordinary because it is the only planet in our solar system where animals and plants can survive. Earth rotates every twenty-four hours. Its movement around the sun creates the seasons.

The other major planets are Mercury, Venus, Mars, Jupiter, Saturn, Uranus and Neptune. Pluto was once called a major planet, but it is now called a dwarf planet.

Work with a partner on this activity.

- Take turns reading the paragraphs aloud with a partner.
- List two words that were difficult for you.
- Compare your words with your partner's. Tell how you decoded each word.
- Check your dictionary to find the meaning of an unknown word.

TEKS 3.1D identify/read contractions; **ELPS** 4C develop/comprehend basic English vocabulary and structures; **5C** spell English words with increasing accuracy; **5E** employ increasingly complex grammatical structures in writing

Phonics

A Game of Contractions   A contraction is two or more words shortened into one. When you make a contraction, you drop a letter or letters and use an apostrophe instead. For example, *don't* is a contraction for the words *do not.* In the contraction *don't,* the *o* was dropped from the word *not* and an apostrophe was put in its place.

do not

don't

was not

wasn't

   Make as many contractions as you can with the words in the box. Write them on a separate sheet of paper. You may use some words more than once.

it	had	are	will	am	not
I	is	he	have	we	

TEKS 3.1D identify/read contractions; **ELPS** 4C develop/comprehend basic English vocabulary and structures; **5C** spell English words with increasing accuracy

Phonics

Take Apart a Contraction

Read the paragraphs below. On a separate sheet of paper, write each underlined contraction. Then write the two words that are used to form it.

Tia wanted to join the softball team, but she <u>wasn't</u> sure she could hit the ball. She asked her dad to help her practice at the park.

Every Saturday Tia and Dad went to the park. <u>He'd</u> pitch the ball to her over and over again. "<u>Don't</u> swing the bat too early!" Dad said many times. He <u>wouldn't</u> ever get impatient, though.

Tia listened to her dad's advice. Finally, after many tries, she whacked the ball straight into the outfield. "<u>That's</u> the way to hit. Great job!" exclaimed Dad.

TEKS **3.1A(iv)** decode using prefixes/suffixes; **3.4A** identify meanings of prefixes/suffixes; **ELPS 4A** learn English sound-letter relationships/ decode; **4C** develop/comprehend basic English vocabulary and structures

Phonics and Vocabulary

Suffixes –y, –ful, –ous A suffix is a word part added to the end of a root word. Adding a suffix makes a new word with a different meaning. The suffixes *–y, -ful,* and *-ous* all mean "full of."

Write the following words on a sheet of paper. After each word, write the root word without the suffix. Read the word pairs aloud to a partner.

1. **joyous**
2. **smelly**
3. **grainy**

4. **forgetful**
5. **humorous**
6. **fruitful**

Suffix Tic-Tac-Toe

Find the winning Tick-Tack-Toe row. It contains only words that end with a suffix meaning "full of." Write the words on a separate sheet of paper.

useful	silly	famous
prescribe	joyous	restore
mountainous	helpful	guilty

TEKS **3.1A(iv)** decode using prefixes/suffixes; **3.4A** identify meanings of prefixes/suffixes; **RC-3(A)** establish reading purposes; **ELPS 1C** use strategic learning techniques to acquire vocabulary; **4A** learn English sound-letter relationships/decode; **4C** develop/comprehend basic English vocabulary and structures

Phonics and Vocabulary

Suffix Word Cards for *-y, -ful, -ous*   Work with a partner to make suffix word cards.

- On the front of a card, write a word that contains one of the three suffixes listed above.

- When you have completed five word cards, switch cards with your partner.

- Look at the word on the front of the card. Figure out its meaning and write the meaning on the back of the card.

- Take turns using the words in sentences.

Word Hunt

Reread this week's selection, *Jump!* Find examples in the story of each of these:

- a root word
- a root word with a suffix

Write the words you find on a separate sheet of paper. Write definitions for each word. Use your dictionary if you need help with the suffixes or word meanings. Then share your words with a partner.

TEKS 3.15A follow/explain written directions; ELPS 4K employ analytical skills to demonstrate comprehension

Comprehension

Make a Snowman   Directions explain how to do something, giving steps to follow in order. Follow the directions below. Draw your snowman on a separate sheet of paper.

1. Draw three circles.

2. Make a face on the top circle.

3. Add arms to the middle circle.

4. Give your snowman a scarf and a hat to keep it warm.

Mixed-up Directions   The directions below list the steps for making a peanut butter sandwich, but the steps are out of order. On a separate sheet of paper, write the directions in the correct order, numbering them 1–4.

• Eat the sandwich.

• Get bread and peanut butter.

• Spread the peanut butter on the bread.

• Ask your mom or dad to cut the sandwich in half.

TEKS 3.15A follow/explain written directions; **ELPS** 2I demonstrate listening comprehension of spoken English

Comprehension

Explain Directions

Read the following directions silently to yourself. Then explain what you have read to a partner. Have your partner pantomime, or act out, each step as you explain it. When you are finished, switch roles.

1. **First, pick up everything on the floor and put each item where it belongs.**

2. **Second, get rid of anything that is trash.**

3. **Third, put dirty clothes in the hamper or laundry room.**

4. **Next, hang up or put away the clean clothes.**

5. **Last, dust and vacuum the room.**

TEKS **3.4C** identify/use antonyms/synonyms/homographs/homophones; **3.24E** spell single syllable homophones; **ELPS 1E** internalize new basic/academic language

Spelling and Vocabulary

Using Homophones   Homophones are two or more words that sound the same but have different meanings and different spellings. Here are some examples:

sun/son   to/two/too

What does each homophone mean? Can you use each in a sentence? The homophones in the sentences below are from this week's selection, *The Science Fair*. On a separate sheet of paper, write the homophone that correctly completes the sentence.

1. (There, Their) wasn't enough time to complete our project.

2. Move in closer or you won't be able to (sea, see).

3. The fair began at (for, four) o'clock in the afternoon.

4. The microphone was set very (high, hi) on the stage, and little Melissa could not reach it.

5. "Hooray, we (one, won)!" the girls shouted.

What Is It?

Work with a partner. Take turns answering the homophone questions below. Then make up new sentences and try to stump your partner.

• Something on a boat OR bargain priced.
• Something on top of your head OR a fast little animal.
• Something that is delivered to you OR a boy.
• Something the wind did OR the color of the sky.
• Someone who wears a coat of armor OR a time when you go to bed.

TEKS 3.4C identify/use antonyms/synonyms/homographs/homophones; **ELPS 1E** internalize new basic/academic language;
4C develop/comprehend basic English vocabulary and structures

Vocabulary Strategies

Which Words Are Homographs?   Homographs are words
that are spelled the same but have different meanings and
sometimes different pronunciations. For example, the
homograph *wind* can be used in these two ways:

Please *wind* up the toy so it keeps moving.

The *wind* is blowing so strongly we'll
have to close the windows.

Look at the words in the box below. On a separate
sheet of paper, write down the words that are
homographs. Then use the homographs in sentences.

lives	call	bear	tick
ask	sit	list	bill

TEKS 3.4C identify/use antonyms/synonyms/homographs/homophones

Vocabulary Strategies

Homograph Challenge

Work with a partner. Think of some homographs. Fold a sheet of paper in half the long way. Write homographs on the left side of the paper. Trade papers with your partner. Write two different meanings and sentences to go with each homograph.

Homograph Tick Tack Toe   Look at the tick tack toe. Can you find a row across or a column down where all the words are homographs? On a separate sheet of paper write the three words from the row or column that makes a homograph tick tack toe.

address	conflict	can
me	sand	house
row	record	close

TEKS 3.4B use context to determine word meaning; 3.4C identify/use antonyms/synonyms/homographs/homophones; **ELPS 1E** internalize new basic/academic language; **4A** learn English sound-letter relationships/decode; **4C** develop/comprehend basic English vocabulary and structures

Vocabulary Strategies

Choose the Correct Homograph   On a separate sheet of paper, write the correct meaning for the underlined homograph in each sentence.

1. Be careful not to <u>tear</u> the paper.
    a. rip
    b. a drop of liquid that comes from your eye

2. Thomas took the <u>lead</u> in the bike race.
    a. a soft, gray metal
    b. a position in front

3. I can't wait to give Grandmother her <u>present</u>.
    a. the time that is happening now
    b. gift

4. Mom hopes you are feeling <u>well</u>.

    a. healthy
    b. a deep hole that contains water

A Different Meaning

Read each sentence below. On a separate sheet of paper, write a new sentence that uses a different meaning of the underlined homograph.

1. I <u>object</u> to eating all those vegetables.

2. Please don't <u>drop</u> the very delicate vase.

3. At the end of the game, I predict Jonas will <u>sink</u> the winning shot.

4. Jill <u>dove</u> into the water and raced across the pool.

TEKS 3.1D identify/read contractions; **3.23C(i)** recognize/use apostrophes in contractions/possessives; **ELPS 4C** develop/comprehend basic English vocabulary and structures

Phonics

What's the Contraction?   A contraction is two or more words shortened into one. When you make a contraction, you drop a letter or letters and use an apostrophe instead. Read the following sentences. What contraction can you make from the two underlined words in each sentence? Write your answers on a separate sheet of paper.

we have

we've

have not

haven't

1. Jake said, "The hoop <u>is not</u> too high for me to make a basket."

2. <u>They are</u> going to play the game at ten o'clock on Saturday morning.

3. "<u>You have</u> been gone for too long," Dad said.

4. "<u>I am</u> sorry I missed dinner," I replied.

5. The dogs <u>can not</u> go to the park with us this time.

Words That Make Contractions

On a separate sheet of paper, write each contraction and the two words that make it up. Then choose three contractions, and write a sentence using each one.

he's	let's
don't	they've
we'll	you're
aren't	

TEKS 3.4C identify/use antonyms/synonyms/homographs/homophones

Vocabulary Strategies

Using Homophones Remember that homophones are words that sound the same but are spelled differently. Read the sentences below. Underline the correct homophone in each one. Then write new sentences for the homophones you did not choose.

Example: I have a (pear/pair) of tickets to tonight's show if you'd like to go.

I'll be ready to go as soon as I eat this pear!

1. The doctor always checks my height and (weight/wait) when I go for a checkup.

2. Kendra got her (hair/hare) cut very short last weekend.

3. Don't use more than two cups of (flower/flour) when you make that cake.

4. Marco told me about a strange dream he had last (knight/night).

5. When the last (guest/guessed) left the party, we cleaned up all of the popped balloons.

6. Every seat on the (plain/plane) was full, so they had to wait for the next flight.

7. I'm hoping for a special package in the (mail/male) this afternoon.

8. (Wear/Where) did you put my favorite blue sandals?

TEKS 3.4C identify/use antonyms/synonyms/homographs/homophones

Vocabulary Strategies

Using Homophones   Make up a story about an exciting adventure you had in the forest. Use as many homophones as you can from the box. Then read the paragraph aloud to a partner. Pause after each sentence containing a homophone. Ask your partner to spell the homophone correctly.

tail/tale

bear/bare

hear/here

meet/meat

their/there

sun/son

sent/scent

eight/ate

through/threw

TEKS 3.1A(iv) decode using prefixes/suffixes; 3.4A identify meanings of prefixes/suffixes; **ELPS** 4A learn English sound-letter relationships/ decode; 4C develop/comprehend basic English vocabulary and structures

Phonics and Vocabulary

Add a Prefix   A prefix is a word part that is added to the beginning of a word. It usually changes the word's meaning. The prefixes *in-* and *im-* mean "not." For example, *imperfect* means "not perfect."

Copy the following chart onto a separate sheet of paper. Read the list of words in the chart aloud. Then write each word's meaning. The first one has been completed for you.

Word	Word's Meaning
immature	not mature
indirect	
impersonal	
incomplete	
impolite	
inconvenient	
impatient	
inaccurate	

ELPS 4A learn English sound-letter relationships/decode

Phonics

Decoding Unfamiliar Words As you read this story, pause and decode any unfamiliar words. First, read the sentence without the word. Ask yourself, *What part of speech is this? What word would make sense here?* Next, look for any familiar word parts, such as prefixes or suffixes. Last, break the word into syllables you can pronounce.

Miguel's New Pet

Miguel pleaded with his parents to let him get a pet. His parents finally agreed. Miguel and his mom walked to the pet store. Miguel was overwhelmed when he saw all the fish and reptiles at the store. He had no idea which pet to pick!

"I'm losing patience," said Mom. "You need to make up your mind!"

"I want that one," exclaimed Miguel, pointing to a black and white snake.

Miguel's mom paid the cashier. When they got home, Miguel tried to put the snake in the cage. It squirmed out of his hands and slithered across the room!

Fortunately, Mom got the snake into the cage before Dad got home. Dad is terrified of snakes!

TEKS **3.1E** monitor decoding accuracy; **3.3** read aloud with fluency/comprehension; **ELPS 3A** practice sounds/pronunciation of English words

Fluency

Work with a Partner

- Take turns reading "Miguel's New Pet" aloud with a partner.

- List two words that were difficult for you.

- Compare your words with your partner's. Tell how you decoded each word.

- Check your dictionary to find the meaning of an unknown word.

TEKS **3.3** read aloud with fluency/comprehension; **3.4C** identify/use antonyms/synonyms/homographs/homophones; **ELPS** **2A** distinguish sounds/intonation patterns of English; **3A** practice sounds/pronunciation of English words

Fluency

Partner Reading   Work with a partner. Select a few pages from this week's story, *The Extra-good Sunday*.

1. **Read the pages to yourself. Make sure you understand how to say all the words.**

2. **Read the pages aloud, alternating paragraphs with your partner.**

3. **As you read, use rate, expression, and phrasing to show the feelings of the author or characters.**

4. **As you listen, think about how your partner uses rate, expression, and phrasing.**

5. **Give your partner feedback. Then read the pages aloud again to improve your fluency.**

Vocabulary Strategies

Synonym Match   Synonyms are words that mean almost the same thing. The words *happy* and *glad* are synonyms. Some of the synonyms in the box below are from this week's selection, *The Extra-good Sunday*. Look at the words in the box. Find the synonyms that match and write them on a separate sheet of paper.

laugh	neat	couch	house
prepare	small	mean	tidy
good	unkind	giggle	sofa
nice	tiny	home	sound
noise	make	sad	unhappy

TEKS 3.1A(i) decode by dropping final "e"/adding endings; **3.22A(i)** use/understand verbs; **3.24B(ii)** spell by dropping final "e" before ending; **ELPS** **4A** learn English sound-letter relationships/decode; **4C** develop/comprehend basic English vocabulary and structures

Grammar

Dropping Final e When a base word has a final *e*, the *e* must be dropped before adding the *–ed* ending. The ending *–ed* makes the word past tense. Look at these words:

| rake | raked |

What happens to the final *e* in *rake* when *rake* is changed to *raked*? It is dropped. Copy this chart. Fill in the blanks in each row with either the root word or the past tense form of the base word. Read the words on the chart to a partner when you're done.

Root Word		dance	bake		like			share
Past Tense Form	saved			stared		moved	carved	

Drop the "e"

Look at the words in the box. Find the words that drop the final *e* before adding the *–ed* ending. Write them on a separate sheet of paper.

dread	hope	shape	trade
desire	call	live	free

TEKS 3.1A(ii) decode by doubling final consonants/adding endings; 3.22A(i) use/understand verbs; 3.24B(i) spell by doubling consonant before ending; **ELPS** 4A learn English sound-letter relationships/decode; 4C develop/comprehend basic English vocabulary and structures

Grammar

Doubling Final Consonants   Look at these words:

top   **topped**

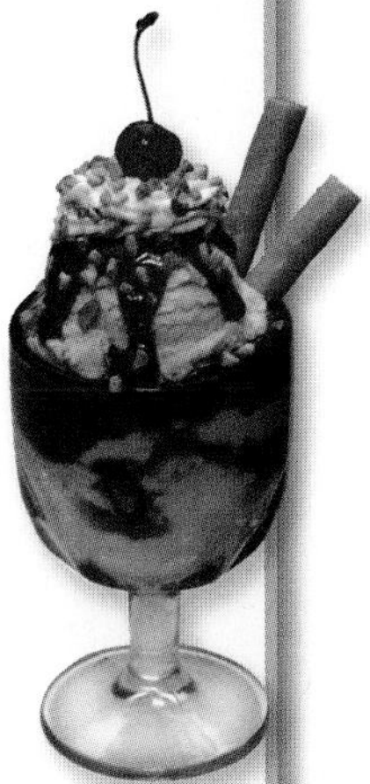

The word *top* is a CVC (consonant, vowel, consonant) word. When the ending *–ed* is added to CVC words, the final consonant is doubled. When the final consonant is doubled, you know that the vowel sound in *topped* is short.

Read the list of words below. Which words follow the CVC pattern? On a separate sheet of paper, write the words that require doubling the final consonant before adding the *–ed* ending. Here's a hint: you should have five words on your paper. Then beside each of the words add the *–ed* ending to make new words.

jog	fold	ship	pick
tan	hop	move	trim

patted

ragged

slipped

Word Cards

Work with a partner to create word cards.

- **Write a word with the *–ed* ending on one side of a card. Make sure you choose a CVC word that requires doubling the final consonant before adding the *–ed*, for example, *patted, ragged, slipped*. Repeat until you have five word cards.**
- **Trade cards with a partner.**
- **On the blank side of each word card, write the base word before the *–ed* ending was added. Take turns reading the word cards aloud.**

TEKS **3.1A(iii)** decode by changing final "y" to "i"; **3.22A(i)** use/understand verbs; **3.24B(iii)** spell by changing "y" to "i" before ending; **ELPS** **4A** learn English sound-letter relationships/decode; **4C** develop/comprehend basic English vocabulary and structures

Grammar

Changing final *y* to *i*   When you add endings such as *–ed* to words that end in *y*, you sometimes have to change the *y* to *i* before adding the ending. Read these examples:

try   tried   carry   carried

You see that in both words *try* and *carry,* the final *y* changed to *i* before the *–ed* was added. Write the following words on a separate sheet of paper. Then write the past tense of each word by adding the *–ed* ending. Remember to change the *y* to *i* before adding the ending. The first one has been done for you.

1. **testify**   **testified**
2. **dry**
3. **supply**
4. **apply**
5. **cry**
6. **marry**

Find the Root Word

All of the words in the box below have the *–ed* ending. Also, all of these words have root words that ended in *y* before the *–ed* ending was added. Look at each word. Then on a separate sheet of paper, write its root word.

spied	buried	fried	tried
rallied	hurried	denied	satisfied

Glossary

This glossary contains meanings and pronunciations for some of the words in this book. The Full Pronunciation Key shows how to pronounce each consonant and vowel in a special spelling. At the bottom of the glossary pages is a shortened form of the full key.

Full Pronunciation Key

Consonant Sounds

b	**bib**, ca**bb**age	kw	**cho**ir, **qu**ick	t	**t**igh**t**, stopp**ed**
ch	**ch**ur**ch**, sti**tch**	l	**l**id, need**l**e, ta**ll**	th	ba**th**, **th**in
d	**d**ee**d**, mail**ed**, pu**dd**le	m	a**m**, **m**an, du**mb**	*th*	ba**th**e, **th**is
		n	**n**o, sudde**n**	v	ca**v**e, val**v**e, **v**ine
f	**f**ast, **f**i**f**e, o**ff**, **ph**rase, rou**gh**	ng	thi**ng**, i**nk**	w	**w**ith, **w**olf
		p	**p**o**p**, ha**pp**y	y	**y**es, **y**olk, oni**on**
g	**g**a**g**, **g**et, fin**g**er	r	**r**oa**r**, **rh**yme	z	ro**s**e, si**z**e, **x**ylophone, **z**ebra
h	**h**at, **wh**o	s	mi**ss**, **s**au**c**e, **sc**ene, **s**ee	
hw	**wh**ich, **wh**ere			zh	gara**g**e, plea**s**ure, vi**s**ion
j	**j**u**dg**e, **g**em	sh	di**sh**, **sh**ip, **s**ugar, ti**ss**ue	
k	**c**at, **k**i**ck**, s**ch**ool				

Vowel Sounds

ă	p**a**t, l**au**gh	ŏ	h**o**rrible, p**o**t	ŭ	c**u**t, fl**oo**d, r**ou**gh, s**o**me
ā	**a**pe, **ai**d, p**ay**	ō	g**o**, r**ow**, t**oe**, th**ough**		
â	**ai**r, c**a**re, w**ea**r	ô	**a**ll, c**augh**t, f**o**r, p**aw**	û	c**i**rcle, f**u**r, h**ear**d, t**er**m, t**ur**n, **u**rge, w**or**d
ä	f**a**ther, k**oa**la, y**a**rd	oi	b**oy**, n**oi**se, **oi**l		
ĕ	p**e**t, ple**a**sure, **a**ny	ou	c**ow**, **ou**t	yo͝o	c**u**re
ē	b**e**, b**ee**, **ea**sy, pian**o**	o͝o	f**u**ll, b**oo**k, w**o**lf	yo͞o	ab**u**se, **u**se
ĭ	**i**f, p**i**t, b**u**sy	o͞o	b**oo**t, r**u**de, fr**ui**t, fl**ew**	ə	**a**go, sil**e**nt, penc**i**l, lem**o**n, circ**u**s
ī	r**i**de, b**y**, p**ie**, h**igh**				
î	d**ear**, d**eer**, f**ie**rce, m**ere**				

Stress Marks

Primary Stress ´: bi·ol·o·gy [bī **ŏl**´ ə jē]
Secondary Stress ´: bi·o·log·i·cal [bī´ ə **lŏj**´ ĭ kəl]

A

a·bil·i·ty (ə **bĭl** ĭt ē) *noun* The quality of being able to do something: *Most cats have the **ability** to land on their feet.*

ad·vice (ăd-**vīs´**) *noun* An idea or suggestion about how to solve a problem: *Rhianna gave me **advice** about writing well.*

af·ford (ə **fôrd´**) *verb* To be able to pay for or spare: *We can't **afford** a new car.*

an·nounce (ə **nouns´**) *verb* To officially make known: *The mayor **announced** the date of the parade.*

anx·ious·ly (**ăngk´** shəs lē) *adverb* Nervously or fearfully: *I waited **anxiously** for the bus on my first day of school.*

ap·plause (ə **plôz´**) *noun* Enjoyment or approval shown especially by clapping hands: *The audience gave the actors a round of **applause**.*

a·shamed (ə **´shāmd**) *adjective* Feeling shame or guilt: *The team was **ashamed** of its poor performance at the soccer game.*

ath·lete (**ăth´** lēt´) *noun* A person who is trained in or is good at physical exercises, games, or sports: *Each **athlete** stretches and runs in place before a race.*

athlete
The word *athlete* comes from the Greek word *athlon*, meaning "prize."

B

bal·ance (**băl´** əns) *verb* To put in a steady or stable condition: *Those kids are **balancing** balls on their heads.*

blast (blăst) *verb* To give off a loud noise: *Suddenly, the loud sound of a siren **blasted** through the air.*

block (blŏk) *noun* A part of a street marked off by the two nearest cross streets: *Everyone who lives on our **block** is coming to the party.*

blur·ry (**blûr´** ē) *adjective* Dim or hard to see: *Everything looks **blurry** if I'm not wearing my glasses.*

bor·der (**bôr´** dər) *noun* Outer parts or edges: *White lines mark the field's **borders**.*

bor·row (**bŏr´** ō) *verb* To get something from someone else and plan to return or replace it later: *You can **borrow** my notebook for an hour.*

C

cer·tain·ly (**sûr´** tn lē) *adverb* Surely; without a doubt: *I will **certainly** be there by noon.*

cer·tif·i·cate (sər **´ti** fi kət) *noun* An official document that gives information or proof: *A birth **certificate** gives proof of where and when you were born.*

ă r**a**t / ā p**ay** / â c**a**re / ä f**a**ther / ĕ p**e**t / ē b**e** / ĭ p**i**t / ī p**ie** / î f**ie**rce / ŏ p**o**t / ō g**o** / ô p**aw**, f**o**r / oi **oi**l / o͝o b**oo**k

cham·pi·on·ship
(**chăm´** pē ən shĭp´) *noun* A contest to determine the winner of a game or contest, accepted as the best of all: *The team that wins the **championship** must win four playoff games.*

chart (chärt) *noun* A sheet that gives information in the form of a table, diagram, or graph: *The numbers on these **charts** show population growth.*

cling (klĭng) *verb* To stick or hold tight to: *Dirt will **cling** to a wet rug.*

col·lect (kə **lĕkt´**) *verb* To gather as a hobby or for study: *I **collect** old movie posters.*

com·pet·i·tor
(kəm **pĕt´** ĭ tər) *noun* A person or group that competes with another or others; opponent: *She is my **competitor** for the role.*

con·tact (**kŏn´** tăkt´) *verb* To get in touch with: *Every parent was **contacted** and invited to the meeting.*

con·tin·ue (kən **tĭn´** yōō) *verb* To keep on or persist in: *The rain **continued** for days, and the ground was flooded.*

con·vince (kən **vĭns´**) *verb* To persuade to do or believe: *Have you **convinced** your sister to go on the trip?*

court (kôrt) *noun* A level area marked for playing a game, as tennis or basketball: *I groaned when my tennis ball sailed out of the **court**.*

cre·a·tive (krē **ā** tĭv) *adjective* Having new ideas; being able to create things: *A lot of **creative** and talented people worked on that mural.*

crew (krōō) *noun* A group of people who work together: *It took a large **crew** to build this skyscraper.*

cross (krôs) *adjective* In a bad mood; grumpy; grouchy: *Mom calls me an old grump when I am feeling **cross**.*

cus·tom·er (**kŭs´** tə mər) *noun* A person who regularly buys goods or services: *Many **customers** were shocked to learn the store was closing.*

cross

D

dart (därt) *verb* To move suddenly and swiftly: *A squirrel **darted** across the path so fast I barely saw it.*

de·gree (dĭ **grē´**) *noun* One of the units into which a measuring instrument, such as a thermometer, is divided: *Water boils at a temperature of 212 **degrees**.*

ōō **boo**t / ou **ou**t / ŭ **cu**t / û **fu**r / hw **wh**ich / th **th**in / *th* **th**is / zh vi**s**ion / ə
ago, sil**e**nt, penc**i**l, lem**o**n, circ**u**s

dis·ap·pear (dĭs´ ə **pîr**´) *verb* To pass out of sight; vanish: *My dog **disappears** when it is time for her bath.*

disappear
Disappear contains the prefix *dis-*, which means "not" or "opposite of." The prefix *un-* also means "not" or "opposite of," as in *unkind*

E

earn (ûrn) *verb* To gain by working or by supplying service: *I **earn** money each week by doing chores.*

ed·u·ca·tion·al (ĕj´ ōō **kā**´ shən əl) *adjective* Giving information or providing a learning experience: *We saw an **educational** film about recycling.*

e·lec·tric (ĭ **lĕk**´ trĭk) *adjective* Of, relating to, or produced by electricity: *An **electric** current runs through the wiring of a house.*

electric

en·tire (ĕn **tīr**´) *adjective* Whole or complete: *I ate an **entire** pint of ice cream.*

e·rupt (ĭ **rŭpt**´) *verb* To burst out violently: *Lava and ash **erupt** from a volcano.*

ex·am·ine (ĭg **zăm**´ ĭn) *verb* To look at carefully: *We **examined** the plant cells under a microscope.*

ex·cite·ment (ĭk **sīt**´ mənt) *noun* The state of being excited: *As the game went on, the **excitement** grew.*

ex·per·i·ment (ĭk **sper**´ ə mənt) *noun* A test to find out or prove something: *Let's try an **experiment** to see if our idea works.*

F

fa·mil·iar (fə **mĭl**´ yər) *adjective* Well known, as from repeated experience: *I heard the **familiar** voice of the announcer.*

fan (făn) *noun* A person with a keen interest in or admiration for someone or something: *My friends are basketball **fans**.*

fes·tive (**fĕs**´ tĭv) *adjective* Merry; joyous: *We were in a **festive** mood at the parade.*

fig·ure (**fig**´ yər) *verb* To work out by thinking: *The guide will **figure** out a way to cross the mountains.*

fine (fin) *adjective* Excellent; of high quality: *This shop sells only **fine** foods.*

fog·gy (**fô**´ gē) *adjective* Full of, having, or covered by fog: *Lighthouses were a big help to ships on **foggy** nights.*

fond·ly (**fŏnd**´ lē) *adverb* Lovingly or tenderly: *Mom always looks at me **fondly**.*

fum·ble (**fŭm**´ bəl) *verb* To feel, touch, or handle in a clumsy way: *I **fumbled** nervously with my keys.*

ă r**a**t / ā p**ay** / â c**a**re / ä f**a**ther / ĕ p**e**t / ē b**e** / ĭ p**i**t / ī p**ie** / î f**ie**rce / ŏ p**o**t / ō g**o** / ô p**aw**, f**o**r / oi **oi**l / ōŏ b**oo**k

G

gadg·et (găj´ ĭt) *noun* A small mechanical device: *A bottle opener is a **gadget.***

gen·ius (jēn´ yəs) *noun* A person who has outstanding mental or creative ability: *My sister is smart, but she's not quite a **genius**!*

guilt·y (gĭl´ tē) *adjective* Having committed a crime or bad deed: *The jury found them **guilty** of stealing.*

H

har·vest (´här vəst) *noun* Crops that are gathered or ready to be gathered: *We pick the corn **harvest** each summer.*

hon·est (ŏn´ ĭst) *adjective* Not lying, stealing, or cheating: *I admire people who are **honest**, and I don't like liars.*

I

il·lus·trate (ĭl´ ə strāt) *verb* To add photographs, drawings, diagrams, or maps that explain or decorate books or magazines: *Let's **illustrate** the book about their journey with a map of their travels.*

i·mag·ine (ĭ măj´ ĭn) *verb* To form a mental picture or idea of: *Can you **imagine** a blue horse with a yellow mane?*

im·pres·sive (ĭm prĕs´ ĭv) *adjective* Having a strong, positive effect on the mind or feelings: *The artist's paintings are so **impressive** that I could stare at them all day.*

in·gre·di·ent (ĭn grē´ dē ənt) *noun* One of the parts that make up a mixture or combination: *Flour is one of the **ingredients** of bread.*

in·ven·tion (ĭn vĕn´ shən) *noun* An original device, system, or process: *The cotton gin was an important **invention**.*

J

jerk·y (jûr´ kē) *adjective* Marked by sudden, sharp motions: *We had a **jerky** ride over the rough road.*

ju·ry (jŏŏr´ ē) *noun* A group of citizens chosen to listen to the facts and proof on cases presented in a court of law: *The **jury** listened carefully as the lawyers summed up their cases.*

L

lab·o·ra·to·ry (lăb´ rə tôr´ ē) *noun* A room or building holding special equipment for doing scientific tests, research, and experiments: *You'll find some test tubes and droppers in the science **laboratory**.*

jerky
The word *jerky* can also be a noun. *Jerky* is meat cut into strips and dried or cured. The noun *jerky* comes from the Spanish word *charqui*, which in turn came from the Quechua word *ch'arki*.

ōō b**oo**t / ou **ou**t / ŭ c**u**t / û f**u**r / hw **wh**ich / th **th**in / *th* **th**is / zh vi**s**ion / ə
ago, sil**e**nt, penc**i**l, lem**o**n, circ**u**s

league (lēg) *noun* A group of sports teams that compete mainly among themselves: *All the teams in our baseball league are here in the city.*

lie (lī) *verb* To take or be in a flat or resting position: *He is lying on the couch and resting.*

loy·al (loi′ əl) *adjective* Faithful: *She is a loyal friend who always helps me.*

M

mist (mĭst) *noun* A mass of tiny drops of water in the air: *Fog is a kind of mist.*

moan (mōn) *verb* To utter a long, low sound as of sorrow: *I moaned to Mom that I didn't feel good.*

mur·mur (mûr′ mər) *noun* A low, continuous sound: *I could hear a murmur of voices from the next room.*

N

nerv·ous (nûr′ vəs) *adjective* Anxious; fearful: *I was nervous about going to the dentist.*

non·sense (nŏn′ sĕns′) *noun* Foolish talk, writing, or behavior: *Your complaints are just nonsense.*

O

oc·ca·sion·al (ə kā′ zhə nəl) *adjective* Happening or encountered from time to time: *Except for an occasional cold, I have been well this winter.*

or·der (ôr′ dər) *noun* An arrangement of things one after the other: *What different orders might you use for a list of city names?*

P

part·ner (pärt′ nər) *noun* One of two or more people working or playing together: *Leah's tennis partner hit the ball to her.*

patch (păch) *noun* A small area: *Only one patch of snow is left on the ground.*

pa·trol (pə trōl′) *verb* To move about an area to watch or guard: *We will patrol the halls to make sure they are empty.*

pause (pôz) *verb* To stop briefly: *The players are pausing because one team has called a time-out.*

peak (pēk) *noun* The top of a mountain: *We can see for miles from the mountain peak.*

plead (plēd) *verb* To make an urgent request; appeal: *The boy pleaded for candy, but his mother said no.*

ă rat / ā pay / â care / ä father / ĕ pet / ē be / ĭ pit / ī pie / î fierce / ŏ pot / ō go / ô paw, for / oi oil / o͝o book

point (point) *verb* To call attention to something with the finger: *The librarian pointed to the sign that said "Quiet."*

pol·ish (**pŏl´** ĭsh) *verb* To make smooth and shiny, especially by rubbing: *We polish the floor weekly.*

pow·er (**pou´** ər) *noun* The force, strength, or ability to do something: *It took all my power to lift the heavy couch.*

pres·en·ta·tion (prĕz´ ən **tā´** shən) *noun* Something that is shared with the public: *During her presentation, Dr. Kim told the audience about her new discoveries.*

prin·ci·pal (**prĭn´** sə pəl) *noun* The head of a school: *Our principal read the new rules to each class.*

pro·fes·sion·al (prə **fĕsh´** ə nəl) *adjective* Making money for doing something that other people do for pleasure or as a hobby: *Some professional baseball players earn huge amounts of money.*

pro·nounce (prə **nouns´**) *verb* To say clearly, correctly, or in a given manner: *I'm afraid I pronounced your last name wrong.*

proud (proud) *adjective* Feeling pleased and satisfied over something owned, made, or done: *You should be proud of your great test scores.*

Q

quiv·er (**kwiv´** ər) *verb* To shake with a slight vibrating motion: *My voice may quiver if I get nervous.*

R

rag·ged (**răg´** ĭd) *adjective* Tattered: *We wore ragged old clothes to paint the house.*

raise (rāz) *verb* To gather together; collect: *We're trying to raise money for a new hospital wing.*

rap·id·ly (**răp´** ĭd lē) *adverb* Swiftly; speedily: *We walked rapidly to the fire exit when the alarm sounded.*

rec·om·mend (rĕk´ ə **mĕnd´**) *verb* To advise: *My dentist recommended that I should floss more often.*

re·mark (rĭ **märk´**) *verb* To say or write casually: *They remarked about the weather.*

re·port (rĭ pôrt) *noun* Give a spoken or written description of something: *Jo will report, on the results of the game.*

re·search (rĭ **sûrch´**) *noun* Careful study of a subject or problem: *Medical research has saved many lives.*

rick·et·y (**rĭk´** ĭ tē) *adjective* Likely to fall apart or break: *Don't sit in that rickety old chair.*

point

ōō b**oo**t / ou **ou**t / ŭ c**u**t / û f**u**r / hw **wh**ich / th **th**in / *th* **th**is / zh vi**si**on / ə
ago, sil**e**nt, penc**i**l, lem**o**n, circ**u**s

root (ro͞ot) *verb* To encourage by or as if by cheering: *We are **rooting** for the home team.*

rude (ro͞od) *adjective* Not considerate of others; impolite: *It is **rude** to break into someone else's conversation.*

rugged

rug·ged (rŭg´ĭd) *adjective* Having a rough surface or jagged outline: *We flew over the **rugged** mountains.*

S

score (skôr) *verb* To gain a point or points in a game, contest, or test: *Did you really **score** ten points in the game?*

scram·ble (skrăm´bəl) *verb* To mix together in a confused mass: *The player **scrambled** the cards before dealing them.*

scrib·ble (skrĭb´əl) *noun* Careless writing or drawing: *Don't hand in homework that has sloppy **scribbles** on it.*

sep·ar·ate (sĕp´ə rāt´) *verb* Divide into parts or sections: *We can **separate** these apples into four piles.*

ser·i·ous (sîr´ē əs) *adjective* Not joking or fooling: *I'm **serious** when I tell you I want to be an astronaut.*

shift (shĭft) *noun* A period of working time: *Dad works the late **shift** at the hospital.*

sig·nal (sĭg´nəl) *noun* A sign, gesture, or device that gives a command, a warning, or other information: *The traffic **signal** was not working properly.*

sketch (skĕch) *noun* A rough drawing or outline: *An artist might do many **sketches** before making a final drawing.*

slam (slăm) *verb* To strike with force; crash: *One of the cars **slammed** into the wall of the racetrack.*

slump (slŭmp) *verb* To droop or slouch: *Her shoulders **slumped** from fatigue.*

snap (snăp) *verb* To bie, seize, or grasp with a snatching motion: *A wild animal may **snap** at you if you touch it.*

soar (sôr) *verb* To rise or fly high in the air: *My kite **soared** into the sky when the wind picked up.*

sort (sôrt) *verb* To arrange by class, kind, or size; classify: *We **sorted** the mail.*

spread (sprĕd) *verb* To open out wide or wider: *The children are **spreading** the blanket on the ground.*

stand (stănd) *noun* The place taken by a witness in court: *An expert witness was called to the **stand** during the trial.*

stands (standz) *noun* The bleachers at a playing field or stadium: *Wild cheers arose from fans in the playing field's **stands**.*

ă rat / ā **pay** / â c**a**re / ä f**a**ther / ĕ p**e**t / ē b**e** / ĭ p**i**t / ī p**ie** / î f**ie**rce / ŏ p**o**t /
ō g**o** / ô p**aw**, f**o**r / oi **oi**l / o͝o b**oo**k

steep (stēp) *adjective* Rising or falling sharply: *We climbed a steep hill.*

stretch (strĕch) *verb* To extend: *Our long telephone cord can stretch from the kitchen to the living room.*

stroll (strōl) *verb* To walk in a slow, relaxed way: *I ran to school but strolled home.*

style (stīl) *noun* A way of dressing or acting: *Our teacher has a special style that makes learning fun.*

T

tense (tĕns) *adjective* Anxious or nervous: *Taking a deep breath can help you relax when you're tense.*

tex·ture (tĕks´chər) *noun* The look or feel of a surface: *Most kinds of velvet have soft, smooth textures.*

tide (tīd) *noun* The regular rising and falling of the surface level of the oceans, caused by the pull of the moon and the sun: *Each high tide carries new seashells to the shore.*

tool (to͞ol) *noun* A device, such as a hammer or an ax, that is specially made or shaped to help a person do work: *Dad's electric screwdriver is one of his favorite tools.*

trac·ing (trās´ĭng) *adjective* Used to copy, or trace, lines: *Try using tracing paper to copy something exactly.*

tri·al (trī´əl) *noun* The studying and deciding of a case in a court of law: *The judge called the trial to order.*

trudge (trŭj) *verb* To walk slowly and with effort; plod: *I trudged through the deep snow.*

tum·ble (tŭm´bəl) *verb* To spill out in confusion, haste, or disorder: *The kids tumbled out of the bus.*

V

va·cant (vā´kənt) *adjective* Not occupied or rented: *The house was vacant for a year.*

W

weak·ly (wēk´lē) *adverb* In a way that lacks strength, power, or energy; feebly: *The sick child asked weakly for a glass of water.*

wor·ry (wûr´ē) *verb* To feel or cause to feel uneasy: *I am worried about my sick dog.*

tide

---

o͞o b**oo**t / ou **ou**t / ŭ c**u**t / û f**u**r / hw **wh**ich / th **th**in / *th* **th**is / zh vi**si**on / ə **a**go, sil**e**nt, penc**i**l, lem**o**n, circ**u**s

Acknowledgments

Main Literature Selections

Aero and Officer Mike: Police Partners by Joan Plummer Russell, photographs by Kris Turner Sinnenberg. (Caroline House, an imprint of Boyds Mills Press, Inc. 2001) Text © 2001 by Joan Plummer Russell. Photographs © 2001 by Kris Turner Sinnenberg. Reprinted by permission of Boyds Mills Press, Inc.

"The Ball Game is Over" from *Good Sports: Rhymes About Running, Jumping, Throwing, and More* by Jack Prelutsky and Chris Raschka. Copyright © 2007 Jack Prelutsky. Reprinted by permission of Alfred A. Knopf, an imprint of Random House Children's Books, a division of Random House, Inc.

Destiny's Gift by Natasha Anastasia Tarpley, illustrated by Adjoa J. Burrowes. Text copyright © 2004 by Natasha Anastasia Tarpley. Illustrations copyright © 2004 by Adjoa J. Burrowes. Reprinted by permission of Lee & Low Books Inc., New York, NY 10016.

"The Extra Good Sunday" from *Ramona Quimby, Age 8* by Beverly Cleary. Copyright © 1981 by Beverly Cleary. All rights reserved. Reprinted by permission of HarperCollins Children's Books, a division of HarperCollins Publishers.

A Fine, Fine School by Sharon Creech, illustrated by Harry Bliss. Text copyright © 2001 by Sharon Creech. Illustrations copyright © 2001 by Harry Bliss. All rights reserved. Reprinted by permission of Johanna Cotler Books, an imprint of HarperCollins Publishers.

"Firefly" from *Flicker Flash* by Joan Bransfield Graham. Copyright ©1999 by Joan Bransfield Graham. Reprinted by permission of Houghton Mifflin Harcourt Publishing Company.

"Giraffe" from *Doodle Dandies: Poems That Take Shape* by J. Patrick Lewis. Copyright © 1998 by J. Patrick Lewis. Reprinted by permission of Atheneum Books for Young Readers, an imprint of Simon & Schuster Children's Publishing Division, and Curtis Brown, Ltd.

The Harvest Birds/Los pájaros del la cosecha by Blanca López de Marscal. English translation copyright © 1995 by Children's Book Press. Reprinted by permission of Children's Book Press, San Francisco, CA, www.childrensbookpress.org

"Homer" from *A Pocketful of Poems* by Nikki Grimes. Copyright © 2001 by Nikki Grimes. Reprinted by permission of Houghton Mifflin Harcourt Publishing Company.

Jump! by Floyd Cooper. Copyright © 2004 by Floyd Cooper. Reprinted by permission of Philomel Books, a division of Penguin Young Readers Group, a member of Penguin Group (USA) Inc. All rights reserved.

Kamishibai Man written and illustrated by Allen Say. Copyright © 2005 by Allen Say. All rights reserved. Reprinted by permission of Houghton Mifflin Harcourt Publishing Company.

Max's Words by Kate Banks, illustrated by Boris Kulikov. Text copyright © 2006 by Kate Banks. Illustrations copyright © 2006 by Boris Kulikov. All rights reserved. Reprinted by permission of Frances Foster Books, an imprint of Farrar, Straus & Giroux, LLC.

"Metamorphosis" from *Honey and Salt* by Carl Sandburg. Copyright © 1963 by Carl Sandburg and renewed 1991 by Margaret Sandburg, Helga Sandburg Crile, and Janet Sandburg. Reprinted by permission of Houghton Mifflin Harcourt Publishing Company.

"Pop's Bridge" by Eve Bunting, illustrated by C.F. Payne. Text copyright © 2006 by Eve Bunting. Illustrations copyright © 2006 by C. F. Payne. Reprinted by permission of Houghton Mifflin Harcourt Publishing Company.

"Python" from *Lizards, Frogs, and Polliwogs: Poems and Paintings* by Douglas Florian. Copyright © 2001 Douglas Florian. Reprinted by permission of Houghton Mifflin Harcourt Publishing Company.

Roberto Clemente, Pride of the Pittsburgh Pirates by Jonah Winter, illustrated by Raúl Colón. Text copyright © 2005 by Jonah Winter. Illustrations copyright © 2005 by Raúl Colón. Reprinted by permission of Atheneum Books for Young Readers, an imprint of Simon & Schuster Children's Publishing Division. All rights reserved.

"The Science Fair" from *Beany and the Meany*, by Susan Wojciechowski, illustrated by Susanna Natti. Text copyright © 2005 by Susan Wojciechowski. Illustrations copyright © 2005 by Susanna Natti. Reprinted by permission of Candlewick Press, Inc. and the author.

The Trial of Cardigan Jones written and illustrated by Tim Egan. Copyright © 2004 by Tim Egan. All rights reserved. Reprinted by permission of Houghton Mifflin Harcourt Publishing Company.

What Do Illustrators Do? written and illustrated by Eileen Christelow. Text and illustrations copyright © 1999 by Eileen Christelow. All rights reserved. Reprinted by permission of Houghton Mifflin Harcourt Publishing Company.

"What is Science?" by Rebecca Kai Dotlich. Text copyright © Rebecca Kai Dotlich. Reprinted by permission of Curtis Brown, Ltd.

Yonder Mountain: A Cherokee Legend told by Robert H. Bushyhead, written by Kay Thorpe Bannon, illustrated by Kristina Rodanas. Copyright © 2002 by Kay Thorpe Bannon. Illustrations copyright © 2002 by Kristina Rodanas. All rights reserved. Reprinted by permission of Marshall Cavendish Corporation.

Young Thomas Edison written and illustrated by Michael Dooling. Copyright © 2005 by Michael Dooling. All rights reserved. Adapted by permission of Holiday House, New York.

Credits

Photo Credits

Placement Key: (t) top; (b) bottom; (l) left; (r) right; (c) center; (bg) background; (fg) foreground; (i) inset.
TOC c Andreanna Seymore/Getty Images; **TOC 4** t VisionsofAmerica/Joe Sohm/Getty Images; **TOC 5** t Provided by Youth Service America, a Washington, DC based **501** (c)**3**; **TOC 5** c Gary Crabbe/Alamy; **TOC 5** b (c) David Bergman/Corbis; **TOC 6** b Kenneth Hamm/Photo Japan; **TOC 7** c Matsuda Film Productions/ courtesy of Digital Meme; **TOC 7** b (c) Bettmann/Corbis; **TOC 8** t Photodisc/Alamy; **TOC 8** bkgd t (c)PhotoDisc; **TOC 8** b Courtesy Woolaroc Museum, Bartlesville, Oklahoma;